ISLAM
in
SOUTH ASIA

A REGIONAL PERSPECTIVE

ASIM ROY

University of Tasmania, Hobart

South Asian Publishers * New Delhi

SOUTH ASIAN PUBLISHERS PVT. LTD.
50 Sidharth Enclave, P.O. Jangpura, New Delhi 110014

ISBN   81-7003-193-1

Typeset at Anjali Computer Typesetting, 50 Sidharth Enclave,
P.O. Jangpura, New Delhi 110014
[Phones: 6925315, 6835713]

Published by South Asian Publishers Pvt. Ltd.
50 Sidharth Enclave, P.O. Jangpura, New Delhi 110014
and printed at
Mehra Offset Press, Chandni Mahal, Daryganj, New Delhi 110002.
Printed in India.

Contents

Preface

MY INTERESTS in Islam stem from my boyhood bewilderment at having to leave our hearth and home in a mofussil town of the name of Ishwarganj in the district of Mymensingh, in present Bangladesh, nee East Pakistan, nee East Bengal in undivided India. One thing leading to another, I ended up in the bosom of History, packing my history curricula with whatever options I could find on general Islamic history or developments concerning South Asian Islam or Muslim. The unquenched thirst impelled me to reinforce my M.A. in Modern History with another Master of Arts degree programme in Islamic History and Culture, on one hand, and some intensive and rigorous exposure to the Farsi (Persian) Language, on the other. All this served as a very useful foil for my major preoccupation, in my research career, with South Asian Islam, with special reference to the Bengali-speaking region.

My sustained research and studies in Bengal – the land of my birth and growth – rewarded me with a paradigm of the regional formulation of Islam, in contradistinction with the widely entertained Islamic centralists notion of a monolithic Islam. The traditional Islamists and the Islamic orientalists uncritically reduced Islam to an undifferentiated mass of a religious and cultural uniformity. The singular absence of serious studies in Islam, in diverse regional contexts, helped to conceal a reality widely experienced by Muslim believers in many parts of the Muslim world, namely, its distinctive regional and local expressions and genius. Underlying the undoubted creedal, doctrinal and ritualistic unity in Islam, the Muslim world, at the micro level, presents a much more complex reality of unquestioned pluralism and diversity. Islamic developments on the soil of Bengal offered me a fertile field of exploration of the richness, creativity and dynamicity of the forces of regional Islam. The primary focus of my fundamental research has, therefore, been broadly related to the issue of unity and variety in Islam, studied basically in the Bengali-speaking region of South Asia. The present publication bears an eloquent testimony to its truth.

It is my great pleasure to bring together, through this particular volume, my salient ideas, thoughts and research findings on South Asian Islam. The level of its endorsement and acceptance by its readers should remain the measure of its strength and relevance. I acknowledge, with due gratitude, the various academic institutions/publications. I am most obliged to Mr Vinod Kumar, Director, South Asian Publishers Pvt. Ltd. for his unqualified trust and confidence in my academic worth,and unbounded patience with my tardiness in getting the material for this publication ready and accessible. Bouts of technical mishaps, ranging from the superficial to the disastrous, tried his patience infinitely more than mine.

Hobart, Tasmania   ASIM ROY
December 1995

Introduction

ISLAM IS not new to serious challenges. Confronting a challenge, Islam in history has always brought to bear on its response a strong degree of resilience and a spirit of accommodation and adaptability. Yet, the contemporary challenge to the world of Islam and Muslims has been of a rather different nature and on an unprecedented scale. Never before has Islam been so comprehensively challenged from so many diverse quarters.

The most fundamental form of external challenge to Islam emanates from the twin pressures of Westernisation under the veneer of globalisation, and a rather complementary process of an effective elimination of the communist "threat" to Western capitalism, in the wake of the Soviet debacle. One seminal effect of such profound global changes is the resurrection of the perceived old Islamic "threat" in the form of Islamic "fundamentalism". The debacle of the Soviet empire has seen Western capitalism and civilization growing anxious to set up their new whipping boy in the so-called fundamentalist Islam, The West, in particular, has raised the spectre of a "militant Islam", sweeping across the world, directly challenging the Western political and cultural dominance, or posed as a civilisational conflict in the eyes of those like Samuel Huntington.

In the last two decades a very large part of the Muslim World appeared indeed to have been in severe ferment. News media never stopped churning out great many stories – important or trivial – about these lands and people. The cues were later taken by the politicians and still later by academics. The phenomenon was variously designated in the Western media and political parlance as Islamic "resurgence", "radicalism", "militancy", or "political Islam". There is no clear perception and understanding of what lay behind all this, except a vague, uncanny and uneasy apprehension of the sinister rise of Islamic "militancy".[1] Khomenian Iran, Palestinian Al-Hamas and Hizabullah, National Islamic Front of Sudan, Islamic Brotherhood of Egypt, Islamic revolutionaries in Algeria, Talibans and other Mujahideen in Afghanistan, Moros of the Philippines, radical Islamists in Pakistan, Bangladesh, India, Indonesia and Malaysia, and religiously concerned and sensitive Muslims in the Western countries, like the USA, UK, and similar groups in other European and Asian countries, as well as Australia – are all systematically churned-out piping-hot stuff for journalistic and political consumption. The Western stereotyping of and pressure on the Muslim world have been conducive to further enhancement of the notion of Islamic militancy.

Interpreting Islamic developments is indeed a daunting task. Secular explanations of religious actions are as important as these are often so problematical. Such scholars often tend to carry their zeal too far to the point of reducing a religious phenomenon to anything but religious. The real challenge in studying religion is to explore and be aware of the non-religious intermingled with the religious, and restore thereby the religious issues and attributes to their legitimate positions and contexts

There is an extraordinary degree of vagueness and confusion about what constitutes this Islamic fundamentalism. An objective enquirer is certain to encounter some strong assumptions and an established pattern of popular mythification. There are several major problems with such uncritical assumptions. First, this represents a monolithic and normative view of Islam which has been found totally inadequate in an empirical, historical analysis of Islamic development in a regional-cultural setting. Until fairly recently we had very little social-scientific knowledge of the regional varieties and formulations of Islam. Serious problem with the form and meaning of "Islamic fundamentalism" does exist, as various Muslim social groups take advantage of its flexibility in order to serve their own interests.

Secondly, even within this limited validity of the religious explanation, this view fails to differentiate between the "appearance" and "reality" the "symbol" and the "substance". One would be naturally inclined, and justifiably enough, to seek religious meaning and significance in all multi-faceted developments in the Muslim countries, and this has precisely been the case. Islamic resurgence, to most, is what it says to be religious in its origins, inspirations and expressions. It is not so much a question of rejecting this popular perception, as revealing its inadequacies and simplistic nature. What appears strikingly religious in both form and meaning may not necessarily be essentially religious in inspiration. It is now widely known throughout the Muslim world that Islam is being systematically pressed into secular use by both Muslim governments, as well as by people and groups who are opposed to those governments. Many people, described as "fundamentalists", are very far from the actual fundamentals of the religion that they claim to espouse. Our concern is that in a political context, these groups are using Islam as a political tool rather than espousing a return to the fundamentals of Islam. As such, Islam has proved itself a powerful political tool. Religion in South Asia, as perhaps elsewhere, has no often been found to conceal secular concerns: transcendental symbols were, in reality, nothing more than convenient covers for not so elevated mundane interests. One could so easily be misled by the religious symbolism of the "Islamic resurgence".

Thirdly, there is very little awareness of the inner divergences and complexities in the religious contents of Islamic resurgence. The Islamic contents of the process of Islamisation underlying Islamic resurgence are rather substantially divergent and dissimilar. The terms indiscriminately used are "fundamentalism", "orthodox", "conservative" etc. There are significant differences in these conceptual terms, and these differences apply just as much to Islam as in other religions. It is possible to see in all this a broad revivalistic spirit and urge, but no agreement about what was to be revived. The interpretations of the "purity" and "simplicity" of Islam are not one and the same. There are many different versions of the "golden age" in Islam. With different groups and interests in Islam, different models and degrees of Islamisation have been canvassed, and each ultimately was designed to suit their particular purpose and interest. Hence the process is often rather "selective". Particular matters of *sharia* are picked up or ignored to justify matters of specific concerns and interests.

We need not go further than South Asia to identify the cross-purposes to which the call of "Islamic fundamentalism" is pressed into service by people in government and outside. Here there is no dearth of examples of Islam being deployed to foster national unity and integration, as well as to suppress, where necessary, legitimate assertions and demands of ethnic nationalism. Islam is also found in this region to legitimise authoritarian regime, and suppress democratic aspirations and movements of the people. Conversely, Muslims in opposition to an undemocratic regime, resort to the Islamic ideology in defence of their objectives. An observer also finds an instrumental use of Islam, in the interests of maintaining or acquiring political power, as is the case, either to win the confidence or neutralise and weaken the Muslim clergy (*ulema*). Above all, the recent surge of Islamic spirit is often co-related to the lure of petro-dollar, and that of augmenting foreign reserve through a massive export of skilled and unskilled labour to the rich and expanding job markets of West Asia.

The social-psychological appeal of a puritanical form of Islam, at a time of saucy-economic stresses and strains, has been underlined in various sociological micro-studies. A massive dislocation of life, in the wake of profound social and economic changes in the developing countries, such as the movement from rural to the urban areas, the pressures and deprivations of a miserable city and slum life and so on, came to enhancetherole of religion as a psychological relief and solace, and also project religious authenticity as a bond of unity and a badge of identity in a strange, harsh and hostile human environment. Idealistic youth often turns to the pure and simple faith as a reaction against the materialistic life style of the affluent and the comfortable classes and against all-round corruption and erosion of values.

And yet, no student of a religious phenomenon is entitled to overlook or ignore the religious concerns underlying the Islamic resurgence. Probing the secular and mundane concerns underpinning resurgent Islam is not to devalue its religious import. The greater challenge is to set the role and relevance of the religion within the frame of a total perspective. Viewed in this light, much of the discontent, disaffection, bitterness, frustration, fury and iconoclasm of the Muslim world today would seem to have been rooted in Islamic history, and an adequate understanding of that history needs to focus on a remarkable nexus in Islam of faith, community, power and history. This raises the most vital issue which concerns not only Islam as a faith and ideology but also Islamic history, and to that extent, today's Muslims concerns as yesterday's.

The close identity of religion and politics in Islam is a common assumption. Lately, some Muslim scholars have questioned its validity, primarily on two grounds. First, the links are no different, as they point out, from that in other religions like Judaism, Christianity, Hinduism, Buddhism and Sikhism. Secondly, except in the early years of Islamic history, the religious and political life of Muslims remained effectively separate. One is prepared to accept the partial validity of this position. But it is difficult to adopt this position fully. To me, a total identity of the faith, its social ideal and the community is a special genius of Islam. The centrality of the community and the social ideal in Islam is as crucial as it is well known: Man alone was given a choice and responsibility which he accepted and must act upon; it is both an individual and a collective discharge of responsibilities and right living, in accordance with God's commands. The historicity of the mission, as well as its gravity and urgency as the last warning and the last chance for the humanity formed additional imperatives. The Islamic mission, to the believers, is mankind's last opportunity to redeem themselves not merely through individual piety but through actualisation of the social ideal in history.

Also there are some vital historical explanations for the intertwining of the temporal and the spiritual in Islam. In Islam, the absence of the "church", which represented the organised community in Christianity, the religious struggle for Muslims, therefore, has not been "between the church and the state, but for the state".[2] Hence this identity of faith and power, religion and state, as well as the very strong appeal of an Islamic State among Muslims. Additionally, and more importantly, the state and religion issue was not really faced by Muslims. Mecca was the most likely place for confrontation between the believers and their temporal and religious opponents, but Muhammad left Mecca for Medina, where the temporal and the spiritual were united in his person, thus avoiding a potential discord between the two orders. Later, history witnessed sweeping success for Islam and Muslims at both temporal and spiritual levels. Islam steadily as a strident and leading civilization. The success was understandably seen by the believers in religious terms. History seemed to have vindicated the faith, especially for those who cherished to believe it. The obvious gap between the ideal and the actual, or faith and history was either overlooked or glossed over, because of this ultimate vindication of the faith, together with the comforting thought and reality that Muslims ruled Muslims. The first serious crisis in Islam – the conquest of the Muslim world by the Mongol infidels, resulting in the fall of Baghdad and the Abbasid Caliphate (1258 AD.) – was conveniently averted, with the conversion of those conquerors to Islam. The current crisis, stemming from the challenge of modernity and the Western colonial dominance, was not to be resolved so easily in the Mongol fashion. One after another the Muslim lands fell like a pack of cards before the onslaughts of Western imperialism. This was not to be brushed aside as a mere political crisis, rather many saw it as a profound spiritual crisis – "an appalling gap between the religion of God and the historical development that He controls".[3] The twin motifs of modern Muslims response to the new challenge have been, on one hand, strong resistance and defence against external aggression and encroachment, as well as scathing attack on internal decadence, corrosion and corruption, on the other. Muslim countries, in the post-World War II period, have been able, by and large, to throw off the foreign yoke, but the problems of the Muslim world persist in new shapes and forms: economic imperialism persists; Muslim collaborators thrive; creation of Israel at the heartland of the Muslim world and the pathetic Muslim helplessness against it burns; the rage against American neo-colonialism, or "coca-colonialism", as it is often derisively called, continues unabated; nationalism, undermining the vitality of the ideal of Islamic unity, and finally, the despotic Muslim rulers of both secular and religious variety and the exploitative Muslim classes have been making a mockery of the Islamic ideal of social justice.

A reason for widespread unrest in the Muslim world is, in Edward Said's words, a tragic betrayal of the Muslim masses by their elites. Committed to their faith and perplexed by the inadequacy of their community and history in the contemporary world, eager to act, yet not knowing what to do, the Muslim masses are often easy prey to every cold and cruel tricks of a skilful manipulator of the secular or religious variety. The crisis of suffering, anguish, and anger, arising from this greatest and continuing tragedy in the history of this community, remain drowned under the roaring waves of the so-called Resurgent Islam.

The issues concerning Islamic fundamentalism are not confined to the area discussed above. Another profoundly significant question, flowing from the growing emphasis attached to the projection of an image of fundamentalist Islam, has been briefly mentioned above, and the question has a critical bearing on my own research interests and studies. The debates and discussions on the so-called fundamentalist Islam, both at the popular and scholarly levels, have conduced to create and foster a monolithic, albeit stereotypical and imaginary, concept of Islam. This is likely to prove incalculably significant for the future development of Islam, as well as for studies in Islam. Sharply opposed to the idea of monolithic Islam propagated through the current debates, historical Islam, as revealed in the intensive research-based studies in regional settings, such as mine in the Bengali-speaking region, remains a very rich and dynamic social-cultural process. The disproportionate emphasis placed on the theme of unity, to the total exclusion of the role and place of variety, in Islam has not only caused a gross distortion of a remarkably protean historical process, but also reduced Islamic process to a simple, flat and linear development. Islam and Islamic studies have, in my view, been poorer for this. A great civilisation is not made within the narrow and rigid frame of a belief and social system. Neither ideology nor life could work in disjunction and separation. It is this infinitely complex and creative forms of interaction between the ideal and actual that made Islam a rich, vital, living and great civilization.

I have, in my humble way, sought to capture the breadth, elasticity, tolerance and creativity in the process of historical development of Islam, as encapsulated in its formulations in the Bengali-speaking region in South Asia. Bengal provides an excellent paradigm of a regional formulation of Islam, and its importance, in a study of the Islamising process in a regional setting, cannot be exaggerated, as expounded in a number of my studies incorporated in the present publication. Of several characteristic features of Islam, here in this region, two seem to stand out most. One relates to the statistical truth of the numerical preponderance of Bengal Muslims. In divided Bengal today, Muslims of Bangladesh alone (over 100 million) are not only the largest Muslim people in South Asia but also the second largest of such groups in the world behind Indonesia (over 150 million). The presence of such a massive proportion of Muslim in Bengal is, undoubtedly, a vital aspect of Islamic development in the region. The second major feature concerns the dominant nature and form of Islam in the land. There has been a virtual unanimity among sundry observers that the dominant version of the religion, as practised by the overwhelming majority of its votaries in pre-modern Bengal, was rather, "tainted", "spurious" or "corrupt".

The explanations for such a development, emanating from these observations, are not only divergent, but also conflicting in nature, and so necessarily inadequate. There seem to be two broad lines of reasoning. The theory of "incomplete conversion" or "semi-conversion" is rather similar in nature to that of "folk Islam", both pointing at the level and the limit of the cultural attainment of the masses of indigenous converts. The theory of "degeneration", on the other hand, offers a much different kind of reasoning. None of these explanations could, however, be sustained either by logic or history, as argued in some of my following essays.

The argument of incomplete conversion and degeneration contradict each other. Degeneration could not have logically followed from a situation which was already regarded inadequate and "incomplete". Besides, the descriptive labels such as "half converts" or "census Muslims" raise serious questions about the place for value judgements in academic pursuits. Finally, the most serious objection to the theory of Islam's degeneration in Bengal is that it is patently unhistorical. There is no historical evidence to suggest that Islam as practised by the masses of its votaries in Bengal, in the declining years of the Mughals, was anything different from what it had been there in the past or that the so-called "corrupt", "degenerate" and "hinduised" Islam, confronted by the Islamic revivalists and reformists since the nineteenth century, was a sharp deviation from a golden or classical age of Islam in Bengal lying in the past. On the contrary, the earliest extant Muslim Bengali literary sources, dating largely from the sixteenth century, provide the clearest possible evidence of the early existence in Bengal of masses of believers who, having been linguistically cut off from the Arabic and Persian sources of Islamic tradition and denied of such tradition in their vernacular Bengali, continued to remain steeped in the locally popular non-Muslim tradition, readily available in the vernacular Bengali. The authors of this early Muslim Bengali literature were themselves instrumental in recasting Islamic tradition in syncretistic moulds, as discussed below.

The conventional perceptions of Islam's Bengali reformulation are indeed grossly inadequate and also misleading. Underlying the problem one is aware of a wider and vital question of perspective appropriate for studying a Muslim group in a regional setting. I have attempted to raise serious doubts about an approach that begins with a "definition" of a religion and accepting and rejecting everything to the extent that it measures up to this standard. A much more meaningful effort is to "find" the religion in the life and world of the believer. Studies in Islam in the context of South Asia are generally remiss in this perspective.

In the absence of much significant empirical research in this area, its study has very largely been dominated by the normative or macro perspective of the traditional Islamists which are firmly rooted in the notion of a monolithic Islam. Proceeding from this deductive position, the empirical realities of Islamic development in a regional and local setting are "judged" by this idealised and abstract norm and hence discarded as "folk" or "popular" aberrations; their practitioners are likewise dumped as "half converts" or "nominal" or "statistical" Muslim. The inescapable implication of this approach in terms of sifting "good" from "bad" Muslims may be endorsed by many as a good religious act, but is likely to be treated by many others as a pointless and bad academic exercise. It is useful to bear in mind as well that individual Bengali Muslims, regardless of such external criticisms, have always taken pride in their Islamic identity.

In its empirical development, no system of beliefs and practices could be divorced from its spatial-social context. The social and cultural mores or the believer invest particular meanings and symbolism into those beliefs and practices as far as possible as a mean of accommodating them to his *weltanschauung*, and leave the rest of his previous cultural baggage to coexist, generally harmoniously, with his new acquisitions. A student of this phenomenon is more meaningfully challenged to unravel this complex interface between the old inheritance and the new acquisition. Islam's encounter with Bengal has its own specific social and cultural contexts which proved determining in recasting Islam into its distinctive regional mould. In this land, Islam has not been a "primary" but a "secondary" culture, that is, exogenous and not indigenous to the region. Also, here in this region, Islam has not been a "single" or the only "great tradition" since it entered a land which was not culturally virgin, and confronted the long-established indigenous great tradition. These are vital considerations in the regional development of Islam.

The Islamic revivalists and other observers encountered a situation in Bengal that resulted, not from a later debasement of Islam, but from the original conditions of culture-contact in the region. Nurtured and nourished by a rich combination of social, cultural, and political circumstances in the history of medieval Bengal, the dominant form of Bengal's Islamic response blossomed, over a long period of time, into a rich syncretistic and acculturated tradition. The so-called degenerate and devitalised Islam in later Bengal was nothing but an embodiment of an earlier perception and formulation by Bengal Muslims of their religion in a syncretistic frame of reference. The syncretistic tradition remained the dominant form of Islamic acculturation in Bengal for several centuries until the nineteenth century witnessed a massive and organised assault on this tradition and on the cultural values and norms necessary to sustain it. The history of Muslim Bengal had then entered its rather dysjunctional new and modern phase. Even in this particular stage, syncretistic values and concerns were scotched but not killed. Some of my studies in colonial Bengal, included in this volume, should bear testimony to its truth. History is not about telling future, and no historian can or should anticipate what lies in the womb of the future. Islam in South Asia has a brilliant track record of creative adaptation and accommodation to its social and cultural environment. Much has happened and has been happening to undermine the mores and morale of this syncretistic genius. And yet, a keen observer cannot miss even today the pull of the undercurrent of the syncretistic tradition, flowing through the course of Islamic development in South Asia. In history success and failure are not eternally defined attributes. Today's success is tomorrow's failure and vice versa.

NOTES

1. Cf. "The Moslem world rekindles its militancy", *The New York Times* (18/6/78).
2. W.C. Smith, *Islam in History* (Princeton, New Jersey: Princeton Univ. Press, 1957), pp. 10ff, 211
3. Ibid., pp. 10ff.

PART ONE

ISLAMISATION AS A SOCIAL-RELIGIOUS-CULTURAL PROCESS

1 The Interface of Islamisation, Regionalisation and Syncretisation The Bengal Paradigm

I

OF THE TWO major characteristic features of Islamic development in Bengal one, by its very nature, remains incontrovertible, and the other is a source of confusion and disputation. The first relates to the statistical truth of the numerical preponderance of Bengal Muslims. In India undivided, the largest concentration of Muslims [about 34 million] was found in Bengal. In divided Bengal today, Muslims of Bangladesh alone [over 100 million] are not only the largest Muslim people in South Asia but also the second largest of such groups in the world behind Indonesia [over 150 million]. The presence of such a massive proportion of Muslims in Bengal is, undoubtedly, a vital aspect of Islamic development in the region.

The second major feature relates to the dominant nature and form of Islam in the land. There has been a virtual unanimity among observers that the dominant version of the religion, as practised by the overwhelming majority of its votaries in traditional or pre-modern Bengal,[1] was rather "lax" and "spurious", though divergent and even conflicting explanations for such a development are found to have emanated from these sources. This particular perception of the dominant form of Islam in the land goes back long in history. As early as the sixteenth century a Mughal Admiral in Bengal, Ihtimam Khan, expressed sentiments belittling the indigenous born in Bengal.[2] In the late eighteenth century, Gulam Husain Tabatabai observed this "deviance" of Muslim Bengal.[3] A late nineteenth-century British resident observer in the Muslim-dominated Eastern Bengal, Dr James Wise, noted "the corrupt Hinduised rites" of Muslims in Bengal.[4] The most graphic depiction and the most venomous condemnation of such "debased" Islam came from the large volume of polemical and didactic writings of the Islamic fundamentalists, revivalists and reformists in the nineteenth century and after.[5] At the beginning of this century Syed Ameer Ali, a distinguished member of the modern Muslim social and intellectual elite, contrasted "the Mahomedan settlers from the West who had brought with them to India traditions of civilisation and enlightenment" with the Eastern Bengali Muslims who were "chiefly converts from Hinduism" and "still observe[d] many Hindu customs and institutions."[6] A little later, William Crooke, a keen British observer of the phenomenon of popular religion in India, regarded the Muslim converts as those who "assimilated Islam only in an *imperfect way* [italics mine]".[7] Contemporary West Pakistani politicians and officials have often made derogatory remarks on the piety of Bengali Muslims. Malik Feroze Khan Noon, the Punjabi Governor of East Bengal in 1952, regarded his wards as "half-Muslims".[8] President Ayub Khan entertained similar attitudes.[9]

The popularity of this view extends beyond the circle of lay observers to include professional scholars. Muhmmad Mujeeb, a South Asian Islamist of repute, considers them "partly converted".[10] Peter Hardy dubbs them "census Muslims" and adds:

> . . . the real challenge to purity of belief and practice in Islam in medieval India was to be found . . . in the convert's countryside – in the ignorance of new Muslims of the requirements of Islam and in the insidious infiltrations of 'creeping Hinduism' into the daily life of the convert.[11]

In an excellent study relating to the early sixteenth-century Bengal, a Bengali Muslim historian of considerable standing, Momtazur Rahman Tarafdar observes:

> Islam, in its simple and austere aspect, does not appear to have characterised the life of the people [of Bengal] . . . a careful study of the literature of the time shows that there prevailed a sort of *folk Islam* [italics mine] having hardly any connection with the dogmas of religion.[12]

Azizur Rahman Mallick, another distinguished Bengali Muslim scholar, refers to Islam in Bengal "where *corrupt and irreligious practices* [italics mine] gained considerable ground."[13] He speaks of the "ignorance" of the "half converted Muslims" and identifies "incomplete conversion" as "a channel through which un-Islamic practices passed" into Islam. "Incomplete conversion in the rural districts of Bengal", Mallick writes, "left these people only *nominal followers* [italics mine] of the Faith . . . ."[14] An interesting aspect of his observations relates to his attempt to offer some curious explanations for this Islamic phenomenon in Bengal. He raises, on one hand, the issue of the Mughal decline and the "loss of political power" which, in his opinion, "undoubtedly contributed to the *degen-*

eration [italics mine] of Islam ...."[15] Elsewhere he writes:

> Thus long years of association with non-Muslims who far outnumbered them,[16] cut off from the original home of Islam, and living with *half-converts* [italics mine] from Hinduism, the Muslims had greatly deviated from the original faith and had become 'Indianised'.[17]

The distinctive nature and personality of Islam as popularised in traditional Bengal would, therefore, seem evident enough. The explanations for such a development, as noted above, are, however, far less acceptable and adequate. There seem to be two broad lines of reasonings. The theory of "incomplete conversion" or "semi-conversion" is rather similar in nature to that of "folk Islam", both pointing at the level and the limit of the cultural attainments of the masses of indigenous converts. The theory of "degeneration", on the other hand, offers a much different kind of reasoning. None of these explanations could, however, be sustained either by logic or history.

To begin with, the arguments of incomplete conversion and degeneration contradict each other. Degeneration could not have logically followed from a situation which was already regarded inadequate and "incomplete". Besides, the descriptive labels such as "half converts" or "census Muslims" raise serious questions about the place for value judgments in academic pursuits. To call a Muslim something less than a Muslim is a value judgment and not a description or analysis of the meaning of being a Muslim from the point of view of one who calls himself a Muslim and claims the religion as his own. Such an attitude is likely to perpetuate dissensions in a religious community on the issue of what constitutes the piety for which no religious community has seemed to have ever developed a consensus. Finally, the most serious objection to the theory of Islam's degeneration in Bengal is that it is patently unhistorical. There is no historical evidence to suggest that Islam as practised by the masses of its votaries in Bengal, in the declining years of the Mugals, was anything different from what it had been there in the past or that the so-called "corrupt", "degenerate" and "Hinduised" Islam, confronted by the Islamic revivalists and reformists since the nineteenth century, was a sharp deviation from a golden or classical age of Islam in Bengal lying in the past.[18] On the contrary, the earliest extant Muslim Bengali literary sources, dating largely from the sixteenth century,[19] provide the clearest possible evidence of the early existence in Bengal of masses of believers who, having been linguistically cut off from the Arabic and Persian sources of Islamic tradition and denied of such tradition in their vernacular Bengali, continued to remain steeped in the locally popular non-Muslim tradition readily available in the vernacular Bengali.[20] The authors of this early Muslim Bengali literature were themselves instrumental in recasting Islamic tradition in syncretistic moulds, as discussed below.

II

The conventional perceptions of Islam's Bengali reformulation are indeed grossly inadequate and also misleading. Underlying the problem one is aware of a wider and vital question of perspective appropriate for studying a Muslim group in a regional setting. In his brilliant comparative study of Islam in Morocco and Indonesia, Clifford Geertz raises very serious doubts about an approach that begins with a "definition" of a religion and accepting and rejecting everything to the extent that it measures up to this standard. Instead, he urges a more meaningful effort to "find" it in the life and world of the believer.[21] Studies in Islam in the context of South Asia mostly fly in the face of Geertz's caution.

In the absence of much significant empirical research in this area, its study has very largely been dominated by the normative or macro vision of the traditional Islamists of the old Orientalist type which is firmly rooted in the notion of a monolithic Islam or a world-Islam, defined essentially in textual terms of the *Sunni* orthodoxy. Proceeding from this *a prioric* position, the empirical realities of Islamic development in a regional and local setting are viewed through the prism of this idealised and abstract norm and hence discarded as "folk" or "popular" aberrations; their practitioners are likewise dumped as "half converts" or "nominal" or "statistical" Muslim. The inescapable implication of this approach in terms of sifting "good" from "bad" Muslims may be endorsed by many as a good religious act, but is likely to be treated by many others as a pointless and bad academic exercise. It is useful to bear in mind as well that individual Bengali Muslims, regardless of such external criticisms, have always taken pride in their Islamic identity.

In its empirical development, no system of beliefs and practices could be divorced from its spatial-social context. The social and cultural mores of the believer invest particular meanings and symbolism into those beliefs and practices as far as possible as a means of accommodating them to his *weltanschauung*, and leave the rest of his previous cultural baggage to coexist, generally harmoniously, with his new acquisitions. A student of this phenomenon is more meaningfully challenged to unravel this complex interface between the old inheritance and the new acquisition. Islam's encounter with Bengal has its own specific social and cultural contexts which proved determining in recasting Islam into its distinctive regional mould. In Bengal, Islam has not been a "primary" but a "secondary" culture, that is, exogenous and not indigenous to the region. Also, here in this region, Islam has not been a "single" or the only "great tradition" since it entered a land which was not culturally virgin, and confronted the long-established indigenous great tradition. These are vital considerations in the regional development of Islam.

The Islamic revivalists and other observers encountered a situation in Bengal that resulted, not from a later debasement of Islam, but from the original conditions of culture-contact in the region. Nurtured and nourished by a rich combination of social, cultural and political circumstances in the history of medieval Bengal, the dominant form of Bengal's Islamic response blossomed, over a long period of time, into a rich syncretistic and acculturated tradition. The so-called degenerate and devitalised Islam in later Bengal was nothing but an embodiment of an earlier perception and formulation by Bengal Muslims of their religion in a syncretistic frame of reference. The syncretistic tradition remained the dominant form of Islamic acculturation in Bengal for several centuries until the nineteenth century witnessed a massive and organised assault on this tradition and on the cultural values and norms necessary to sustain it. The history of Muslim Bengal had then entered its new modern phase. In the following pages we should endeavour to explore the social-structural and cultural contexts of Islamic acculturation in this region with special reference to its syncretistic formulation.

III

A striking feature of Bengal Muslim history has been a close correspondence between the human geography of the land and many significant aspects of its historical development. Much explanation for the historical developments in deltaic Bengal is found in the physical nature of its deltaic constitution. The geographical distribution and the demographic patterns of the Muslim population are as much conditioned by physical and historical forces as those are vital determinants in the regional transformation of Islam. Ever since the startling revelations, in the first census of Bengal (1872), of a preponderant number of Muslim in the northern, eastern and southern parts of the land and also of their predominantly rural character, gradual, though occasionally grudging, recognition has been gained in favour of the view that the overwhelming majority of Bengal Muslims were local converts and their descendants, and also belonged to the lower rungs of the social ladder.[22]

Eastern and southern Bengal, on one hand, and northern Bengal, on the other, where two-thirds and three-fifths respectively of the inhabitants were Muslims according to the Census Report of 1901, present a typically rural landscape and have been compared even in recent times to "a huge sprawling village".[23] The demographic landmark of this deltaic region has always been the clustering of certain predominant social groups, all occupying lower positions in the social hierarchy of a primarily agricultural society. The Hindu *Mahisya*, *Pod* and *Namasudra*, and the Muslim agriculturists, known locally as *Sek* or *Sekh* (*Shaikh*) and *Jola* (*Julaha*) respectively, formed the great bulk of the people in this region. The strong anthropometric correspondence between *Namasudra* and various Muslim groups in these areas had been observed.[24]

This demographic pattern fitted quite well into a significant pattern of physical changes in the deltaic Bengal. The entire network of river-systems in

Bengal has undergone great changes through the course of centuries, the most consistent and significant feature of which has been a gradual shift in the location of fertile soil from the moribund west of the delta to its mature eastern and southern parts. Eminent geographers, O.H.K. Spate and A.T.A. Learmonth underline "the well-known contrast between the decayed west, scarred with silted or stagnant bhils, the *disjecta membra* of dead rivers, and the active east . . .".[25] This physical change, combined with the pressure caused by the steady influx of upper caste immigrants to the settled western region of Bengal, forced the aboriginal and pioneer agriculturists and settlers from the old to the new productive "frontiers" of the delta. The upper Ganga (Ganges) valley seemed to have already undergone development of this nature. The higher castes were found to live in contiguity throughout the Ganga valley, while the unprivileged *Bhar*, *Pasi*, *Chamar* and *Dosadh* of the upper plain lived in scattered clumps of houses on the brink of marshes and swamps, just like their *Mahisya*, *Pod*, *Namasudra* and *Sekh* counterparts in the lower delta.[26]

The lower delta is subjected to heavy rainfall and precariously open even now to the constant threat of cyclonic catastrophies. The loss and suffering in both human and material terms, resulting from such frequent natural disasters could "hardly be estimated or exaggerated."[27] The rainfall there is between 60 and 95 inches, while in the rest of Bengal, excluding the northern submontane region, it is between 50 and 60 inches. The region along the Padma and the lower Meghna is backed by the Madhupur jungle, a much-dissected older alluvial terrace rising considerably above the general level. This interruption of the slope down to the sea, the ponding back of the local water by the main Ganga-Brahmaputra current, and the high rainfall combine to make the Meghna-Surma embayment perhaps the most amphibious part of Bengal during the rains. The lower tracts are flooded to a depth of 8-15 feet, and the homesteads are built on earth platforms 15-20 feet high.[28] Here, in the lower and the most active part of the delta, the inhabitants – agriculturists, wood-cutters, fishermen, boatmen and the like – were indeed pitted against a Nature that was at once rich and bountiful, menacing and cruel. They had to live and fight against a mighty array of adversaries – fierce floods, storms, brackish waters, snakes, crocodiles and tigers. The experience of material existence in this environment was reflected in the religious beliefs characteristic of the region. It is not accidental that the cult of the Tiger-god, Daksin-ray, emerged and flourished in this region. In the popular religious tradition of this region, the goddess Ganga was represented as the presiding deity of the crocodiles. It is highly significant that the Hindu tradition of Daksin-ray and the Muslim tradition of Gazi and his associate Kalu, both popular in the region, found these popular heroes involved in a contest for control of territories in the region which ended happily with territorial divisions arbitrated by God, appearing in a meaningful form of half-Hindu and half-Muslim. Further, both Daksin-ray and Gazi were invested with command over tigers and crocodiles.[29] In the course of time, the fertility of the new deltaic regions and their gradual settlement through the strenuous efforts of the pioneers and adventurers drew representatives of the higher culture from the western and northwestern parts. Though the western and northern Bengal continued to remain the major seat of the hieratic brahmanical culture, the new delta came inevitably to be subjected to the process of sanskritization with a view to bringing it under the ambit of high Hindu culture. Attempts were made, on one hand, to superimpose Brahmanical social and ritual hierarchies, giving rise to a rather loose *varna* social structure for which Bengal is generally noted; a simultaneous process, on the other, of brahmanical or upper-caste assimilation of local cultures was set on foot. This is clearly evidenced by the development of the cult of the Tiger-god which eventually made its way into the religious domain of the upper caste.[30] A wide range of the medieval Bengali literature, called *mangal-kavya*, glorifying the cults of particular gods and goddesses, evinces clearly the vigour and tenacity with which they fought for recognition from the higher sections of the society.[31]

There was another unique feature of life in the most active part of the new delta. The very nature of the lower delta precluded settled authority in the region which had major attributes of a "frontier society". Its history down to the British period was largely marked by turbulence and rioting linked with the conditions of local geography. The frequent flood waters there destroyed all marks or boundaries between the fields and were indirectly a constant source of social disorder.[32] Taken together, the ferocity of nature and the anarchical conditions in the lower delta, aggravated by the conditions of institutional inadequacies in social and cultural terms, underlined the dire need of some binding foci of authority, stability and assurance in a largely unstable physical and social situaion. It is these specific leadership roles linked with the distinctive needs and demands of this frontier society that were rather successfully appropriated by a number of Muslim adventurers and settlers who earned the admiration and respect of their grateful clienteles in the form of popular canonisation as saints or *pirs*. One of the basic explanations for the Muslim preponderance in the most active parts of deltaic Bengal must be sought in the special circumstances of these regions. The provision for the material and spiritual needs of the areas was a crucial element in the process of Islamic conversion as well as of pirification. A number of shrines and traditions were found in this area, relating to some popular *pirs*, who would seem to have performed such specific deltaic roles.[33]

IV

The indigenous, low-class, rural and mass conversion of the Muslim masses in Bengal, as well as the dominant social rather than religious considerations underlying their conversion, were determinants in the regional formulation of Islam. The main features of Islamic conversion in Bengal seem to correspond closely to the general pattern of conversion movement in the subcontinent. Conversion, in the South Asian context, has been noted as being more meaningful in social terms rather than in spiritual – more in a social sense of "moving out of one community to another" or a "shifting of camps" and less in a spiritual sense of being a change of inner religious consciousness and experience. Conversion here, in other words, scarcely involved an immediate spiritual experience and transformation, and meant "more a change of fellowship than conduct of inner life – although the latter may in time occur." The convert joined a new social group that largely defined its identity on the basis of the limit on intermarriage, inter-dining, and also partly ritual observances.[34]

That the Islamic conversion of the Bengali masses did not result from much "spiritual" considerations is clearly evidenced by the earliest available Bengali Muslim writings which speak of the existence of a large body of Bengal believers who reamained steeped in the pre-existing non-Muslim tradition of the land, as mentioned before. These writers reveal, on one hand, an anxiety to illumine those masses of co-religionists with the essentials of Islamic tradition, and a consensus, on the other, that the root of the lack of mass awareness lay in their inability to follow the works on Islamic tradition in the Arabic and Persian languages. The realization impelled them to take it upon themselves to provide such works in the local Bengali language. The decision involved a bold defiance of the orthodox opposition to reducing the sublime religious truth, enshrined in the noble languages of Arabic and Persian, to a "profane" and "vulgar" local language.

There was much more than a simple religious inhibition involved in this opposition which stemmed basically from a deep social cleavage among Muslims in Bengal. There, as elsewhere in India on a vastly smaller scale, the Muslim population comprised both immigrants and indigenous converts, occupying, respectively, the higher and the lower rungs of the social ladder, and locally popular, respectively, as *asraf* (sing. *sarif*) and *ajlaf* or *atraf* (often its Bengali corruption *atrap*). *Asraf*, meaning "noble" or "persons of high extraction", included, according to the Report of the Bengal Census of 1901, "all undoubted descendants of foreigners and converts from the higher castes of Hindus", and "all other Muhammadans including the functional groups . . . and all converts of lower ranks, are collectively known by the contemptuous term 'Ajlaf', 'wretches' or 'mean people'." [35] The two sections were considered "structurally alien" to each other in Bengal even in modern times.[36]

History, myth, and popular ignorance all contributed to the perpetuation of this ethnic cleavage between *asraf* and *atraf*. Despite its egalitarianism, Islam "strengthened the traditional aristocratic proclivities of the Arabs by providing a new and, to the Muslim, unimpeachable basis for social distinction, the closeness to the prophet in blood and in faith." [37] Beyond the confines of Arabia, Islam brought similar changes in the estimate of what constituted a claim to honour.[38] Bengal was no exception. Among Bengal Muslims, ancestry traceable to the west, to Arabia, Persia, Afghanistan, or Central Asia, broadly extending over the Muslim world of *Arab* and *Ajam*, and sometimes even to northern India, was reckoned as *sarif* ancestry. The west is nearer to Arabia and, therefore, nearer to the Prophet and his religion. In the Muslim society of Bengal, according to a recent survey of some Muslim aristocratic families in then East Pakistan, nobility was

> determined by immigration from the west in direct proportion to the nearness in point of time and distance in point of land of origin from Bengal to [sic] Arabia.[39]

The social importance attached to foreign extraction gave rise to a natural tendency to claim fictitious foreign ancestry by aspirants to social position. This particular form of social mobility was further facilitated by other usual concomitants of nobility such as wealth, land-control, or feudal status.[40]

The social chasm between these two estates was further widened by the massive cultural barrier placed between them. The extra-territorial cultural ethos of the *asraf* was both observed and endorsed by Muslims with *sarif* leanings in Bengal even in the nineteenth and the present centuries,[41] while the same became a target for social satire and lampoon by Muslim Bengali writers.[42] The exaggerated importance attached to alien origin so permeated Bengal Muslim society that Muslims in Bengal fell logical victims to their own myth, claiming for themselves an alien culture, if not origin, and being so regarded by all others. In many parts of Bengal, rural and urban, a Hindu had always enjoyed the prerogative of being regarded a "Bengali", and a Muslim had simply been a "Musalman".

A vital component of the *asraf*'s alien cultural orientation was their contemptuous disregard for and hostility to the local Bengali language in favour of Arabic, Persian, and later, the composite language of Urdu. William Hunter, in 1871, mentioned the Bengali language "which the educated Muhammadans despise."[43] As late as 1927 a Bengali Muslim complained of many co-religionists who were "ashamed and humiliated to recognise Bengali as their mother-tongue" in fear of undermining their prospects for an "aristocratic status".[44]

The pioneering Bengali Muslim writers on Islamic tradition came up against these deep-seated and dominant *asraf* prejudices and values against the regional culture, and left clear traces of tensions arising out of this dichotomous situation. Shah Muhammad Sagir/Sagir fought against his feeling of "sin, fear and shame" associated with his attempt at writing religious books in Bengali.[45] Another prolific *pir*-writer of great standing among his followers and following generations, Saiyid Sultan, who showed great concern for the helpless people "born in Bengal and unable to follow Arabic", found himself "blamed", for having composed his *magnum opus* in Bengali, *Nabi-vamsa*, or the Succession of the Prophets, a history of the creation and of the prophets from Adam to Muhammad. For his critics the attempt amounted to making the book "hinduised".[46] Shaikh Muttalib also fought against his feeling of "sin" for having rendered a book on Muslim religious laws, *fiqh*, into Bengali.[47] Abd un-Nabi/ Abd al-Nabi, who spoke of the "mental anguish of the people, unable to follow the story of Amir Hamza in Persian", was also rather "apprehensive about incurring the wrath of the lord" for having rendered "Islamic matters into Bengali".[48] Shaikh Paran, father of Shaikh Muttalib and a contemporary of Saiyid Sultan, wrote, "on the basis of a Persian work", a compendium on "one hundred and thirty" Islamic mandatory observances, *farz*, "for the people to follow in Bengali".[49] Haji Muhammad also alluded to the contemptuous attitude of some sections of Muslims towards the Bengali language.[50]

The dire consequences following from the deep social and linguistic cleavage in the Bengal Muslim society are clearly evidenced in the early Muslim Bengali literature. It reveals the vital linkage between the denial of access, for the masses of Bengal believers, to the Islamic tradition contained in the Arabic and Persian languages, and the pervasive influence and dominance of the prevailing non-Muslim tradition on their lives. "There is", wrote Saiyid Sultan, "no dearth of *kitabs* in Arabic and Persian" which were "for the learned alone, and not for the ignorant folk." The latter, "unable to grasp a single precept of their religion", remained "immersed in stories and fictions" of local origin. "Hindus and Muslims, in every home" took themselves "with avid interest" to the Hindu epic, the *Mahabharata*, rendered into Bengali by Kavindra-paramesvara in the second quarter of the sixteenth century, and "nobody thought about *Khoda* and *Rasul*." [51] The appeal of the other Hindu epic, *Ramayana*, in the middle of the sixteenth century is also known: the story of Rama was "heard respectfully even by the yavanas [Muslims]", and they were "in tears to hear about the predicament of Sri Raghunandana [Rama] at the loss of Sita [Rama's wife]." [52] The picture of Bengal Muslims, wallowing in "sinful activities" in consequence of unfamiliarity with non-Bengali Islamic religious books, *kitabs*, is clearly depicted in this literature.[53] Writing in the eighteenth century about his own village in North Bengal, where his "forefathers were settled from a long time", one writer expressed his concerns:

It pains me day and night to see that none knows much about religious commandments in my village. They do not grasp the truth of the religion (*din*) and have no knowledge of the Koran, kitabs and other provisions for guidance in all situations. With this daily experience, I have set upon myself to write the message of din in the name of Alla/Allah.[54]

A deep structural and cultural chasm long revealed in the historical development of Bengal underlay, in the ultimate analysis, the *asraf-atraf* dichotomy. Following closely on the line of a sharp social division between a small range of upper castes and a vast multitude of lower castes and outcastes, the cultural order in pre-Islamic Bengal is effectively conceptualised in terms of "great" and "little" traditions. "High" or "sanskritic" Hinduism, alongside the popular Yogic-Tantric *Nath*, *Dharma*, and *Sahajiya* cults, in addition to hosts of other popular objects of veneration and supplication, constituted Bengal's religious complex. The perpetual contact and the fundamental continuity between the great and the little traditions, stemming from the primary and the indigenous nature of the cultures, presented a marked contrast to the nature of Islamic contact with Bengal. The intrusive and exogenous character of orthodox *Sunni* Islam in the cultural milieu of Bengal forced a breach in the cultural continuum of the great and little traditions – a breach that was further widened by the *asraf*'s social and cultural exclusiveness, reinforced by the linguistic apartheid. The total absence of culture contact and communication between those two major segments of the Muslim community contained the potential for a very serious structural threat to Islam and the Muslim dominance. The danger inherent in the situation found clear expression much later in the writing of a *sarif*:

> The refusal or inability of the higher Mosalmans to adopt the Bengali has already affected the relation between them and the lower Mosalmans. We do not learn the Bengali – whilst our lower orders cannot learn the Persian . . . . There are thus no means of fellow-feeling or of acting together.[55]

The break of cultural continuity between the great and little, or between the elite and the folk traditions of Islam in Bengal called for urgent action and mediation. Robert Redfield identified the distinct role of "the cultural specialists devoted to mediating between Great Tradition and Little." [56] Milton Singer, in his analysis of the structure of Hindu tradition, underscored the role of leaders who, "by their identification with the great tradition and with the masses", were in a position to "mediate the one to the other." [57] The sixteenth and seventeenth centuries in Bengal saw the emergence of a number of Muslim "cultural mediators" engaged, consciously or unconsciously, in the great task of mediating Islam to the masses of its Bengali believers. To these mediators Bengali Muslims owed not only their earliest literature in Bengali but a very rich legacy of highly creative and varied syncretistic tradition as well.

Undoubtedly, the mediators comprised a proportion of Muslims of non-Bengali or non-Indian lineage as well as of diverse social and economic persuasions such as religious guides (*pirs*), middle-ranking or minor office holders - both secular or religious – and others. They were, perhaps, set apart from the typical *asraf* society by their lower economic standing, by their shared concern for the souls of their less comfortable classes of co-religionists, by their common diagnosis of the source of the malaise in terms of both religious and linguistic polarisation, and finally, by their courageous attempt to force a break with the

dominant alien cultural orientation of the *asraf* orthodoxy by having chosen to
adopt the indigenous Bengali language as the cultural vehicle for the majority of
the local Muslims.[58] Many of these mediators, especially the *pir*-writers among
them, brought a sense of pious religious obligation to bear upon their task. Saiyid Sultan addressed himself to the Bengali Muslim folk in a somewhat grandi-
ose style:

> Muslims of Bengal, listen to me. May you all be engaged in pious deeds to
> please the Lord. . . . The learned who live in the land but do not expound the
> truth for you are destined to be castigated to hell. Should people commit
> sins, the learned will be taken to task in the presence of Alla/Allah. I am born
> in the midst of you and so I must talk to you about religious matters. Alla
> shall accuse: 'all you learned ones, there, did not stop people from
> commiting sins.'. . . When God calls for you about your good and bad deeds,
> you may very well plead before Him that you resorted to the guru who failed
> to warn you. God shall chastise me much more than you. I am ever haunted
> by this fear, and driven by this; I composed Nabi-vamsa to take people away
> from sin.[59]

The transcendental and moral urges notwithstanding, the situation involved, as already noted, a danger more immediate and mundane than an appre-
hended indictment on the day of judgment. Popular religious leaders like Saiyid
Sultan, having direct concern with and knowledge of the Muslim masses in their
capacity as *pirs*, could not but become increasingly anxious about the situation,
and try to prevent their community (*umma*) from falling apart. Besides, there is
evidence that the pressure often built up from below, and subsequent development was a mere recognition of the same. We have it on the authority of Shaikh
Muttalib that he wrote his colossal work on Muslim canonical law in Bengali at
the instance of Maulawi Rahamatullah/Rahamat-Allah who, earlier on, was ap-
proached, at the end of a congregational prayer, by the assembly to have such a
manual written in that language in order that they could "perform duties according to scriptures."[60]

It required formidable moral courage on the part of this mediator-*literati* to
defy this crushing weight of power and orthodoxy. Only a few among them
could shake it off completely, while most of them were apologetic for their deviation or sought to rationalise it. Shah Muhammad Sagir needed to take a "firm
resolution" against the feelings of "sin, fear and shame" relating to his task, as
mentioned above. He found Muslims "afraid" of writing religious books (*kitab*)
in Bengali and also apprehensive about being "blamed" for it. He reassured himself: "I have thought about this subject and have come to realise that such fears
are false. If what is written is true, it does not matter what language it is written
in."[61] Shaikh Muttalib failed to achieve the same degree of conviction:

I am sure that I have committed a great sin in that I have written the Muslim scriptures in Bengali. But this I am sure of in my heart that the faithful will understand me and bless me. The blessings of the faithful shall involve great virtue, and merciful *Alla* will forgive my sin.[62]

A similar lack of conviction resulting from a sense of conflict was revealed also in Haji Muhammad:

Do not do anything that is forbidden . . . . I am not entitled to write in the Hindu script but made an effort to impart some knowledge to the people. . . . Do not ignore it because of its Hindu script. Why should you ignore the precious matters revealed in Bengali letters? These matters have been expounded by *pirs* and here is a fragment of that knowledge for people to seek at any cost at any time. Do not feel sick to see it in Bengali language.[63]

Abd un-Nabi moved a little further:

I am afraid in my heart that God may be angry with me for writing Muslim scriptures in Bengali. But I reject the fear and firmly resolve to write in order to do good to the common people.[64]

Saiyid Sultan took a firm stand based both on reason and the scripture. He said that the language that God gave to one was one's "precious gem", and added:

I know from *Alla* that He wills to reveal the truth in the particular language of a land. The prophet speaks one language and the people another. How are we to follow the dialogue, then?[65]

But the most resolute defence of the Bengali language came from Shah Abdul/ Abd al-/Hakim:

Whatever language a people speak in a country, God understands that language. God understands all languages, whether the language of Hindus or the vernacular language of Bengal or any other. . . . Those who, being born in Bengal, are averse to the Bengali language [*Bangabani*] cast doubt on their birth. The people, who have no liking for the language and the learning of their country, had better leave it and live abroad. For generations our ancestors have lived in Bengal, and instruction in our native language is, therefore, considered good.[66]

The flood-gates of Muslim Bengali literature were thrown open by these new

Muslim cultural mediators, and through them poured waves of literary works of religious import to fertilise the minds of Bengali Muslims for the following centuries. Bengali forced its recognition as the local vehicle, while Arabic and Persian continued to draw the traditional respect associated with Islamic religion and culture. One of the greatest Muslim champions of the Bengali language, Abdul Hakim left no doubt about the place of Arabic and Persian in the Muslim world:

> Arabic learning is the best of all. If you cannot learn Arabic, learn Persian to become aware of what is good in the end. Should you find yourself unable to master Persian, you must study the scriptures in your own language.[67]

The language alone was not capable, however, of bringing the alien religion closer to the masses. If the medium of cultural communication was to be intelligible to the people, its idioms, symbols, imageries and nuances should be no less so. Islam, in its austere doctrinal forms, came to consist in the minds of the Bengali masses of certain essential beliefs and observances, with little or no emotional content. These could scarcely satisfy the manifold popular demands on a religion, especially in a land where history and fiction, myth and legend, faith and superstition, supernatural and real, spirit and matter were all intermingled and interchangeable. The problem, then, was not merely confined to making available to the masses, manuals for formal religious observances in their own language. They needed more from their religion: they needed a religion that could become the central focus of their *weltanschauung*. The religious perceptions at this social and cultural level were dominated by an instinctive search for divinity, godliness or religiosity in the supernatural and the fantastic. The greatness, for them, was not in what remained, like themselves, subjected to the processes and laws of nature. The truth of their religion was to be vindicated, not so much through its dogmas or doctrines as through the ability of its heroes and heroines to rise to superhuman and supernatural heights. They longed to hear about the glorious and miraculous exploits of the champions of their religion. They knew next to nothing about their new idols, who remained prisoners in the "ivory tower" of Arabic and Persian literatures, whereas the entire cultural atmosphere of Bengal was saturated with the highly popular traditions of the *Mahabharata*, the *Ramayana*, Nathism, and the *mangal-kavyas*, centring round the exploits of Manasa, Chandi, Dharma, Siva and so on. The masses of Muslim converts could not live in a cultural void, and they held on to what was already there for them – the inexhaustible source of traditional Bengali ballads and folklore, and religious and mythological traditions of diverse kinds. Hence the mediators' task demanded much more than Bengali renderings of Perso-Arabic works. This would have been a comparatively easy and a fairly mechanical undertaking. The more daunting task, which lay ahead of them, was to make their religious traditions available to the Bengal Muslim masses in terms familiar and intelligible to them. This meant breaking sharply with the uncompromising and non-adaptive conservative approach, and bringing Islam into line with the regional cultural tradition of the people.

Although presented as mere works of translation, it does not take more than a casual glance to recognise how deeply these are permeated by indigenous elements. Works primarily of a liturgical and didactic nature did not naturally provide much scope for re-creation. Such works dealt with matters like prayers (*namaz*), ablutions (*wadu'*), the ceremonial bath (*ghusal*), fasting (*roza*) in the month of Ramadan, purification by sand (*tayammum*), funerals (*janajah*), and so on. These conformed closely to standard Islamic prescriptions of the *Hanafi* school of law, very widely followed by the *Sunni* majority in the Indian subcontinent.[68] All other categories of the mediators' writings were strikingly syncretistic in both form and content, thoroughly permeated by indigenous religious and cultural notions, values and even practices. The whole gamut of this literature bearing on the Islamic syncretistic tradition reveals various facets. For the purposes of this paper we shall use two vital as well as popular areas of this literature as illustrative material, namely, historical-mythical and mystical-esoteric writings.

V

Judged by the volume and wide popularity of the historical-mythical literature, the Bengal Muslim *literati* as cultural mediators and as authors of the syncretistic tradition seemed to have been most attracted to this area of popular interest. An internal examination of this particular strand of their literary contributions clearly reveals its close correspondence in both form and spirit to the traditional long and continuous narrative poems in Bengali known variously as *mangal-kavya*, *vijay*-kavya, *panchalika* or simply *panchali*. Of the two general forms – the lyrical and the narrative – found with the old and middle Bengali literature, the Muslim writers adopted both. To them are attributed the short lyrical *pada*-compositions of esoteric-mystic import as well as the long narrative poems with historical, mythical, and romantic content. Bengali narrative poems were composed either in short couplets (*payar*) or long couplets with two caesura (*tripadi*). The *payar* compositions were musically recited by the principal singer, called *bayati* or *mul-gayen* in the eastern Bengal. The songs in *tripadi* and also in *payar*, known as *nachari* or dance-style, were sung by the principal singer, supported by the associated singers, known as *dohar* or *pali* or *pal-dohar*.[69]

Of the three variants of the Bengali narrative poems – the religious, historical and the romantic – the grand religious narrative poems received far greater attention than the other two which are known to have been introduced in Bengali by the Muslim writers. The Muslim narrative historical-mythical writings were, however, prompted by the same religious impulse as what underlay the Hindu *mangal-kavyas*, celebrating and vindicating the popular deities. The Muslim narrative writer sought to transmit to the Bengali Muslim masses the cultural heritage of Islam, woven around the activities of Islamic historical, legendary and mythical heroes and heroines. His object seemed to wean Muslim away from *mangal*-literature by creating for them in Bengali an Islamic substitute based on Muslim history and myth. In effect the Muslim idols were either substituted for *mangal*-deities, or found their rightful place in the familiar world of the *mangal*-pantheon. This led to literary ventures, centred around the prophet, his descendants and followers, mostly in imaginary terms designed to cater to the popular demand for the supernatural, miraculous and fantastic. The lives of Muhammad, his daughter Fatima, his grandsons Hasan and Husain, and his followers were embroidered lavishly with fictitious adventures and exploits to reduce them to some replicas of their *mangal* counterparts. Saiyid Sultan's monumental work, *Nabi-vamsa*, containing a biographical account of the prophets from Adam to Muhammad, was perhaps intended as a national religious epic for the Bengali Muslims in which history and myth freely coalesced. Muhammad Khan, one of Saiyid Sultan's disciples, carried the work of his master forward by bringing down the story to the tragedy of Karbala, in which the prophet's grandson, Husain, lost his life. There was also outright recourse to legendary and mythical heroes. A semi-historical person named Hanifa, believed to be a son of Ali, the prophet's son-in-law, became the centre of many heroic and supernatural exploits which attained great popularity in Bengal.[70] Amir Hamza, an uncle of Muhammad, emerged as another popular hero whose imaginary military exploits provided much religious-cultural nourishment to those believers.[71]

If the Muslim writers of narrative poems cherished the ulterior objective of reconstructing a distinctive religious-cultural tradition for Bengali Muslims, they were able to advance their cause further by their pioneering contribution, as mentioned above, to romantic narratives in Bengali based on Perso-Arabic and even Indian materials. The romantic narrative poems on popular Perso-Arabic themes like Yusuf-Zulaikha, Laila-Majnun, Saif al-Muluk -Badi al-Jamal, Lal-mati-Saif al-Muluk, Gul-i Bakawali, Zeb al-Muluk-Samarokh, and also on Indian themes such as Padmavati, Vidya-Sundar, Sati Mayna-Lor-Chandrani, and Manohar-Madhumalati remained as popular in the Middle Bengali period as later in the nineteenth and twentieth centuries, when they were turned out on a large scale by the cheap Bengali press of *Bat-tala*.[72]

A detailed analysis of this particular type of the mediators' writings reveals conscious and subtle attempts on their part to present Islamic tradition in terms meaningful to the world of the Bengali believers. An interesting part of the endeavour was to reduce the Islamic struggle against infidelity in general to that against Hinduism. Prophet Muhammad's mission in Arabia was presented as an anti-Hindu call. His antagonistic uncle, Abu Jehal/Jahl, appeared as "the chief of the Hindus" and addressed his God as "Brahma", "Visnu" and "Niranjan".[73]

The attempt to bring the characters of Muslim tradition closer to the relig-ious-cultural milieu of Bengal also took the form of searching for parallels in the Hindu puranic and epic traditions. The simplest device for making the figures of Muslim tradition known to the local people was to introduce them along with their Hindu parallels. The motive underlying this attempt was often to vindicate the Muslim idol, drawn within a comparative framework. But the dominant ob-jective seemed to make both Muslim and Hindu characters appear natural in the context of the regional religious-cultural tradition.[74] The most significant part of the attempt to reduce the polarity between the indigenous and exogenous tradi-tions relates to the anxiety of the mediators to bring the prophet himself into line with the comparable symbols of Hindu tradition. A striking attempt was made to identify the Islamic concepts of *nabi*, a receiver of the divine message, and *rasul*, who received from God a book in addition to the message, with the concept of *avatara*, an incarnation of God himself. The Qur'anic recognition of *nabi* being born in different lands in different times provided a semblance of identity be-tween the Islamic and Hindu concepts. They, however, compromised a great deal to reconcile the two. And yet, there was no attempt to impose the total meaning of the one onto the other. They sought to achieve their goal by inter-changing the contents of the concepts of *nabi* and *avatara*. While, on one hand, God was represented as creating Muhammad out of "his own self",[75] the Hindu *Avatara* Krisna, on the other, was boldly depicted as God's messenger. The iden-tification of *nabi* and *avatara* was further designed to incorporate some of the popular Hindu incarnations of God, such as Krisna and Rama, among the proph-ets who preceded Muhammad. Innovations of this nature could not but pose seri-ous theological problems for a Muslim mediator, such as the iconic character of the Hindu *avatara* and the love-dalliances of Krisna extolled in the *Vaisnava* tra-dition. The mediator sought to resolve these problems by a creative reconstruc-tion of the Hindu myths or even creation of new myths. Saiyid Sultan's rather ingenious treatment of the Krisna-myth provides a fine example of an Islamic syncretistic myth-making.[76] The intended effect of identifying the two concepts was further heightened by the presentation of Muhammad within the chrono-logical framework of Hindu mythology. The Hindu concept of the four ages (*yuga*) found ready acceptance among these Muslim writers, and the Arab prophet of Islam emerged in Bengal as "the *kali-avatara*" or "the *avatara* of the *kali-* age" to redeem the fallen people.[77]

Finally, the process of acculturation of Muslim tradition was further aug-mented by the mediators' attempts to set the character, situations and stories in the natural geographical, social and cultural milieus of the land. The entire at-mosphere of these narrative works was saturated with local fragrance. The local landscape, flora and fauna, food and dresses, music and amusements, customs and values – all conjured up the image of Bengal and imparted an air of congruity, reality and familiarity to their stories. The West Asian landscapes of these stories were modelled on the natural phenomena typical of the Bengali scene. The food was no more alien to the local tastes. The cosmetics and dresses of the alien characters in these stories were identical with those locally known. The locally familiar social etiquettes were freely attributed to the alien Muslims of these stories. The social ceremonies like marriage were often cast in the local mould. The similes, metaphors, idioms, imageries and motifs used in these writings were also characteristically familiar in the Bengali literary tradition.[78]

VI

Matters of mystical-esoteric import expounded largely by the *pir*-mediators revealed another major and significant facet of Islamic syncretistic development in Bengal. As observed in the foregoing analysis of the historical-mythical ideas and beliefs, the mystical concerns of these writers offered a total impression of accord and identification with their corresponding non-Muslim local tradition. A critical evaluation of the local impact on the mystical ideas and practices revealed in this literature is rendered a little difficult by the fact that, on one hand, all mystical approaches share some things in common, and, on the other, the issue of communication and interaction between the Indian and Islamic mystic systems is not beyond dispute.[79] A student of Bengali Muslim mystical thought is, however, in an envious position of not being needed to be forced into these controversial areas. The Islamic and the indigenous elements in these writings remain very clearly distinguishable and self-evident. There is very little scope for any confusion and disputation concerning the sources of the two sets of mystical concepts and practices, as clearly revealed in this literature, one classical Islamic and the other Yogic-Tantric. One does not, for instance, expect serious confusion between the established Sufic concepts of *manzil* (stage) and *maqam* (station), on one hand, and the Yogic-Tantric concepts of *chakra* (nerve-plexus), *nadi* (nerve), *asan* (posture), and *mudra* (gesture), on the other. The mystical thoughts of the Bengali mediators were indeed largely presented in such clearly identifiable forms. We are able to discern two broad facets of their attempts in this area: (1) Local dilution: introduction of classical sufic ideas often considerably diluted with indigenous matters (2) Direct appropriation: a direct, outright and total absorption of locally popular mystical formulae, symbols and techniques of Yogic-Tantric origin. The writings cover both speculative aspects of the mystical discipline as well as its rather elaborate practices and techniques.

It is characteristic of the Muslim Bengali mystical writings that the classical Islamic terminologies for mysticism (*Tasawwuf*) and mystics (*Sufi*) found no single mention. *Darwesi, Faqiri,* and *Tariqat/Tariqa* were terms most commonly used by these writers. Of greater significance is the free and extensive use of the indigenous terminological equivalents not only to designate the mystical path but also to underscore its supreme importance and superiority to the exoteric or scriptural approach (*Shari'a*). The term frequently used to refer to esoterism is *Agama*, a Hindu Tantric name for the secret truth. The terms *Yoga-pantha* (the Yogic way), *Siddhi-pantha* (the path leading to the attainment of the Yogic goal), and *Ulta-* or *Bimukh-pantha* were also used. Both *ulta* and *bimukh*, meaning "reverse", have reference to the "regressive culture" advocated by the popular Yogic-Tantric cults in Bengal. *Shari'a*, representing the exoterical and formal aspects of islam, was identified with the Hindu *sastra* or scripture, and the *Qur'an* and the Hindu *puranas* were cited as example of this.

The *Qur'an*, *puranas* and *sastras* were considered incapable of leading a mystic practitioner to the truth of *Yoga*, which was called "the command of God". One could "memorise the whole of the *sastras*, read the *Koran* for a hundred years", and yet could "not hope to match the true *Faqir*'s piety and purity." Even "the doyen among the learned and scholars (*pandits*) " was no more than "a servant of a Faqir." The mystical truth was kept hidden because of its "supreme merit" and also for the complexities involved in understanding the nature of "the regressive way" which demanded a realization of the essential identity and inter-changeability of what appeared as exact opposites to each other such as "right and wrong, sadness and happiness, front and rear, high and low, fire and water, . . . Man as God and God as Man."[80]

Despite the strong emphasis placed on the esoteric truth, the importance of formal knowledge (*ilm*), revelation, adherence to *Shari'a* , and the essential in-terdependence between *Shari'a* and *tariqa* were clearly noted. *Shari'a* lay "at the very root" and is "essential to the realisation of the Agamic truth." True *Faqiri* was "not divorced from the prophet's rules of conduct". An uninitiated Muslim who was "unable to distinguish between the right and the wrong, and between the sanctions (*halal*) and prohibitions (*haram*)" was in no position to "recognise God" and doomed to a "spiritually barren life". Knowledge was "either open (*za-hir*) or hidden (*batin*)." The former was compared to milk and the latter to butter produced from it. The essential oneness (*wahadat*) of being found an effective expression:

The fruit grows from the tree,
And the tree again from the fruit. . . .
The egg comes from the bird,
And the bird again from the egg.
All is one' – is the essence of truth. . . .
Sari'at and *Ma'rifat* are essentially one.[81]

A highly exalted and venerable status, often purported to be of divine nature, attributed to the mystic guide is another major facet of this mystical literature. The mystic preceptor and initiator, called *pir*, *mursid*, *shaikh*, *sah* or *saha*, was more frequently introduced in his local name, *guru* . The preceptor-disciple relationship, popular as *pir-muridi* in Islam, found its Indian parallel in the widely prevalent institution of *guru-sisya* or *guru-chela* relationship. It was not the name *guru* but the content of the change that seemed of greater significance. The Sufic attitude towards the mystic guide, even in its most liberal expression, was limited to the viewing and use of the guide as a medium of contemplation by the practitioner, intended to bring about a total identification and merger of the disciple's individual ego and self-consciousness into that of the mentor as an essential step towards the ultimate mystic communion with the deity. In Sufic parlance, the pursuit of the mystic object in the first stage was called *rabita* and that in the second was *muraqiba*, while the attainment of the first was known as *fana fi-shaikh* and the second was *fana fi-Allah*. A *guru* in Hinduism, on the other hand, was a divine incarnation and hence worshipped. The Bengal Muslims' adoration of the *pir*, as reflected in this literature, was unqualified and boundless, and provided a strong parallel with the local non-Muslims' resort to the *guru*. Prophet Muhammad was presented as the final repository of the esoterical truth, and his son-in-law, Ali as receiving secret instruction from him as an example of the perfect disciple. It may be more than of passing interest to note that the Hindu god Siva is regarded in the Hindu esoteric tradition as the primal source of the secret truth of *Agama*, and his consort, Parvati as its first recipient.[82]

As with speculative mysticism, so with mystical techniques, classical Sufic notions found their place alongside syncretistic notions, based either on local dilution of exogenous materials or direct absorption and assimilation of indigenous matters primarily of Yogic-Tantric origin, as mentioned above. The wide popularity of the Yogic-Tantric mystical ideas and practices among the Bengal Muslims is evidenced not only by the literature under study but also by two other Muslim compositions, in which the respective authors resorted directly to Hindu religious tradition influenced by the Yogic-Tantric disciplines. One is Shaikh Faizullah's/ Faiz-Allah's *Goraksa-vijay* [83] which is a direct contribution to the Nath tradition. The other is Shaikh Chand's *Hara-Gauri Samvad* [84] which makes a thorough exposition of the Yogic-Tantric ideas, adopting the Tantric and Nathist motif of revelation of the esoteric truth by Hara or Siva to his consort Gauri or Parvati.

It is rather difficult to identify the channel through which these ideas influenced the minds of these Muslim writers. Medieval Bengal witnessed the emergence and nourishment of various cults and sects such as the *Bauddha-sahajiyas*, the *Nath-panthis*, the *Vaisnava-sahajiyas*, and the *Bauls*, who were influenced by the Yogic and Tantric ideas. Naturally enough, there was much that these cults held in common, for example, the supreme importance attached to the mystic initiator (*guru*), the importance of the human body as the microcosm of the universe (*dehatattva*), and the resultant psycho-physiological culture (*kaya-sadhana*). And yet it appears that the Yogic-Tantric ideas of the Muslim writers were largely derived through the Nathist channel, as evidenced by a large stock of Nathist terminologies in their writings. We have also noted above that one of the earliest and the most popular works on the *Nath* tradition was written by a Muslim, Shaikh Faizullah. In addition, the Nathist emphasis on the Yogic psycho-physiological exercises, in contrast with the *Sahajiya* preoccupation with Tantric sexual symbols and techniques, drew Bengali Muslims generally closer to Nathism than to other esoterical disciplines in Bengal.

The Nathist literature in Bengali was the most powerful agent for the popularity of the *Hatha-yogic* ideas in the region. While other forms of *Yoga* are rather philosophical, the primary emphasis of *Hatha-yoga* is on the psycho-physiological culture, conducive to immortality, initially in a perfect body (*siddha-deha*) and finally in a divine body (*divya-deha*). The Yogic texts contain the promise and prescription for a state of perfect (*siddha*) body, free from disease, decay, and death, the attainment of which is called *siddhi* or immortality, and forms the supreme object of Yogic exercises. In the realization of the supreme Yogic goal, a perfect control over the mental processes is considered an indispensable pre-condition. From this particular need follows a host of patent Yogic psycho-physiological exercises, relating, on one hand, to control of nerves (*nadis*), nerve-plexuses(*chakras*), ducts, sinews, and muscles, and on the other, to retention of *semen virile* (*virya*) with the help of respiratory techniques (*pranayama*), physical postures (*asana*), gestures (*mudra*), and other Yogic-Tantric practices.

Dominating the entire background of the esoteric disciplines in medieval Bengal was, therefore, the idea of the supreme importance of the human body exalted as a microcosm, and the consequent emphasis on the psycho-physiological culture. An all-embracing and elaborate structure of homologies – cosmic, theological, natural and physical – was effectively used to illustrate the subtle truth of the mystic physiology. The mystical ideas in particular reference to the techniques and practices of the discipline, as found in the Muslim mediators' writings, show the strong influence of many of these ideas and practices of indigenous bio-mental culture. The *pir*-mediators located in the body the sun, the moon, the stars, earth, heaven, nether region, air, fire, twelve houses of the zodiac, seven days, rivers such as the Ganga, the Bhagirathi and the Sindhu/Indus and also those of Hindu and Muslim traditions.[85] Four traditional Hindu ages, and the four *Vedas* were identified in the human body, along with the four revealed books and the four Sufic stations (*maqam*).[86] In Adam's body, seen as a microcosmos, was located four parts of the "moon" (*chari-chandra*) – a Nathist concept.[87]

The Yogic-Tantric concepts and formulae of mystic-physiology with esoteric significance attached to nerve-plexuses, veins, limbs, breath-control, and retention of *semen virile* found great favour with the Muslim cultural mediators. The "piercing" or "penetration" (*bheda*) of the six nerve-plexuses (*chakras*), known as *sat-chakra-bhed,* was the central concept in all Yogic-Tantric systems. One of the writers chose a rather suggestive title for his mystical work, *Chari-maqam-bhed* ("The Piercing of Four Mystical Stages"), and called the entire mystical process *Yoga.* There were frequent references to the "sun" and the "moon", and to *pingala, ingila* and *ida* in the Yogic-Tantric mystical sense of the two important nerves respectively on the right and the left in the body.[88] The union of these two, meaning the union of the two currents of the vital wind, called *prana* (inhalation) and *apana* (exhalation), was considered a Yogic ideal. The important Yogic practices of retention of inhaled air (*kumbhaka*),[89] the well-known Nathist practice of "stealing the ambrosia" (*ksechari-mudra*),[90] the role of *khema* or *khemai* in the Nathist system as the vigilant sentinel of the body against all illusions and temptations, and finally, various physical postures (*asana*) and gestures (*mudra*),[91] popular among Yogic-Tantric groups – all found their way in the mediating efforts of the Bengali *pir*-writers.

VII

A large corpus of lyrical compositions of the *Vaisnava pada* (short song) style is another dimension of the mystic strand of the Islamic syncretistic tradition in Bengal. Unlike the mainstream Muslim mystic literature in Bengali discussed above, the nature of these lyrical compositions has given rise to serious controversy. The Hindu commentators on this particular literature had, generally speaking, not only regarded these compositions as direct Muslim contributions to the *Vaisnava* tradition but also taken their authors as *Vaisnavas* themselves.[92] Undeniably, the entire atmosphere of this literature is saturated with characters, places, objects, images, symbols and nuances, characteristic of the tradition of Vaisnavism and of *Vaisnava* lyrical literature. Nevertheless, any facile assumption of the *Vaisnava* identity of either this literature or their authors is totally unwarranted for several reasons. First, a significant proportion of the Muslim *pada* writers seems to have used *Vaisnava* symbolism to express their own mystical urges and concerns. Secondly, one is not entitled to establish a necessary correlation between these writers' literary pursuits and personal faiths. Some of the greatest Hindu *pada* writers themselves, like Vidyapati and Badu Chandidas, were not followers of the *Vaisnava* faith. Thirdly, certain Muslim Bengali writers chose to write on other Hindu traditions without becoming converts to the particular faiths. Finally, some Muslim writers, chose more than one Hindu tradition as literary themes. Shaikh Faizullah wrote on both Vaisnavism and Nathism.

The Muslim commentators on this literature, on the other hand, are content to attach nothing more than allegorical and symbolic meanings to its *Vaisnava* expressions. Enamul Haq does not only regard the Muslim *padas* essentially Sufic in spirit; he also makes a rather sweeping and uncritical assertion that the entire Bengali literature on Bengal Vaisnavism is "fully impregnated with the spirit of the *Sufi* literature" under "a Hinduistic veneer."[93]

None of the two extreme views – the *Vaisnava* and the Sufic – on the nature of the Muslim *padas* are, therefore, adequate and tenable. Y.M. Bhattacharya sought to resolve the problem with the help of a six-fold categorisation of this literature. His categories, also adopted by E.C. Dimock, Jr., lack clear definition and seem considerably overlapping.[94] Consequently, a particular *pada*, taken by Bhattacharya and Dimock for an example of "pure *vaisnava* poetry" of their first category has been used by Haq as a fine specimen of Sufic mysticism using *Vaisnava* symbolism.[95]

The universality of the mystical urges and the eclectic and syncretistic ethos of the mediator-writers often made it hazardous to determine the nature of these lyrical compositions. One cannot, however, ignore the obvious truth of their Muslim authorship. Without positive evidence to the contrary, it is unreasonable to question the truth of their mystic concerns as Muslims, expressed through *Vaisnava* symbolism. A careful analysis often reveals the Islamic allegiance of their authors.[96] The Sufic or the *Vaisnava* allegiance and inspiration of the authors are often betrayed by their attitudes to the deity as the beloved. Theologically, Bengal Vaisnavism recognises a measure of duality between God as Krisna and the individual (*jiva*). The relation between the two is identity as well as difference, which is metaphysically described as incomprehensible (*achintya*) and dualism in non-dualism (*advaita-dvaita-bhava*). The theological concept of dualism, however, prevails, and all poetical and metaphorical descriptions of love seem to be based on this theological speculation.[97] The Sufic concept of love in its popular *Wujudi* form in Bengal, on the other hand, practically assumes an ontological monistic position in the doctrine of annihilation of self in God (*fana fi-Allah*).[98] This subtle difference in the theological formulation of love in Bengal Vaisnavism and Sufism is related to two different types of Bengali *pada* writings. With the former, man (*jiva*) has no part to play in the eternal and cosmic love-process (*prema-lila*) between Krisna and his cosmic partner of feminine energy in the form of Radha. *Jiva* has no more to do in this than remain a spectator, enjoy its bliss, and proclaim (*kirtana*) this *lila* in words and music. The *Vaisnava* lyrics of Bengal are, therefore, conspicuous by the absence of a human longing for union with Krisna. The Sufic lyrics, on the other hand, relatively unrestricted by any theological demands, discovered in Radha's longing for Krisna, a channel in which to direct the poets' personal feelings, longings and emotions. Their writings, hence, tended to become allegorical and assumed symbolic character. An effective mode of differentiating between the *Vaisnava* and the Sufic spirit in the *pada* literature is provided in the colophon. On strict theological grounds the Vaisnava poet is unable to identify himself with or participate in the cosmic love process of Krisna and Radha, and so his colophon assumes a distinction betwen the object in the divine love and the humbler observer in the poet. The Sufic leanings, on the other hand, are expressed in the poet's unmistakable effort, in the colophon, to substitute himself for Radha, longing for Krisna. This differential attitudes to the deity, in practice, cut across the religious affiliations of the lyricists. Not an insignificant number of compositions adopting the *Vaisnava* mode of expression of love can be attributed to some Muslim lyricists, just as there are many *padas* of Hindu authorship composed in the monistic spirit of the *Wujudi* variant of the Sufic mysticism. This distinction may help to explain the prevailing confusions relating to the attempts either to seek *Vaisnava* affiliation of the whole body of Muslim *pada*-composers or to read merely allegorical and symbolic meanings in the whole range of Muslim *pada* literature.[99]

Even with poems with undoubted Sufic affiliation and using *Vaisnava* symbolism, what strikes as significant is that the Muslim mystical poets adopted the locally popular Radha-Krisna motif of the Bengal *Vaisnava* tradition. Unlike the Muslim mystic poets elsewhere in India and outside, their Bengali counterparts were marked by their indifference to the popular Islamic motifs such as Yusuf-Zulaikha, Laila-Majnun, Sirin-Farhad, Saif al-Muluk-Badi al-Jamal, Gul-i Bak-awali, Haft-Paikar, and so on. Bengali Muslim writers no doubt made use of almost all of those themes, as noted before, but with a crucial difference. They stripped these stories of their mystical content and presented them in the form of secular romantic narrative poems – a literary genre which Bengali Muslims had the distinction of introducing into the corpus of Bengali literature.[100]

VIII

A study in the historical process of Islamisation in pre-modern Bengal raises, directly or indirectly, a number of significant issues concerning the specificity of regional formulations of Islam, but more importantly, it confronts us with a seminal concern about our approach and perception of such developments within the larger frame of Islamic History.

One would have expected that the macro and normative approach of the traditional Islamists, looking to find, as though, "Arabs in the diaspora" in Islamic developments throughout the world, have been largely discredited and discarded as the result of considerable advance made in the past decades on greater and deeper understanding of the process of Islamisation in divergent geo-cultural and social settings. But vestiges of such attitudes and expectations survive in both academic and non-academic perceptions, as indicated at the beginning of this essay. In his review of my book on the Islamic syncretistic tradition in Bengal, Ali Asani of the Harvard University focuses on the same issue:

Most studies of Islam in the Indian subcontinent concern themselves largely with those aspects of classical Islamic civilisation in the area which are also found in the rest of the Islamic world. Consequently, the rich diversity of rituals, beliefs and literary genres belonging to the so-called 'popular' tradition and hence specific and unique to the Indo-Pakistan are either ignored or dismissed as 'aberrations' and 'corruptions' of a 'pure' Islam, unworthy of scholarly interest. This attitude towards popular and regional forms of Islam is unfortunate for frequently these forms, by revealing the adaptations made by the Islamic tradition to diverse cultural milieus, hold the keys to furthering our understanding of the process of Islamisation.[101]

The *aprioric* normative approach is riddled with problems and open to manifold objections, as pointed out at the outset. It is methodologically inadequate and inappropriate to the extent that it is both unable and unwilling to explore the distinctiveness of the Islamic response in a variety of social-cultural environments. It is academically deficient, on one hand, in not seeking to discover the particular meanings of an adopted religion in the existential social and cultural world of the converts. On the other, it seems a much less academic concern than religious to attempt to determine the quality of one's faith, devotion and piety in terms of one's approximation to the "normative definition" of a "true" religion.

The interaction between an intrusive religion and the social and cultural mores of the groups of believers is, by its very nature, a rather complex and creative process. This is more so in the case of Bengal, where Islam penetrated culturally a strikingly rich land and with entrenched traditions, and hence lacked both the initial advantages of being a "primary" or indigenous and a "single" or the only great tradition. Besides, consistent with the general pattern of religious conversion in South Asia, the Islamic conversion was a group "social" experience rather than "spiritual" or even "cultural", essentially embodying a change in commensal and connubial relationship – a mere change in "social camp". In the particular circumstances of Bengal, it meant drawing mass converts from the vast majority of rural and socially depressed elements of the population. The intrusive and alien ethos of Islam, perpetuated by the social and cultural exclusiveness of the dominant *asraf*, broke, naturally, the cultural continuity between the indigenous great and little traditions of the converts, but remained both indifferent and unable to build the new bridge and provide necessary cultural sustenance to the masses of converts. The potential crisis inherent in the situation set the stage for the emergence of the Bengali Muslim *literati* as cultural mediators and bridge builders. They pulled down the language barricade to create a rich Islamic tradition for Bengali Muslims in syncretistic and hence more locally meaningful terms. This proved not only necessary for the cultural sustenance of the Muslim masses but also vital for the maintenance of their Muslim identity.

This raises some important questions relating to the nature and role of the Islamic syncretistic tradition *vis-a-vis* the issue and the process of Islamisation.

For reasons discussed above, it is not difficult to see why religious developments of the syncretistic nature within a religion generally meet the opposition and condemnation of the "purists". Viewed in its historical context, as expounded in this paper, Islamic syncretism in Bengal appears, on the contrary, a necessary and crucial stage in the process of Islamisation in the region. Until the fundamentalists' and revivalists' challenge in the nineteenth century the syncretistic tradition, which maintained its considerable popularity uninterrupted for several centuries, performed a significant historical function in the dissemination of Islam, in catering for the particular needs and demands of Bengali Muslims, and most importantly, ensuring thereby the survival of the large community by having held their continued allegiance to Islam. Syncretism, therefore, remained as integral to the process of Islamisation in Bengal as the subsequent fundamentalist, revivalist, and reformist contributions.

Viewed historically, the Islamic identity of the Bengali converts acquired changing attributes in time, and may be seen to have developed in three broad stages. In its earliest stage, Islamisation was no more than a change of commensal and connubial relations of the converts in a social sense, while culturally, the dichotomy between exogenous Islamic great tradition and indigenous little traditions of the converted masses broke the cultural continuum and arrested the cultural process. This, in the second stage of Islamisation there, necessitated the emergence of the cultural mediators and the construction by them of a syncretistic model of Islamic great tradition with a view to restoring the broken continuity. The syncretistic model of Islamisation held its ground until in the third stage of Islamisation, beginning from the early nineteenth century, the fundamentalist and revivalist forces in Islam, stirred by a massive combination of diverse factors, sharply focused on the need for a deeper Islamic consciousness, and launched a vigorous assault on the syncretistic and acculturated tradition. Bengal Muslims were gradually drawn towards the heterogenetic model of classical Islam as an answer to the whole range of religious and secular problems and challenges facing the community in contemporaneous Bengal, with the consequence of widening the hiatus that already existed between the exogenous Islam and the indigenous Bengali culture and of deepening the crisis of Bengali Muslim identity.

There is a final issue concerning the nature of the syncretistic tradition expounded in my studies. Its conceptualisation involves two interrelated critical elements the lack of a clear appreciation of which may result in, and has actually caused some confusion about the rationale underlying this conceptualisation. The first concerns the important question of the syncretistic tradition being "Islamic". The "Islamic syncretistic" tradition, for the purposes of this study, means precisely what it says, that is, the phenomenon of Islamic reformulation in syncretistic terms. The focus of my study in the syncretistic developments in the area of Bengal has been Islam and Islam alone. Any one, with the slightest degree of familiarity with the cultural world of medieval Bengal, should know about the pervasive nature of beliefs, superstitions, and practices shared in common among the people. It has not been my purpose to concern myself with this general area of common beliefs and practices obtained in medieval Bengal. Instead, I scanned the diverse and rich pioneering Bengali works of the Muslim *literati* and generations of their successors, and came to realise the range and depth of their significant contributions to the making of an Islamic tradition of syncretistic import, explicitly intended for the Bengali Muslims.

This brings me to the other important question about the making of this tradition. Richard Eaton, in his review of my book on the Islamic syncretistic tradition, expressed reservations about "Roy's mediators" being engaged "quite self-consciously and deliberately" in "concocting their syncretic brew for the masses", and added:

> Possibly much of Roy's literature reflected not so much the product of a conscious selection . . . as the survival of a purely Bengali substratum of values and ideas . . . .[102]

The specific objectives underlying my studies in Islamic syncretistic tradition, as just explained above, should partly allay Eaton's doubts. There were of course much, coming from their long historical past, that the Bengalis, like any other people, held in common. The purpose of my study has neither been to deny such developments nor to explore them. My specific concerns have been to "find" and explain the presence of such indigenous matters in the literary efforts of the mediators which clearly evince their anxiety to foster the Islamic consciousness of the teeming masses of Bengal Muslims with attempts to win the latter's allegiance to a reconstructed Islamic tradition in the vernacular Bengali, couched in familiar and populr syncretistic forms and symbolisms. The problem set for my investigations has been as limited and specific as perhaps the objectives of "my mediators". It was precisely because of the converts continuing to be steeped in non-Islamic cultural heritage of Bengal that the Muslim *literati* were compelled to construct a tradition which Bengal Muslims could call and claim as their own. Saiyid Sultan bemoaned the fact that Bengali Muslims "in every home", denied of any comparable Islamic alternative in the Bengali vernacular, resorted to the Hindu epics, the *Mahabharata* and the *Ramayana*.[103] This prompted him to compose his *magnum opus*, *Nabi-vamsa*, to wean Muslims away from the Hindu epics, *puranas* and *mangal-kavyas*. His subtle and purposive tampering with and construction of new myths about Krisna to vindicate the mission of Muhammad[104] provides, among many others, a clear and incontrovertible evidence of the mediators' "self-conscious and deliberate" role in constructing a popular and meaningful tradition for Bengali Muslims.

NOTES

1. Although aspects of traditional Muslim religious-cultural life persisted through later years to our own times, our concern in this study is limited essentially to the eighteenth century which, with good reason, may be taken as the divide between the traditional or pre-modern and the modern periods of Islam in Bengal and also of Indian Islam. The nineteenth century saw the beginning of a qualitatively new phase of Muslim religious-cultural as well as political responses, under pressures of the British colonial rule.

2. Mirza Nathan, *Baharistan-i Ghaybi*, English tr. by M.I. Borah, (Gauhati, Assam: Dept of Historical and Antiquarian Studies, Govt of Assam, 1936), vol. I, p. 51; see Asim Roy, *The Islamic Syncretistic Tradition of Bengal* (Princeton, New Jersey: Princeton U.P., 1983; or its Indian edition, New Delhi: Sterling Publishers, 1987), pp.58ff; also his "Social factors in the making of Bengali Islam", *South Asia*, No. 3 (August, 1973), p. 26.

3. Siyar ul-Muta'akherin, cited, Qazi Abdul/ Abd al-/ Wadud, *Hindu-Musalmaner Birodh* [in Bengali] (Santiniketan: Visva-Bharati, 1936), p.16.

4. James Wise, *Notes on the Races, Castes and Trades of Eastern Bengal* (London: Harrison & Sons, 1883), p. 6; Roy, Syncretistic Tradition, p. 4.

5. Roy, ibid., Preface, ix-x, xiii-xxi.

6 . *The Moslem Chronicle* (Calcutta), 28 January 1905, p. 193.

7. Ja'far Sarif, *Qanun-i Islam*, Eng. tr. by G. Herklot, ed. by William Crooke (Oxford UP, 1921), Introduction.

8. Cited in Anthony Mascarenhas, *The Rape of Bangladesh* (Delhi: Vikas Publications, 1971), p. 18. Among the "major points of discontent" between the Bengalis and West Pakistanis Mascarenhas mentions "the absurd denigration of the piety of the Muslims in the east wing by those in the west". [Ibid. p. 14] He reminisces about a Punjabi military officer, placed in an East Pakistan district during the Bangladesh crisis, who grabbed a handful of the "the rich, black earth" of the place and exclaimed, "My God, what couldn't we do with such wonderful land", and then added: "But I suppose we would have become like them." [Ibid., p.11]

9. M. Ayub Khan, *Friends Not Masters* (London: Oxford U[niversity] Press, 1967), p. 187.

10. Muhammad Mujeeb, *The Indian Muslims* (London: Allen & Unwin, 1967), p. 22.

11. Peter Hardy, *The Muslims of British India* (London & New York: Cambridge U.P., 1972), p.27.

12. Momtazur Rahman Tarafdar, *Husain sahi Bengal, 1494-1538* (Dhaka: Asiatic Socity of Pakistan, 1965), pp. 163-64.

13. Azizur Rahman Mallick, *British Policy and the Muslims in Bengal 1757-1856* (Dhaka: Asiatic SP, 1961), p. 3.

14. Ibid., pp. 7-8.

15. Ibid., p. 9.

16. One cannot overlook here that while Muslims formed a minority in the Indian subcontinent, they were a majority of the Bengal population.

17. Mallick, *British Policy*, p. 29.

18. Roy, *Syncretistic Tradition*, p. 6.

19. The reference here is to the vast corpus of Muslim Bengali writings in manuscript (some of it is available in print) which constitute the primary sources for my studies in the syncretis-

tic tradition of Islam in pre-modern Bengal. These were collected by the untiring efforts of late Munsi Abdul Karim, and now held as a collection in his name at the Manuscript Section of the Dhaka University Library. These holdings are catalogued, largely on the basis of brief descriptive notes of the collector himself, by his nephew and an eminent scholar of the Bengali literature, Ahmad Sarif. This has been published as Ahmad Sarif (ed.), *Punthi-parichiti* [in Bengali] (Dhaka: Dhaka U.P., 1958), and its later English edition, Husain, S. Sajjad Husain (ed.), *A Descriptive Catalogue of Bengali Manuscripts in Munshi Abdul Karim's Collection by Munshi Abdul Karim and Ahmad Sharif* [hereafter *DCBM*] (Dhaka: Asiatic Society of Pakistan Publication, no. 3, 1960). All references to the Dhaka Manuscripts [hereafter DMs.] in this study, quoting the manuscript number followed by the serial [hereafter sl] number, are as given in the *DCBM*, or as otherwise indicated.

20. Roy, *Syncretistic Tradition*, p. 7. See also below.

21. C.Geertz, *Islam Observed: Religious Development in Morocco and Indonesia* (New Haven & London: Yale UP, 1968), p. 4.

22. H. Beverley, *Report on the Census of Bengal, 1872* (Calcutta: Bengal Secretariat Press, 1872), pp. 131-33, also Table ib, vb, xxxii, xccv; E.A. Gait, *Report* [on Bengal], *Census of India, 1901* (Calcutta: Bengal Secretariat Press, 1902), vol. VI, pt 1, pp. 166, 171, 450, also vol. VIa, pt 2, Table xiii, p. 288; H. Risley et al (eds), *The Imperial Gazetteer of India* (Oxford: Clarendon Press, new rev. ed., 26 vols, 1931), vol. I, p. 475; Khan Bahadur Diwan Fuzli Rubbee, *The Origins of the Musulmans of Bengal* (Calcutta: 1895), pp. 4ff.; *The Moslem Chronicle*, 17 January 1895, p. 20; Muhammad Abdur Rahim, *Social and Cultural History Bengal* (Karachi: Pakistan Publishing House, 2 vols, 1963-67), vol.I, pp.56ff; Roy, *Syncretistic Tradition*, pp.19-57.

23. Govt of Pakistan, *East Pakistan: Land and People* (Karachi:Govt of Pakistan, the People of Pakistan Series, no. 2, n.d.), p. 23. Cf. also: The Muslims in Bengal "appear to take less readily to a town life than the Hindus; but elsewhere the reverse is the case and in the United and Central Provinces, in Madras, and in many of the adjoining states the proportion of the Muhammadans in towns is double that of Muhammadans in the population at large." [Risley, ibid., p. 455; also Gait, ibid., p. 484].

24. D.N. Majumdar and C.R. Rao, *Race Elements in Bengal. A Quantitative Study* (Calcutta: Statistical Publishing Society, 1960), p. 96; also Roy, *Syncretistic Tradition*, pp. 26-28.

25. O.H.K. Spate and A.T.A. Learmonth, *India and Pakistan: A General and Regional Geography* (London: Methuen, 3rd edn, 1967), p. 574; also R.K. Mukerjee, *The Changing Face of Bengal - A Study in Riverine Economy* (Calcutta: Calcutta UP, 1938), pp. 4, 7-9.

26. Mukerjee, ibid., pp. 19-23.

27. Spate and Learmonth, *India and Pakistan Geography*, p.575.

28. Ibid., pp. 575, 583. See also N.G. Majumdar, *Inscriptions of Bengal* (Rajshahi: Varendra Research Society, 1929), III, pp. 146, 194; Abu'l Fadl, *A'in-i Akbari*, English tr. by H. Blochmann and H.S. Jarrett, revised and annotated by J.N. Sarkar (Calcutta: Royal Asiatic Society of Bengal, 1949), II, p. 132; J.N. Sarkar, "Journey to Bengal (in Persian), 1608-9 by Abdul Latif", *Bengal Past and Present* (Calcutta), 35 (April-June 1928), p. 144; L.S.S. O'Malley, *Bengal, Bihar and Orissa, Sikkim* (Calcutta: Govt of India, 1917), pp. 8-9.

29. Krisnarama-das, *Ray-mangal*, ed. by S.N. Bhattacharya (Bardhaman, 1956); and Abdul Karim, *Kalu-Gaji* (*Gazi*)-*Champavati* (Calcutta, n.d.); Roy, *Syncretistic Tradition*, pp. 46, 53, 235-41.

30. Krisnarama-das, the most popular and perhaps the earliest poet of this cult belonged to an upper caste. See Sukumar Sen, *History of Bengali Literature* (New Delhi: Sahitya Academy, 1960), pp. 141-42.

31. "Popular Bengali poetry represents these goddesses as desiring worship and feeling

that they are slighted: they persecute those who ignore them, but shower blessings on their worshippers, even on the obdurate who are at last compelled to do them homage. The language of mythology could not describe more clearly the endeavours of a plebian cult to obtain recognition." [Charles Eliot, *Hinduism and Buddhism. An Historical Sketch* (London: Routledge & Kegan Paul, 3 vols, 1962), vol. II, p. 279. See also T.W. Clark, "Evolution of Hinduism in medieval Bengali literature': Siva, Candi, Manasa", *Bulletin of the School of Oriental and African Studies* (London), XVII (1955), pt 3, pp. 503-18; E.C. Dimock, Jr, "The goddess of snakes in medieval Bengali literature", *History of Religions*, I, no. 2 (1962), pp. 307-21; P.K. Maity, *Historical Studies in the Cult of the Goddess Manasa* (Calcutta: Puthi Pustak, 1966), pp. 169-82.

32. Mukerjee, *Changing Face of Bengal*, pp.27-28; Roy, *Syncretistic Tradition*, pp. 49-50

33. Roy, ibid., pp.52-54.

34. G.A. Oddie (ed.), *Religion in South Asia. Religious Conversions and Revival Movements in South Asia in Medieval and Modern Times* (New Delhi: Manohar, 1977), p. 4; also Hardy, *Muslims of British India* , p. 8; Roy, ibid., pp. 38-41.

35. E.A. Gait, *Bengal Census Report*, 1901, p. 439; also Reuben Levy, *The Social Structure of Islam* (Cambridge: Cambridge UP, 1957), p. 68; also Govt of Pakistan, *East Pakistan*, p. 34.

36. A.K. Najmul Karim, "The Modern Muslim Political Elite in Bengal", Ph.D thesis (London University, 1964), p. 225; also his *Changing Society in India and Pakistan* (Dhaka: Oxford UP, 1956), *passim*.

37. G.E. Von Gruenbaum, *Medieval Islam: A Study in Cultural Orientation* (Chicago: Chicago UP, 1946), p. 199.

38. Levy, *Social Structure of Islam*, p. 68.

39. A. Majed Khan, "Research about Muslim aristocracy in East Pakistan. An introduction", in Pierre Bessaignet (ed.), *Social Research in East Pakistan*, Appendix, p. 22, also p. 28; also Najmul Karim, *Changing Society*, p. 134.

40. Gait, Bengal Census Report, 1901, pp. 170 ff.; also Kunwar Muhammad Ashraf, *Life and Conditions of the People in Hindostan* (New Delhi, 2nd edn, 1970), p. 107; Karim, ibid., p. 132; Levy, *Social Structure of Islam*, p. 68.

41. See Syed Ameer Ali in *The Moslem Chronicle* (Calcutta), 28 January 1905, p. 193; also Maulawi Abdul Wali, "Ethnographical notes on the Muhammadan castes of Bengal", *Journal of the Anthropological Society of Bombay*, VII, no. 2 (1904), pp. 98-113; Roy, *Syncretistic Tradition*, pp. 63-64.

42. Editor, "Samaj-kalima", *Islam Pracharak* (Calcutta), V, no. 5 [Bhadra 1326 B.S. II, no. 2 [Jyaistha 1299 B.S. (*Bangla Sal*/ Bengali Calendar)/ 1892]; Hamid Ali/ Ali, "Uttar Banger Musalman sahitya", *Basana* (Rangpur), II, no. 1 (Baisakh 1316 B.S./ 1909); Abdul Malik Chaudhuri, "Banga-sahitye Srihatter Musalman", *Al-Islam* (Calcutta), II, no. 6 (Asvin 1323 B.S./ 1916); Muhammad Maizur/Ma'iz al-/ Rahman, "Samaj-chitra", ibid., V, no. 5 (Bhadra 1326 B.S./1919); Maniruzzaman/Manir al-Zaman/ Islamabadi, "Samaj-sanskar", ibid., no.8 (Agrahayan, ibid.); Maulawi Safiuddin/ Safi al-Din/ Ahmad, "Abhijatya gaurav (*asraf-atraf*)", *Samya-vadi* (Calcutta), I, no. 1 (1329 B.S./ 1922). See also Mustafa Nurul Islam, *Bengali Muslim Public Opinion as Reflected in the Bengali Press 1901-1930* (Dhaka: Bengali Academy, 1973), pp. 248-52; Roy, ibid., p. 64.

43. William Hunter, *The Indian Mussalmans* (Calcutta, reprint of 3rd edn of 1876, 1945), p. 178.

44. Tassadaq Ahmad, "Sabhapatir abhibhasan", *Shikha* (Dhaka), I (Chaitra 1333 B.S./ 1926). For further evidence on the *asraf-atraf* linguistic cleavage, see William Adam, *Reports on the State of Education, 1835-1838*, ed. by Anath N. Basu, Three Reports (Calcutta:

Calcutta UP, 1941), Third Report (1938), pp. 149, 213-14; Muhammad Na'imuddin/ Na'im al-Din, *Zobdatul Masayel/ Zubdat al-Masa'il* (Calcutta, 1873), vol.I, Introduction; James Wise, "The Muhammadans of Eastern Bengal", *Journal of the Asiatic Society of Bengal*, LXIII, no. 1, pt 3 (1894), p. 62; Syed Ameer Ali, quoted in *The Nineteenth Century* (London), XII (1888), p. 200; Yaqinuddin Ahmad, quoted in *The Moslem Chronicle*, 11 April 1896, p. 165; Roy, *Syncretistic Tradition*, pp. 65-67.

45. *Yusuf-Zulaikha*, quoted, Muhammad Enamul Inamal-Haq, *Muslim Bangla Sahitya* [hereafter *MBS*] (Dhaka: Pakistan Publications, 1965), p. 58. The Muslim Bengali sources have been cited in their printed version, wherever possible, rather than in their manuscript form, unless my own reading of the manuscript is in clear disagreement with the printed version.

46. Saiyid Sultan, *Sab-i Mi'raj* (DMs 433: sl 490), fol. 259. The ms. used by me does not support Enam-ul Haq's rendering (*MBS*, p. 161), accepted by all, that Saiyid Sultan was stigmatized a "hypocrite" (*monafek/munafiq*) by his critics. Instead of "I am called a *monafek*..." (*monafek bale more*...) as Haq reads it, I have "the *monafek* calls me..." (*monafeke bale more*...).

47. Shaikh Muttalib, *Kifayatul Musallin/ Kifayat al-Musalli*, in *DCBM*, p. 61; also *MBS*, p. 198.

48. Abdunnabi/ Abd un-Nabi/Abd al-Nabi, *Hamza-vijay*, in *DCBM*, p. 3; also *MBS*, pp. 214-15.

49. Quoted in *MBS*, p. 163. Our ms. attributed to Shaikh Paran (DMs. 193: sl 94) is without a title. This has been introduced as *Kaidani Kitab* or a Book on Islamic Observances in *DCBM* (p. 80), and as *Nasihat Nama* in *MBS* (pp. 163-64).

50. Haji Muhammad, *Nur Jamal* (DMs. 374: sl 260), fol. 2 mc (microfilm).

51. Saiyid Sultan, *Nabi-vamsa*, in *MBS*, pp. 142, 161.

52. Vrindavana-das, *Chaitanya-bhagavat*, quoted in Sukumar Sen, *Madhyayuger Bangla o Bangali* (Santiniketan: Visva-Bharati, Visya-vidya Sangraha, no. 44, 1962), p. 48.

53. Haji Muhammad, *Nur Jamal*, fol. 2 mc.; Khondkar Nasrullah/ Khwandkar Nasr-Allah/ Khan, *Musar Suwal* (DMs. 68: sl 338), fol. 2 mc; Muhammad Khan, *Maqtal Husain*, in *MBS*, p. 190; Muttalib, *Kifayat*, fol. 7a; Abdul Hakim, *Sihabuddin/ Sihab al-Din/Nama* (DMs. 406: sl 246), fol. 77b; Saiyid Alawal, *Sayful Muluk - Badiujjamal*, in Ahmad Sarif (ed.), *Alawal-birachita Tohfa / Tuhfa* (Dhaka: Bengali Dept, Dhaka University, 1958), p. 62; Muzammil, *Nitisastra-varta*, ed. by Ahmad Sarif, (Dhaka: Bangla Academy, 1965), pp. 5-6.

54. Heyat Mamud/ Hayat Mahmud, *Hitajnana-vani*, ed. by Mazharul Islam in *Kavi Heyat Mamud* (Rajshahi: Rajshahi UP, 1961), p. 7.

55. "Saeed", *The Future of the Muhammadans of Bengal* (Calcutta, 1880), quoted in *The Calcutta Review*, LXXII (1881), pt 2, no. 7, vii; also Roy, *Syncretistic Tradition*, pp. 70-71.

56. Robert Redfield, "The social organization of tradition", *The Far Eastern Quarterly*, XV, no. 1, (1955), p. 15.

57. Milton Singer, "The cultural patterns of Indian civilization", *ibid.*, p. 24. Cf. Arnold Toynbee's concept of the "cultural broker" in the intelligentsia that emerges "to solve the problem of adapting its life to the rhythm of an exotic civilization to which it has been forcibly annexed or freely converted." ["Disintegration of civilizations" in his *A Study of History* (New York: Oxford UP, 1962), vol.V, pp. 154-58]. For an illuminating discussion on this issue, with particular reference to Modern Bengal and its "cultural intermediaries between the foreigner and their own people", see David Kopf, *British Orientalism and the Bengal Renaissance. The Dynamics of Indian Modernization, 1773-1835* (Berkeley & Los Angeles: California U.P., 1969), pp. 1-2, 279.

58. Roy, *Syncretistic Tradition*, pp. 72-75.

59. *Sab-i Mi'raj*, fols. 258-59.

60. Muttalib; *Kifayat*, fols. 6-8.

61. Sagir, *Yusuf-Zulekha*, in *MBS*, pp. 58-59.

62. *Kifayat*, fol. 102.

63. *Nur Jamal*, fols. 2ff.

64. *Vijay-Hamza*, in MBS, pp. 214-15.

65. Sab-i Mi'raj, fol. 259.

66. *Nur Nama*, in *MBS*, pp. 205-206.

67. *Sihabuddin Nama*, in *DCBM*, p. 250; also *MBS*, pp. 208-209.

68. Among works of this type the following seem typical: Afzal Ali, *Nasihat Nama* [ed. by Ahmad Sarif (Dhaka: Bangla Academy, 1969); Shaikh Paran (untitled); Nasrullah Khan, *Musar Sawal/ Suwal*, and also his *Hedayatul/ Hidayat al-/Islam* (DMs. 689: sl 565) and *Shari'aNama* (cited in *MBS*, pp. 175-76); Muttalib, *Kifayat*; Alawal,*Tuhfa*; Khondkar/ Khwandkar/ Abdul Karim, *Hazar Masayel/ Masai'i* (DMs. 109: sl 569); Abdul Hakim, *Sihab*; Hayat Mahmud, *Hitajnana*; Muhammad Ali, *Hairat ul-Fiqh* (DMs. 646: sl 558/ a Bengali composition in Arabic script); Muhammad Jan, *Namaz Mahatmya* (DMs. 189: sl 239); Muhammad Qasim, *Hitopades* (DMs. 140: sl 559); Saiyid Nuruddin/ Nur al-Din, *Musar Sawal/Suwal* (DMs. 188: sl 196); also his *Qiyamat Nama* (DMs 526: sl 81) or *Rahatul/ Rahat al-/Qulub*, *Hitopades* or*Daykat* (DMs. 387: sl 202). See Roy, *Syncretistic Tradition*, p. 11 for some confusion about Nuruddin's works.

69. Abbas Ali, *Gulzar-i Islam* (Dhaka, 1288 B.S./A.D. 1881),p. 61; also M. Islam, *Kavi Heyat*, p. 201; Roy, *ibid.*, pp. 87-88.

70. Muhammad Khan, *Muhammad Hanifar Ladai* (DMs. 286: sl 357); Abdul Alim, *Muhammad Hanifar Ladai* (DMs. 101: sl 369); Amanullah/Aman Allah, *Muhammad Hanifar Ladai* (DMs. 175: sl 368); Saiyid Hamza, *Jaiguner Puthi* (DMs. 135: sl 147), and also its printed version (Calcutta, 1878); Faqir Gharibullah/ Gharib-Allah, *Sonabhan* (DMs. 570: sl 538).

71. Abdun Nabi, *Vijay-Hamza* (DMs. 342: sl 2); Saiyid Hamza, *Amir Hamzar Qissa* (DMs. 711: sl 10); Faqir Gharibullah, *Amir Hamzar Puthi* (Calcutta, 1867).

72. Shah Muhammad Sagir, *Yusuf-Zulekha /Zulaikha* (DMs. 125: sl 12); Abdul Hakim, *Yusuf-Zulekha* (DMs. 425: sl 15); Faqir Gharibullah, *Yusuf-Zulekha* (DMs. 557: sl 17) and its later printed edition (Calcutta, 1880); Daulat Wazir Bahram Khan, *Laili-Majnu/Laila-Majnun*; Saiyid Alawal/ Ala'wal, *Sayful Muluk – Badiujjmal / Saif al-Muluk – Badi al-Jamal*(DMs.179: sl 572); Dona Gazi, *Saif al-Muluk- Badiujjamal*(DMs. 319: sl 524); Tamizi, *Lalmati-Tajul Muluk* (DMs. 651: sl 451); Sarif Shah, *Lalmati-Sayful Muluk* (DMs. 321: sl 448); Abdul-Hakim, *Lalmati-Sayful Muluk* (DMs. 321: sl 448); Muhammad Muqim, *Gule/Gul-i /Bakawali* (DMs. 417: sl 97); Muhammad Nawazis Khan, *Gul-i Bakawali* (DMs. 427: sl 98); Saiyid Muhammad Akbar Ali, *Zebul Muluk - Samarokh* (DMs. 418: sl 142); Saiyid Alawal, *Padmavati* [ed. by Saiyid Ali Ahsan, (Dhaka: Student Ways, 1968)]; Daulat Qazi, *Sati Mayna o Lor-Chandrani* [ed. by S.N. Ghosal in *Sahitya Prakasika* (Santiniketan), pt 1, 1362 B.S./1955]; Muhammad Chuhar, *Azab Shah-Samarokh* (DMs. 358: sl 11); Saiyid Hamza, *Madhu-Malati*, (ed. by Saiyid Ali Ahsan, Chattagram 1380 B.S./A.D. 1973); Shaikh S'adi, *Gada-Mallikar Puthi* (DMS. 573: sl 106).

73. Sultan, *Sab-i Mi'raj*, fols 22, 92; also Roy, *Syncretistic Tradition*, pp. 90-92.

74. Roy, ibid., pp. 92-95.

75. Sultan, *Nabi-vamsa* (DMs 574: sl 220), fol. 22 mc; his *Sab-i Mi'raj*, fols 151-52 mc; also Enamul Haq, "Kavi Saiyid Sultan", *Sahitya-Parisad Patrika* (Calcutta), no. 2 (1341 B.S./A.D. 1934), p. 50.

76. Sultan, *Nabi-vamsa* (DMs. 90: sl 221), fols 313-39; Roy, *Syncretistic Tradition*, pp. 96-98.

77. Sultan, *Nabi* (DMs 574: sl 220), fol. 133; his *Sab*, fol. 257; also Hayat Mahmud, *Hita-*

jnana, pp. 3, 33, 155.

78. Roy, *Syncretistic Tradition*, pp. 104-10.

79. R.C. Zaehner, following Tholuck, Von Kremer, Dozy, Goldziher, and Max Horten, notes effective Indian influence on Sufism. [Zaehner, *Hindu and Muslim Mysticism* (London: London UP, 1960), pp. 86ff.]. A.J. Arberry [*Sufism. An Account of the Mystics of Islam* (London: Allen & Unwin, 1950), passim], on the other hand, concurs with Nicholson, Massignon and Moreno in repudiating this claim. Aziz Ahmad [*Studies in Islamic Culture in the Indian Environment* (London: Oxford UP, 1964), p. 118] goes further in observing the "general trend of exclusiveness of Sufism in India from Hindu mystical schools, with which it had so much in common" and also "the merely occasional, more negative than positive contact of the two mystical systems on the indian soil."

80. Shaikh Mansur, *Sirr Nama* (DMs.569:sl460), fols.9,13; also Roy, *Syncretistic Tradition*, pp142-44.

81. Ali Raja, *Agam*, fols 24-25; Roy, ibid., 146-49.

82. Roy, ibid., pp. 159-63.

83. Shaikh Faizullah/ Faiz-Allah, *Goraksa-vijay*, ed. by Munsi Abdul Karim (Calcutta: Bangiya Sahitya Parisad Granthavali, no. 64, 1324 B.S./A.D. 1917).

84. Shaikh Chand, *Hara-Gauri Samvad* (DMs. 559: sl 556); also ed. in Ahmad Sarif, *Banglar Sufi Sahitya* (Dhaka: Bangla Academy, 1969), pp. 27-40.

85. Shaikh Zahid, *Adya-parichay*, ed. by M.M. Chaudhuri (Rajshahi: Varendra Research Museum, 1964), pp.1ff.; Mansur, *Sirr*, fols 24a-27a. The rivers of Hindu tradition are *Iksu*, *Ratnakara*, *Navani*, *Ksiroda* and *Dadhi*, and those of the Islamic tradition are *Rud* (Oxus), *Nil* (Nile), *Saihun* (Jaxartes), *Jaihun* (Bactrus) and *Kulsum*.

86. Zahid, ibid.; Shaikh Chand, *Talib Nama* (DMs.694: sl 171), fols 8b-10a/ also ed. by Ahmad Sarif, *Sufi Sahitya*, pp. 43-86; Saiyid Sultan, *Jnana-pradip* (DMs.365: sl 152), fols 9b-10a/ also ed. by Sarif, ibid., pp. 14-20; Saiyid Murtaza (untitled ms., catalogued as *Yoga-Qalandar* /DMs. 547: sl 394), fols 1a-9b/ also ed. by Sarif, ibid., pp. 94-116. The four traditional Hindu ages are *satya*, *treta*, *dvapara* and *kali*. The four *Vedas* are the *Rig*, the *Sama*, the *Yajur* and the *Atharva*. The four revealed books are the Psalms, the Old Testament, the New Testament and the Qur'an. The four Sufic stations are *nasut*, *malkut*, *jabrut* and *lahut*.

87. Shaikh Chand, ibid.

88. Abdul Hakim, *Chari-maqam-bhed* (DMs. 408: sl 247), fols 2a-2b.

89. Ibid.

90. The Nathist practice of turning the tongue back to the root of the cerebral region, reaching the source of the divine ambrosia.

91. Sultan, *Jnana-pradip*, fols 11a-11b.

92. Svami Bhumananda, "Vaisnava Musalman", *Bangasri* (Calcutta), Chaitra, 1344 B.S./A.D. 1937, p. 387, and Baisakh, 1345 B.S./1938, p. 502; R.K. Sastri, "Krisna-bhakta Musalman", *Pratibha* (Calcutta), XI (Kartik, 1328 B.S./1921), p. 265; P.L. Das, "Musalman Vaisnava kavir dharmamat", *Arghya* (Calcutta), IV, (1324 B.S./1917), p. 425; S.B. Dasgupta, "Banglar Musalman Vaisnava-kavi", *Visva-Bharati Patrika*, (Magh-Chaitra, 1363 B.S./1956).

93. *MBS*, pp. 50-53; also Muhammad Enamul Haq, *A History of Sufism in Bengal* (Dhaka: Asiatic Society of Bangladesh, 1975), pp. 268-81.

94. Yatindra M. Bhattacharya, *Banglar Vaisnava-bhavapanna Musalman Kavi* [in Bengali] (Calcutta: Srihatta Sahitya-Parisad Granthamala, no. 6, 1336 B.S./1950); Edward C. Dimock, Jr., "Muslim Vaisnava poets of Bengal", in Kopf (ed.), *Bengal Identity*, pp. 25-40.

95. Original in Bhattacharya, *ibid.*, song no. 40, English tr. by Dimock, *ibid.*, p. 27; *MBS*, p. 52.

96. Roy, *Syncretistic Tradition*, pp. 196-97.

97. Shashi Bhusan Dasgupta, *Obscure Religious Cults of Bengal as Background of Early Bengali Literature* (Calcutta: Calcutta UP, rev. ed., 1962), p. 175; R.G. Bhandarkar, *Vaisnavism, Saivism and Other Minor Religious Systems* (Varanasi: Indological Book House, latest ed., 1965), p. 85.

98. L. Massignon in M. Th. Houtsma et al (eds), *Encyclopaedia of Islam* (Leiden & London, E.J. Brill and Luzac, 4 vols, 1913-34), vol. IV, p. 684; D.S. Margoliouth in ibid., vol.II, p. 362; S.A.A. Rizvi, *Muslim Revivalist Movements in Northern India* (Agra: Agra UP, 1965), pp. 37, 43-53, 62-64.

99. Roy, *Syncretistic Tradition*, pp. 195-202.

100. Ibid., pp. 202-203.

101. Ali Asani, "Review" of *The Islamic Syncretistic Tradition of Bengal*, in *Journal of the American Oriental Society,* CV, no. 2, (April-June 1985), p. 363.

102. Richard M.Eaton, "Review" of *ibid.*, in *Journal of Asian Studies*, XLIV, no. 2 (February 1985), p. 443.

103. See above, pp. 6-7; also Roy, *Syncretistic Tradition*, p.69.

104. Ibid., pp. 96-98.

2. Islamisation in South Asia with Special Reference to the Bengali-Speaking Region A Conceptual and Historical Revaluation

RECENT STUDIES in Muslim societies, both historical and empirical, have brought about rather significant modifications and revisions in the understanding and perception of the process of Islamisation in a given situation. Being and becoming a Muslim appears now, in the light of their findings, infinitely more complex and variegated a process and a pattern than what is conveyed by its conventional appreciation and interpretation. There is a steadily growing academic awareness and recognition that a wide range of diverse phenomena remain lumped together under the amorphous label of "Islamisation." [1]

I

It is a far cry today, from the very early stage of association of the meaning of Islamisation with the essence of politico-military Islam, until Thomas Arnold turned the focus on the religious and social dynamics of Islamic expansion.[2] Arnold's significant contributions on "preaching" and "conversion" provided the basis of a rich corpus of scholarly studies in the peaceful penetration of Islam in Asia and Africa.[3] One of the most significant revelations of such studies in the context of South Asia in particular concerns the very nature of "conversion" as well as its interrelations with, and implications for "Islamisation". The South Asian mass conversion movements to Christianity and other non-Islamic religions have generally been found in greater accord with the "social" rather than the "spiritual" meanings of conversion. In its commonly accepted spiritual sense, conversion involved an immediate spiritual experience and transformation – a change of inner religious consciousness, while socially, its meanings did not extend a great deal more beyond "moving out of one community to another", or a "shifting of camps" – in short, "more a change of fellowship than conduct of inner life – although the latter may in time occur." The convert in this sense joined a new social group that largely defined its identity on the basis of the limit on inter-marriage, inter-dining, and also partly ritual observances.[4]

Islamic mass movements in this region revealed clear affinity with the so-cial meanings of conversion. Reasons other than strictly spiritual largely under-lay the mass conversion process in South Asia, and Islamisation in this context could, therefore, be deemed coterminous with conversion not so much in its usual spiritual sense as social.[5] The reasons for such mass or group conversions were perhaps many and varied, though scarcely illumined by contemporary or even later historical sources. But, in the light of rather well-documented experi-ences of Christian proselytising mission in South Asia, the close correspondence between "caste" and "conversion" should be strongly underlined. In trying to ex-plore the reasons for the trickle of conversions becoming a flood of mass move-ments into Christianity in the latter half of the nineteenth century, especially among the ranks of the depressed groups, the Protestant missionaries discov-ered, to their amazement, that "caste links could help rather than hinder evangeli-sation.[6] The group converts often preferred to preserve family and kinship ties, which not only provided much needed support and protection but were also ex-tremely important for the purposes of marriage, commensality, and social com-munication.[7] The absence of "horizontal group solidarity" and the "unusually fragmented character" of the depressed social groups rendered "collective ac-tion" on their part for amelioration of social conditions highly difficult. The tra-ditional anti-caste protest, as expressed in medieval devotional (*bhakti*) sectarian movements, fell far short of the demands of positive social actions. "Sanskritisa-tion" for most of them remained perhaps the most accessible means and some hope for social improvement. And yet, sanskritisation for these groups at their particular social level turned out no better than "a cul-de-sac" because of "con-certed and efficacious rebuffs from the higher castes."[8] More importantly, sanskritisation had been a fiercely competitive process, and one depressed group undergoing sanskritisation impeded another competing group, forcing the latter often to look outside the Hindu world.[9] This provides the wider context of the phenomenon of Islamisation as a social alternative for mass conversion in South Asia.

The salient features of Islamic conversion in Bengal correspond closely to the general pattern of conversion movement in the subcontinent. From the evi-dence of the earliest extant Muslim literature in Bengali, it is reasonable to dis-count "spiritual" attractions underlying Islamic mass conversion in the region.[10] Conversion, in reality, brought no significant alterations in the converts' social position, as evidenced by subsequent and persistent caste and social discrimina-tions in the Bengal Muslim society.[11] Nonetheless, its significance lay, as with other mass conversion movements, in the fact that it was like "a kind of group identity crisis," in which the group passes through a negative rejection of its lowly place in Hindu society to a positive affirmation of a new social and religious identity. This new identity does not depend on its acceptance and recognition by the higher castes; indeed, it has been chosen and is sustained despite their refusal to accept it.[12]

No less determining than the caste factor was another vital explanation for the greater social rather than spiritual input to Islamic conversion, especially in the situation of Bengal. This has reference to our growing understanding of the critical linkage between the expanding physical and economic frontier of eastern and southern Bengal and the corresponding expansion of Islamic demographic boundary in the same region.[13] Much explanation for the historical developments in deltaic Bengal is found in the physical nature of its deltaic constitution.

Eastern and southern Bengal, on one hand, and northern Bengal, on the other, where two-thirds and three-fifths respectively of the inhabitants were Muslim according to the Census Report of 1901, present a typically rural landscape and have been compared even in recent times to "a huge sprawling village."[14] The demographic landmark of this deltaic region has always been the clustering of certain predominant social groups, all occupying lower positions in the social hierarchy of a primarily agricultural society. The Hindu Mahisya, Pod and Namasudra, and the Muslim agriculturists, known locally as *Sek* or *Sekh* (*Shaikh*) and Jola (*Julaha*) respectively, formed the great bulk of the people in this region. The strong anthropometric correspondence between Namasudra and various Muslim groups in these areas had been observed.[15] This demographic pattern fitted quite well into a significant pattern of physical changes in the deltaic Bengal. The entire network of river-systems in Bengal has undergone great changes through the course of centuries, the most consistent and significant feature of which has been a gradual shift in the location of fertile soil from the moribund west of the delta to its mature eastern and southern parts.[16] This physical change, combined with the pressure caused by the steady influx of upper caste immigrants to the settled western region of Bengal, forced the aboriginal and pioneer agriculturists and settlers from the old to the new productive, though harsh and challenging "frontiers" of the delta.

The lower delta is subjected to heavy rainfall and precariously open even now to the constant threat of cyclonic catastrophies. The loss and suffering in both human and material terms, resulting from such frequent natural disasters could "hardly be estimated or exaggerated."[17] Perhaps the most amphibious part of Bengal during the rains, the lower tracts are flooded to a depth of 8-15 feet. Here, in the lower and the most active part of the delta, the inhabitants – agriculturists, wood-cutters, fishermen, boatmen and the like – were indeed pitted against a Nature that was at once rich and bountiful, menacing and cruel. They had to live and fight against a mighty array of adversaries – fierce floods, storms,

brackish waters, snakes, crocodiles and tigers. The experience of material existence in this environment was reflected in the religious beliefs characteristic of
the region. It is not accidental that the cult of the Tiger-god, Daksin-raya,
emerged and flourished in this region. In the popular religious tradition of this region, the goddess Ganga was represented as the presiding deity of the crocodiles.
It is highly significant that the Hindu tradition of Daksin-raya and the Muslim
tradition of Gazi (Ghazi) and his associate Kalu, both popular in the region,
found these popular heroes involved in a contest for control of territories in the
region which ended happily with territorial divisions arbitrated by God, appearing in a meaningful form of half-Hindu and half-Muslim. It is no less meaningful
that both Daksin-raya and Gazi were also invested with command over tigers and
crocodiles.[18]

There was another unique feature of life in the most active part of the new
delta that was quite characteristic of its "frontier" nature. The very nature of the
lower delta precluded settled authority in the region. Its history down to the British period was largely marked by turbulence and rioting linked with the conditions of local geography. The frequent flood waters there destroyed all marks or
boundaries between the fields and were indirectly a constant source of social disorder.[19] Taken together, the ferocity of nature and the anarchical conditions in
the lower delta, aggravated by the conditions of institutional inadequacies in social and cultural terms, underlined the dire need of some binding foci of authority, stability and assurance in a largely unstable physical and social situaion. It is
these specific leadership roles linked with the distinctive needs and demands of
this frontier society that were rather successfully appropriated by a number of
Muslim adventurers and settlers who earned the admiration and respect of their
grateful clienteles in the form of popular canonisation as saints or pirs. One of the
basic explanations for the Muslim preponderance in the most active parts of deltaic Bengal must be sought in the special circumstances of these regions. The
provision for the material and spiritual needs of the areas was a crucial element as
much in the process of Islamic conversion as of pirification. A number of shrines
and traditions were found in this area, relating to some popular pirs, who would
seem to have performed such specific deltaic roles.[20]

II

The strong social urges underpinning conversion, as delineated above, not only
reveal the special meaning of Islamisation in relation to conversion but also add a
further dimension to Islamisation in relation to social mobility of Muslim
groups. The "use [of] the term Islamisation to cover . . . an upward cultural and
social . . . mobility in the status of groups" has been noted by social scientists.[21]
The cultural symbolisms, style of life and customs of the *Ashraf* Muslims possessed significance as a "reference model" for the lower Muslims, and the latter

tried to improve their social position by borrowing the customs and adopting the names of the *Ashraf*, earning thereby the dubious distinction of "pseudo-Ashrafs".[22] In the words of Yogendra Singh:

> . . . Islamisation as a process of social mobility within the social structural framework has many sociological equivalents with Sanskritisation. In both the processes, mobility in status is sought through adoption of names and customs of culturally high-placed groups.[23] In both situations, the economic status of the 'reference model' is and has been traditionally of a superior nature. Finally, both in Sanskritisation and in Islamisation aspiration for mobility is preceded by some degree of betterment in the economic status of the aspirant group. This goes to suggest that what we call Sanskritisation in one case and Islamisation in another is, in fact, the manifestation of an existential situation – the attempt to climb higher in status scale by lowly placed groups through manipulation of the most accessible resources involving least resistance.[24]

This particular facet of the Islamising process as social mobility is also borne out by empirical studies in other Muslim groups in South Asia, such as Mattison Mines's findings about the Tamil-speaking Muslims which reveal further complexities in the processes and patterns of Islamisation in relation to social mobility. In seeking explanations of "why they [the Tamil-speaking Muslims] are undergoing a process of Islamization in Tamilnadu's northern cities despite their close identification with and integration into local society", Mines discovers a situation of Muslims "act[ing] out their social lives on two stages simultaneously" – a dualistic existence between their rural and urban milieus. "In villages", he observes, "Tamil Muslims do not differentiate themselves so much from the rural social structure", while in the cities "rural-based caste-like identity is replaced by non-corporate ethnic identity."[25] Islamisation, therefore, in this particular context of social mobility among Tamilian Muslims, "relates closely not just to vestigial caste structures but to a systematic movement from rural-based, caste-like identity to urban-based non-corporate ethnic identity arising from the need to acquire status among fellow Muslims."[26] Further, "Muslim ethnicity," Mines reiterates, ". . . arises from internal needs to acquire status among Muslims more than it arises from the need for a boundary to regulate external relations and thereby to occupy a niche."[27]

III

Satish Misra's effort at conceptualising "Islamisation" in contradistinction to what he designates "indigenisation" raises a hornet's nest. His view is based on the assumption of a polarity between these two processes, stemming essentially from the problems of "adaptation" of those whom he presents as "foreign" and "Indian" members of "the Muslim communities in India." In his not-so-revealing words:

> These trends are not peculiar to Islam in India; they inhere in any process of adaptation by which a socio-cultural framework is moulded to suit a particular environment a process during which is itself affected and affects the setting as well.[28]

He views these processes as "pulls" in "opposite directions", the "foreign" Muslims being subjected to the process of "indegenisation", while "the Indian Muslim communities" were drawn by "the pull" of Islamisation "in another direction."[29]

To the extent that his attempt does reject the over-prevalent , macro-, and normative perception of a monolithic pattern of Islamic development, Misra's position is in clear accord with the recent academic views on the subject. His perception and notion of a totally dichotomous relationship between some "foreign" and some "Indian" components of the Indian Muslim life does also reflect the position variously held by those whom I should like to characterise as the proponents of the old and orthodox view of Islamisation. Inherent in this position are assumptions which are being subjected to a critical and expanding process of empirical investigations and found either wrong or inadequate.

In my own inquiries into the process of Islamisation in Bengal I became acutely aware of its complex and variegated nature, with particular reference to its strong interconnection with a syncretistic formulation, in the vernacular Bengali, of a rich corpus of Islamic tradition by the Bengal Muslim *literati*. The "syncretiisation" of Islamic tradition – rather analogous, by its implications, to Misra's cultural process of "indigenisation" – has not, in my study, been juxtaposed in opposition to Islamisation, as has been the case with Misra and hosts of other Islamists. To quote the most relevant part of my conclusion that bears on this issue:

> The interrelationship between syncretism and Islamisation emerges as another significant issue from this study. The syncretistic developments in Islam have been generally condemned, particularly at the level of the religious "purists", fundamentalists, and revivalists, as hindrances to Islamisation. Viewed in its historical context, Islamic syncretism in Bengal would seem, on the contrary, a necessary stage in the progress of Islamisation in the country. It has been our purpose to explore the making of the syncretistic tradition by the conscious efforts of the Bengali Muslim cultural mediators, with a view to disseminating Islam in a more locally familiar and meaningful form. This tradition continued to dominate the

religious-cultural perception of the Bengali Muslim masses until the emergence of vigorous and even militant Islamic revivalist and purificatory movements in Bengal, as elsewhere within and without India, since the beginning of the nineteenth century, which sharpened the Islamic consciousness among Bengali Muslims, strongly condemned the syncretistic tradition, and urged suppression of non-Islamic accretions. Until the revivalist challenge the syncretistic tradition performed a significant historical function in the dissemination of Islam in Bengal, and was not, therefore, an antithesis of Islamisation but a necessary stage in its historical development in Bengal. Syncretism remained as integral to the process of Islamisation in the land as the subsequent revivalist, reformist and fundamentalist contributions.[30]

The growing revelation and realisation of a growing hiatus between this conventional orthodox and the new revisionist perspectives on the notion and process of Islamisation has been the most seminal concern of this chapter.

IV

A deep structural cleavage in a society tends to express itself in its cultural formations. South Asian societies are no exceptions. The commonly perceived inner divergences in the religious-cultural domains of South Asia, variously labelled as "high" and "low", "elite" and "folk", "intellectual" and "popular", do seem to correspond largely to their broad societal divisions. In his study in "popular" Hinduism, Louis O'Malley observes:

> It has been found in countries where there are two distinct classes, the one intellectual and learned, the other illiterate and ignorant that the common religion which they profess has two sides, the one higher and the other lower, the one more or less esoteric and the other popular.[31]

Tarachand reiterates very similar ideas:

> There have always been two distinct strata of society in India, the one higher and the other lower; the first small in numbers, but in possession of highly developed religions, social ideas and institutions; the second comprising the great mass of the people who occupy a humbler rung on the cultural ladder. The first provides the intellectual and aristocratic and the second the folk element in India's culture. These two in their interactions have supplied two strands of the pattern . . . .[32]

In a very recent contribution on South Asian Islam, Ali Asani's identification of two distinct Muslim traditions in this region closely follows the same lines. He characterises the diffrence in terms of a "rustic tradition," which

> we may, on the basis of its appeal and popularity among the rural, illiterate masses, characterise variously as the folk, low or little tradition. Contrasting, or perhaps some would say, complementing this rustic tradition is the more sophisticated, intellectual facet of Islamic civilisation that developed in urban areas under the cultural influence of the immigrant Muslim elite of Persian or Central Asian origin.[33]

The inner divergences in Indian Islam are of course evident from sundry historical sources from the medieval times, especially through the occasional outbursts of "purist'" sentiments and reactions of both the religious and non-religious elites.[34] Since the late eighteenth century, and particularly in the nineteenth century, not only the Muslim revivalist writings but also much fuller accounts of Muslim beliefs and practices such as those of Ja'far Sharif,[35] Garcin de Tassy,[36] and Mrs Mir Hasan'Ali,[37] revealed the true measure of the dichotomy between the "scriptural" and "living" Islam in South Asia. The report on the Indian census of 1901 records that "the Musulman religion is an exotic one in India and consequently does not contain a great number of *pure Moslems*."[38]

As regards Bengal, there has been a virtual unanimity among observers that the dominant version of the religion, as practised by the overwhelming majority of its votaries in traditional or pre-modern Bengal was rather "lax" and "spurious".[39] This particular perception of the dominant form of Islam in the land goes back long in history. In the late eighteenth century, Ghulam Husain Tabatabai observed this "deviance" of Muslim Bengal.[40] A late-nineteenth-century British resident observer in the Muslim-dominated Eastern Bengal, Dr James Wise, noted "the corrupt Hinduised rites" of Muslims in Bengal.[41] The most graphic depiction and the most venomous condemnation of such "debased" Islam in Bengal came from the large volume of polemical and didactic writings of the Islamic fundamentalists, revivalists and reformists in the nineteenth century and after.[42] At the beginning of this century Syed Ameer Ali, a distinguished member of the modern Muslim social and intellectual elite, contrasted "the Mahomedan settlers from the West who had brought with them to India traditions of civilisation and enlightenment" with the Eastern Bengali Muslims who were "chiefly converts from Hinduism" and "still observe[d] many Hindu customs and institutions." [43] To contemporary West Pakistani politicians and officials are often attributed derogatory remarks on the piety of Bengali Muslims. Malik Feroze Khan Noon, the Punjabi Governor of East Bengal in 1952, regarded his wards as "half-Muslims."[44] President Ayub Khan also was known to hold similar views.[45]

V

The common perception of the dichotomous nature of Indian Islam is obvious. It is, however, the understanding and explanations of, and attitudes to the divergences, primarily at the academic level, that have been steadily emerging as dubious and deficient. The predominant attitude and approach seem to have been – in the proverbial ostrich style – not to face the question with any degree of academic seriousness, and discard everything that fail to measure up to the norms and prescriptions of "scriptural" Islam, into the shadowy and bottomless pit of "folk" or "popular" Islam, which again is, in its turn, traced to the most specious logic of "incomplete conversion."

"At the *popular level*,"[46] accordng to Aziz Ahmad, "Indian Islam represents a mosaic of *demotic, superstitious* and *syncretistic beliefs*. . . ." Further, "*Animism* in Islam, as in other religions throughout the world, is to some extent rooted in popular beliefs," while in India "it may have been influenced to some uncertain extent by Hinduism."[47] All this, for him, mean nothing more than "add[ing] colour to the bizarre pageantry of India."[48] In Muhmmad Mujeeb's perception they were only "partly converted."[49] Peter Hardy dubbs them "census Muslims" and adds:

> . . . the real challenge to purity of belief and practice in Islam in medieval India was to be found . . . in the convert's countryside – in the ignorance of new Muslims of the requirements of Islam and in the insidious infiltrations of 'creeping Hinduism' into the daily life of the convert.[50]

Francis Robinson refers to them as "half-Islamised peoples."[51] In a recent contribution Richard Eaton spoke of the two variants of Islam in Mughal Bengal –"the folk Bengali variant" and "the North Indian 'ashraf' variant."[52] The case of Imtiaz Ahmad is particularly significant in this context, underlining the depth, magnitude and complexity of the problem. He has been one of the strongest protagonists of the varieties and diversities in South Asian Islam as well as an opponent of the monolithic perception of "orthodoxy" in Islam. He identifies three separate and somewhat "autonomous" strands or "levels" in South Asian Islam: first, the scriptural, "derived from the Islamic religious texts"; the second, comprising "values," "beliefs" and practices, "not derived from the Islamic literature," and not "always" in "accord with", rather sometimes "opposed and antithetical" to the norms of the first, though "they are regarded by the Muslims who hold them as truly Islamic"; and the third, representing the "pragmatic" concerns of believers, such as "supernatural theories of disease causation, propitiation of Muslim saints, and, occasionally at least, deities of the Hindu pantheon and other crude phenomena as spirit possession, evil eye, etc." It is Ahmad's own attitudes to this "level" of Muslim's beliefs and practices that bring him closer to others mentioned above. He opines:

As a matter of fact, one would be perfectly justified in excluding them almost completely from considerations under Islam, except that those who observe them are *nominally Muslims* and are so regarded by others. [53]

Some Bengali Muslim historians also largely share a common ground on this issue. Momtazur Rahman Tarafdar observes:

Islam, in its simple and austere aspect, does not appear to have characterised the life of the people [of Bengal] . . . a careful study of the literature of the time shows that there prevailed a sort of folk Islam having hardly any connection with the dogmas of religion.[54]

Rafiuddin Ahmed, likewise, takes the conventional position of differentiatiating between an "Islamic orthodoxy" and "folk beliefs and practices," and writes:

The adherence to folk beliefs and practices, however, should not be interpreted to mean that the orthodox traditions had no place in Bengali Islam. On the contrary, a large proportion of urban Muslims as well as the mullahs and other religious preachers often tried to remain as 'Islamic' as possible.[55]

Azizur Rahman Mallick's is perhaps the strongest and the most rigid restatement of the orthodox position. He mentions Islam in Bengal "where *corrupt and irreligious practices* gained considerable ground."[56] He speaks of the "ignorance" of the "half converted Muslims" and identifies "incomplete conversion" as "a channel through which un-Islamic practices passed" into Islam. "*Incomplete conversion* in the rural districts of Bengal", Mallick writes, "left these people only *nominal followers* of the Faith. . . ."[57] He raises the issue of the Mughal decline and the "loss of political power" which, in his opinion, "undoubtedly contributed to the *degeneration* of Islam . . . ." [58] Mallick, in an intriguing statement, betrays his inclination not even to count "the half-converts from Hinduism" among "Muslims":

Thus long years of association with non-Muslims who far outnumbered them,[59] cut off from the original home of Islam, and *living with half-converts from Hinduism, the Muslims had greatly deviated* from the original faith and had become 'Indianised.' [60]

There seem to be two broad lines of reasoning in all this for the Islamic divergences. The theory of "incomplete conversion" or "semi-conversion" is rather similar in nature to that of "folk Islam", both pointing at the level and the limit of the cultural attainments of the masses of indigenous converts. The theory of "degeneration", on the other hand, offers a much different kind of reasoning. None of these explanations could, however, be sustained either by logic or history.

To begin with, the arguments of incomplete conversion and degeneration contradict each other. Degeneration could not have logically followed from a situation which was already regarded inadequate and "incomplete". Besides, the descriptive labels such as "half converts," "census Muslims," or "nominal Muslims" raise serious questions about the place for value judgments in academic pursuits. To call a Muslim something less than a Muslim is a value judgment and not a description or analysis of the meaning of being a Muslim from the point of view of one who calls himself a Muslim and claims the religion as his own. Such presumptuous views on the nature and profundity of piety of individual believers seem more akin to a religious posture than academic objectivity. Religious life is a complex whole – a baggage full of myriad and diverse objects, all drawn from their complex and heterogeneous source itself, that is, life. And very much in the sense of "the web of life," there is an underlying unity, coherence and purpose that, in the ultimate analysis, could only have been meaningful in the minds of the believing individuals. Finally, the most serious objection to the theory of Islam's degeneration in Bengal is that it is patently unhistorical. There is no historical evidence to suggest that Islam as practised by the masses of its votaries in Bengal, in the declining years of the Mughals, was anything different from what it had been there in the past or that the so-called "corrupt", "degenerate" and "Hinduised" Islam, confronted by the Islamic revivalists and reformists since the nineteenth century, was a sharp deviation from a golden or classical age of Islam in Bengal lying in the past.[61] On the contrary, the earliest extant Muslim Bengali literary sources, dating largely from the sixteenth century, provide the clearest possible evidence of the early existence in Bengal of masses of believers who, having been linguistically cut off from the Arabic and Persian sources of Islamic tradition, and denied of such tradition in their vernacular Bengali, continued to remain steeped in the locally popular non-Muslim tradition readily available in the vernacular Bengali.[62] The authors of this early Muslim Bengali literature were themselves instrumental in recasting Islamic tradition in syncretistic moulds.

VI

It is possible to detect several strands in the formulations of the orthodox position, academic or otherwise. One of them is to treat religious heterogeneities in a Muslim society as "aberrations," "anomalies," and "accretions" to be overlooked and ignored, being of little importance and consequence; or as "festers" that ought and can be "cured." Mushirul Haq seeks a rather dubious solution by totally leaving out "outwardly socio-religious practices" from the domain of "religion".[63] Aziz Ahmad's prescription for a "proper perspective" in which the "folk-beliefs should be viewed" is that these "should not be over-emphasised or over-rated." He assures us:

> They are specific to microscopic Muslim communities and are generally *the exception rather than the rule*. They were challenged by the fundamentalist, orthodox and modernist movements alike in the nineteenth and twentieth centuries. They have *completely ceased to exist in the Westernised upper class and nearly so in the orthodox lower middle classes*. In the predominantly Muslim regions which now constitute West Pakistan their hold was not very strong even in the lower classes, and *fundamentalism is now rooting them out*.[64]

Another distinctive, and academically popular, effort in bringing together the two large religious complexes of Islam within the broad conceptual frame of "great" and "little traditions," conflated with the corresponding concepts of "orthodoxy" and heterodoxy." In his "summary" statement, relating to the workshop on Islam in Southern Asia, held in Heidelberg (December 1974), Imtiaz Ahmad reports on "the *general trend* of opinion" favouring conceptualisation of Islamic diversities "in terms of a dichotomy of orthodoxy and heterodoxy in religious affairs." Though striking a somewhat discordant note by his subsequent reference to "some participants," the point he wishes to make is unmistakable:

> Using the concept of the Little and Great Traditions as defined by cultural anthropology, some participants contended that the theological and philosophical principles enshrined in the Islamic scriptures and other sources of [the] religion constituted the orthodox religious tradition and the local or regional beliefs and practices represented a heterodox tradition . . . . The process of Islamisation, understood as an increasing tendency amongst Muslims towards new identity formation based on *an increase in conformity to orthodox Islamic principles in social and cultural life and a conscious rejection of syncretic elements* that previously persisted as remnants of their pre-conversion orientations and beliefs, was said to link the orthodox and heterodox religious complexes, resulting in a *gradual shrinkage of the sphere of the heterodox complex of the little tradition*.[65]

Ziaul Hasan Faruqi is another to adopt the great-little-tradition model. He shows awareness of the important contributions made by "recent sociological and anthropological researches" on the "regional communities to show that they are mutually distinct and different in many respects."[66] In regard, however, to the vital question of interrelationship between the great and little traditions, and the corresponding one between orthodoxy and heterodoxy, Faruqi's position, as well as the view reported by Imtiaz Ahmad at the Heidelberg Conference of 1974, as quoted above (especially its italicised portion), diverge very little from the lines of the orthodox scholarship. Faruqi maintains that

> . . . Muslim communities belonging to the Little tradition, with all their distinct cultural traits, have always aspired to relate their social and cultural values to those of the Islamic Great Tradition . . . .[67]

The assumption underlying this particular academic stance concerns the core area of difference between the orthodox and revisionist perspectives on Islamisation. The traditional understanding of the operative process of Islamisation has, as shown above, been rather simple, unifom, unilineal and unidirectional; that is to say, an invariable and continuous process of transition and transformation from "heterodoxy" to "orthodoxy", or from "little" to "great" tradition. This particular position has now become totally indefensible in the light of many recent studies. As early as the late 1960s, I came to realise the relevance and appropriateness of Robert Redfield's concepts of great and little traditions for my purpose, and was *perhaps* the first to apply this model to a comprehensive study of a South Asian Muslim society.[68] One of my basic contentions in this and later studies has been the interrelationship between the great and little traditions of Islam in Bengal. In Bengal, Islam has not been a "primary" but a "secondary" culture, that is, exogenous and not indigenous to the region. Also, here in this region, Islam has not been a "single" or the only "great tradition" since it entered a land which was not culturally virgin, and confronted the long-established indigenous great tradition. Islamic conversion forced a break in the pre-conversion cultural continuity between the great and little tradition of the would-be converts. To remedy the situation, the Bengal Muslim *literati* constructed a rather rich alternative model of great tradition for the Bengal Muslim masses in the Bengali language and on a syncretistic model, and restored thereby the broken continuity between the great and little traditions of the converts. The obvious implication of this finding has been to reveal the inadequacies of a simple and uniform model of great and little tradition relationship.

VII

The emerging revisionist perspective canvasses, on one hand, a non-dichotomous and complementary rather than conflicting, and on the other, a complex rather than flat and uniform pattern of interrelationship between the great and little tradition as well as between the so-called orthodoxy and heterodoxy in Islam.

This view is being steadily reinforced by many empirical investigations into the South Asian situations. Their findings are full of implications for a fuller appreciation of the process of Islamisation in the South Asian setting. The weight of the evidence, first of all, is clearly against "the conceptualisation of religious beliefs, values and practices in terms of a dichotomy of orthodoxy and heterodoxy altogether . . . ." [69] The boundary of "orthodoxy," howsoever well defined in Islamic scriptural works or by the religious professionals, does not appear often to coincide with the one that is locally determined. Quite often, elements of the little tradition, "rather than being rejected or eliminated", are actually accepted through Islamisation, either in their original or somewhat modified form, and "incorporated into the corpus of the orthodox religious complex." Imtiaz Ahmad finds that "beliefs and values . . . . not derived from the Islamic literature" and not necessarily " always [in] accord . . . with orthodox Islam," are "regarded by Muslims who hold them as truly Islamic." He concludes:

> Popular Islam in South Asia is not merely the heterodox side of the Great Tradition of Islam. Looked at from the viewpoint of those who subscribe to its corpus of beliefs and values, it is as much orthodox as the Islamic beliefs derived from the religious texts. [70]

In her illuminating studies in the Tamil-speaking south Indian Muslims called Labbais, Susan Bayly raises some seminal issues concerning the "actual meaning" of the terms "purist" and "syncretic" as well as their "usefulness" as analytical "categories." She also queries "the relationship between 'purist' and 'syncretic' religious behaviour within individual Muslim communities," in particular reference to "the idea of a confrontation between distinct sets of 'purist' maritime Muslims and 'syncretic' peasant or rural Muslims – the sort of people who are so often dismissed as 'half-Islamised' or even degenerate, 'backsliding' or simply 'bad Muslims'."[71] Her findings and observations are emphatic endorsement of the revisionist critique. She totally rejects the "notion of distinct and opposing realms of Muslim worship, of 'high' and 'low' or 'scriptural' and 'non-standard' Islam . . ." [72] Closely paralleling Ricklefs' attempt to set Javanese Islam in the wider contexts of the indigenous social and religious systems, Bayly sought "to trace some of the ways in which the Islam practised by Tamil Muslims was shaped and moulded by an equally complex local religious system." [73] On the basis of her findings, she warns us:

> . . . it is no longer satisfactory to conceive of the Tamil country – and indeed many other parts of south and southeast Asia – in terms of separate and distinct religious cultures confronting one another across rigid communal boundaries. Surely the traditions and practices enacted at these Labbai centres indicate that there has long been a close and subtle relationship

between religious traditions which are often thought of as distinct and mutually exclusive. Certainly the population of this region cannot be divided into the old bald categories of purist/ maritime traders ('santri') and 'syncretic' hinterland peasants ('abangan')[74]

She writes further,

> . . . it must not be thought that this Tamil Muslim trading elite had evolved by the eighteenth century into a population of 'Islamised' Muslims who had divorced themselves from the values, culture and religious motifs of the wider society . . . . It is clear that the maraikayyar [*maraikkayar*/the Tamil maritime traders] retained very complex links to a world of elite and exclusive Muslim piety, but they also pursued much wider ranging religious connections.[75]

Islamisation, contrary to earlier assumptions, is no longer considered unil-ineal, unidirectional or even continuous. It has not always advanced "orthodox Islamic beliefs and practices at the cost of little traditional ones." [76] Aziz Ahmad, whom we quoted earlier as speaking so vehemently about the eradication of "folk beliefs," concedes that "movements of mass reform . . . have tried to erase" those "demonic, superstitious and syncretic beliefs," but *not with complete success*." [77] "In the lower classes of East Pakistan [now Bangladesh]," he writes, "*some folk-beliefs* still persist despite the fundamentalist Fara'idi movement's success in the nineteenth century, and the Jama'at-i Islami's growing influence on religious life today."[78] Ismail Lambat's investigations into the conditions of the Sunni Surati Vohras (Bohras) reveal an intensification, in recent years, of a "struggle between custom and religion," but "the customary rites and ceremo-nies," he adds, "continue to hold a very strong hold on the group and have not been replaced by alternate [sic] religious practices."[79] Partap Aggarwal's find-ings on the Meos of Rajasthan and Haryana, reveal that they continued to op-pose, in the face of sustained pressures of Islamisation on the community, preferential cousin marriage, as prescribed in the *shari'a*.[80] Likewise, Muslims of Tamilnadu, as observed by Susan Bayly, were inclined to the Tamil system of patrilocal *murai* marriage or preferred marriage to father's sister's daughter. Not permitted under "orthodox" Muslim law, *murai* marriages are "common among Muslims in inland Tamilnadu." In the trading ports, which harboured Islamic "orthodoxy," "marriage is based on a distinctive matrilocal system which is un-known elsewhere in the region."[81] Mattison Mines, in his studies on Tamil Mus-lims, notes that they "marry among themselves and only rarely marry Mulims from other groups." According to Mines, this is "largely a result of Tamilians' marriage preference for kinsmen . . .," [82] and thus, "what is considered orthodox by Pallavaram's Muslims is influenced by local beliefs."[83] In villages, he finds

Tamil Muslims do not differentiate themselves so much from the rural social structure. There they accept and practice customs which are anathema to them in their urban based orthodoxy . . . village behaviour provides a striking contrast to urban behaviour. [84]

Mines's study, with this significant exposition of a differential response of the Tamilian Muslims to Islamisation in rural and urban settings, adds a new dimension to the problem under study that Islamisation cannot also be seen as a continuous process. The greater propensity for Islamisation in the urban, rather than rural setting, has been noted in other South Asian regions as well.[85] Mines, however, provides cogent explanations of this differential response to Islamisation. He stresses on the difference in "the structural basis" of these two settings as well as that of their identity. Hierarchy defined by interaction and closed corporate status defined by birth are two major features of village social structure. "Descent, interaction and displays of wealth" establish "religious identity and status in the village," and "an identity based on orthodoxy . . . contributes little to the Muslims' identity and status in the village. Urban structure, in contrast, is "relatively open," and identity in open urban context "cannot be based on corporateness, because fellow villagers are dispersed." Religious identity is "all that remains and orthodoxy helps to establish and maintain this identity," and so they found it "necessary to create a new group sense through Islamisation."[86]

Lina Fruzzetti and Jean Ellickson's studies relative to the Bengali-speaking Muslims, likewise, clearly reveal the coexistence and interpenetration of the twin religious complexes of orthodoxy and heterodoxy. Fruzzetti's perceptive study of the *rites de passage* and rituals among Muslims of Bishnupur in West Bengal leads her to the conclusion:

Bengali Muslims adhere simultaneously to the fundamental orthodox principles of Islam and to a Bengali culture. They state that one can be a 'Muslim' and a 'Bengali' without creating any contradiction or conflict between the two spheres, though both the boundaries are sharply defined by their ideology and practice . . . the universalistic aspect of Islam is not the only concern of the Muslims; in everyday practical life, the Muslims share in a 'Bengali culture,' which is common to both Hindus and Muslim Bengalis. [87]

Besides "the prescribed Islamic rules" concerning life cycle rites, Fruzzetti notes that "a number of local rules, loosely defined as *desher adat* (customs of the land) accompany the rituals." Both the Islamic and local culture are "maintained and followed by the Muslims . . . ." [88] They seemed to have "forged a unique culture" based on a combination of "Islamic precepts" with "the experience of everyday life . . . and the elements that come from a non-Islamic culture."

They see "no contradiction between strictly Islamic and non-Islamic practices," and

> ... whatever does not fit into the one fits into the other. Whatever is not in the Koran is *niom* [*niyam*] (Bengali), complementing though never contradicting, the spirit of Muslim *dharam* [religion].[89]

While Fruzzetti's evidence came from the Hindu-majority area of West Bengal, Ellickson's field study embraced the Muslim-majority area of Bangladesh, and the findings of both reinforced each other. Ellickson reports a substantive conflict between Islamic personal laws and the customary practices of the rural Muslims, who perceived no serious violation of Islamic injunctions in their customary acceptance of inheritance by a grandson.[90] The same perception is corroborated by their customary attitudes to divorce. Here again, Ellickson reports no perceived sense of conflict between the family laws of the *shari'a* and the dominant social values obtained locally, disfavouring divorce by wife. In the words of the locals: "According to *our religion*, 'a woman cannot divorce her husband'."[91] The underlying rationale, which Ellickson offers for this position, is a clear vindication of the revisionist model of a shifting boundary between orthodoxy and heterodoxy. In her opinion:

> The argument was couched in terms of what a good Muslim should do ... and all that is required is general local consensus as to what 'good Muslims' do.[92]

VIII

The revisionist perception does indeed uncover the variety, subtlety, complexity, and dynamism of the highly protean process of Islamisation in South Asia. This it does, as shown above, primarily by pulling down the time-honoured notional barricade between the so-called "orthodox" and "heterodox" Islam, raised and sustained uncritically by the academic orthodoxy on South Asian Islam. In its existential, historical and living ramifications, the regional Islam commanded a great deal more elasticity, plurality, tolerance and accommodation than fathomed by its orthodox observers.

Such views are, however, not exclusive to the world of South Asian Islam. Clifford Geertz's conventional and dominant notion of a dichotomy between a "high," "orthodox," and "purist" santri Islam and its "low," "heterodox," and "syncretic" abangan version,[93] as well as a logical extension of this notion that "the typical mode of Islamisation" involves a "lineal" and "unidirectional" progression of the transformative effects of the Islamising process,[94] have been countered in some recent studies. John Legge does not consider it "a very precise model...." He points out that the abangan tradition of the village community is

> a compound of Islamic as well as earlier traditions, and that the Indonesian peasant finds no great difficulty in combining in varying mixtures his obligations as a Muslim with his acceptance of older beliefs and customs.[95]

In Deliar Noer's opinion,

> this division into the putihan [or santri] and abangan in Java at the turn of the century was not of a hostile character. It merely distinguished one's particular type of devotion to Islam. They all called themselves Muslims, wong selam....[96]

Similar views, suggesting a more subtle process of interplay and interpenetration between Islam and *adat*, in the context of *Indonesia*, have been offered by others like Ricklefs, Christine Dobbin and Peter Carey.[97] In Ricklefs' study the new perception finds a strong articulation in the Southeast Asian context:

> ... it [Islam] was tolerant. It gave greater richness to Javanese religion without requiring the complete abandonment of older ideas. Thus Java came to be a Muslim society, but one in which Islam was only part of the vast cultural heritage.[98]

And yet, like all revisionist views, this new perception, in the context of South Asia, did not emerge in a void. Students of South Asian Islam could not have been unaware of several long-known linkages between the elite and folk levels of Islam. The tenacious persistence of castes, caste analogues and caste values right across the Muslim community in the region, in direct violation of clear Islamic norms, has been a common knowledge for long. Its wide prevalence in the area of Bengal has been noted above.[99] Buchanan-Hamilton, in the early nineteenth century, observed "a practical ascendancy" of the idea of caste over Muslims in Bengal and Bihar.[100] In 1896, Maulavi Muhammad Khan, a Muslim observer of Bengal, noted:

> Certainly Islam does not recognise class distinctions ... yet paradoxical though it may seem, people among Muhammadans do ask 'so and so what caste is he?' ... There are some classes who hold in great regard the custom of early marriage. Forced widowhood although prohibited by religion is rather the rule than the exception.[101]

In no inconsiderable way social and socio-religious practices and values such as "caste", "child marriage" and "forced widowhood" straddled the barrier between the *ashraf* and *atraf* or elite and folk Muslim societal divisions. But the most obvious and effective linkages between the twin social-religious complexes in the South Asian Muslim world are found in the common resort to the cults of saints (*pirs*) and shrines (*dargahs*) and in the extensive range of shared magical and supernatural beliefs and superstitions. Aziz Ahmad, a champion of the "purist" Islam concedes:

> . . . at the popular level Sufism itself became distorted, and even orthodox orders developed irreligious (*bi-shar'*) off-shoots, and most of them absorbed at that level *malami* (blameworthy) features. [102]

In the same context he provides a detailed account of the "heterodox variants" of the orthodox *sufi* orders in South Asia, and adds:

> A number of practices, which from the fundamentalist viewpoint appear heterodox, were common even among the orthodox Sufis . . . . Amulets, (*ta'widh*) containing verses of the Qur'an or other pious formulae, were prepared and distributed in the Sufi hospices. Shah Wali-Allah and Shah 'Abd-al-'Aziz deal with them in their writings with pious credulity. Amulets are still very much in use in India, as indeed in other parts of the Muslim world . . . as a charm against misfortune or disease. By the end of the eighteenth century there was an extensive variety of these amulets suitable for almost every conceivable calamity and misfortune. . . . Even the great Sufis of the thirteenth and fourteenth centuries believed in magic and witchcraft as a cause of illness. . . . Tombs of orthodox Sufis were, and are, held in veneration by mystics, the elite and the common people. [103]

Referring to the beliefs among Muslims in "the evil eye" and its "antidote" in the "concealment or multiplication of names," Ahmad informs us that the "Mughal emperors were sometimes given as many as three names. . ."[104] Further,

> In medieval and pre-modern India, belief in astrology and magic was quite common among Muslims. Astrologers thrived even under the pious and puritan Aurangzib. In the early nineteenth century, Tipu Sultan, otherwise an orthodox Muslim, had recourse to esoteric practices prescribed by Hindu astrologers."[105]

Susan Bayly explicates the "mixed and overlapping religious traditions" of the shrine cults, even of the "purist" Muslim trading towns on the Coromandel coasts.[106] She notes:

> Devotees from almost every class and community . . . flocked to . . . [these]

towns to venerate their dargahs, to obtain blessings, amulets and spiritual counsel from their pirzadas, and to take part in the shrines' ecstatic . . . festivals. . . . Their donors and worshippers clearly did not make any rigid distinctions between acceptable and unacceptable or Islamic and un-Islamic forms of worship: what mattered most was that their dargahs were universally revered as repositories of miraculous and transforming divine power, or barakat . . . these expanding networks of devotion and cult worship are not to be seen as elements of a parochial, debased or unlettered 'folk Islam.'[107]

The strong beliefs in the saint and shrine cults, divination, astrology, charm, and witchcraft among the pre-Mughal as well as Mughal rulers and elites in Bengal are clearly evidenced by the interesting account of Mirza Nathan, a Mughal naval official under Governor Islam Khan (1608-13), and also by other sources. On his authority we know that his father Ihtimam Khan, also a Mughal official, when ordered by Jahangir to proceed to Bengal, made his preparations "at an auspicious astrological hour," and that he kept under his employ a physician who was also "very expert in the science of astrology."[108] As the imperial fleet under his command entered the river Karatoya, writes Mirza Nathan:

On account of great tumult raised by the sailors, the sound of the victorious trumpets and the artillery, the fish of the river, jumping out of the water, began to fall on the boats. This was taken to be a good omen for the conquest of Bhati, and suppression of the rebels.[109]

He also spoke about his experiences in Ghantaghat which was "notorious for magic and sorcery." The people there could make any one "produce the voice of a fowl from inside his stomach," and could also turn mango leaves into fish by "breathing words of magic and sorcery" on them, which, if eaten, resulted in death. Muhammad Zaman was reportedly "bewitched by some person so that for two or three days he used to produce sounds of beasts, like dogs, cats and other animals of that class, and thus he died."[110] Mir Shams, "an expert in the science of necromancy," used "magic spells" to kill Shaikh Kamal, as a result of which "lumps of blood began to come out of his stomach and throat," and "after a week he expired."[111] Buzurg Ummed Khan, son of Nawab Shaista Khan of Bengal, started his march against the Firinghis and Maghs, according to Shihab ud-Din Talish, "at a moment auspicious for making a beginning."[112] He also spoke of the belief that Mir Jumla's fatal sickness, following upon his conquest of Koch-bihar and Assam, was "the result of witchcraft practised by the Rajah of Assam."[113] When Nawab Shuja' ud-Daula, who built "a magnificient garden" at Dehpara, was told about "the fairies," coming down there "for picnics and walks, and to bathe in its tanks," he, "dreading mischief" from them, "filled up the tanks with earth and discontinued his picnics in that garden."[114]

IX

The linkages between the two broad strands of Islam have indeed been there if one is looking for them and caring to read serious meanings into them. As amply evident from our discussions above, many writers – consciously or unconsciously – attest, either historically or empirically, to the presence of such contacts, but scarcely stop to probe deeply the nature of their interrelationship and their meanings. In "Sections V and VI" above, we examined the variety of orthodox academic positions in this matter, the central assumptions underlying them being a common acceptance of their dichotomous relationship – a dichotomy that, in their perceptions, should either be ignored as inconsequential, or must be remedied by means of "purging," "transforming," and "purifying" the folkish "aberrations," "anomalies," "accretions" or "degenerations". There is undeniably a normative, monolithic, and macro-perception of Islam that informs the rationale of such orthodox positions. The inadequacy, rigidity and even hollowness of this as an analytical model have been clearly exposed in many recent studies, as analysed above. The issue is clear: it is patently a simplistic and flawed academic exercise to resort to the convenience of denying every thing in the Islamic developments that one is unable to accommodate easily within the framework of an "ideal monolithic orthodoxy," defined essentially in Sunni scriptural terms. The Islam as practised by teeming millions of believers in South Asia, clearly emerges in our study with much greater elasticity, flexibility, tolerance, accommodative spirit, richness and diversity than what is encapsulated in this rather limited and doctrinaire view of Islamic orthodoxy. One cannot help feeling that this narrow and idealistic perception of Islamisation seeks, paradoxically, to save Islam from what they regard as its weaknesses by turning away from where the real strengths of Islam lay – its dynamism and creativity at the operative level on the world stage. Imtiaz Ahmad expresses similar sentiments when he says:

> . . . while Muslim fundamentalist may assert and maintain that there is one, and only one, version of what is orthodox from the Islamic point of view and whatever does not conform to it is to be dismissed as heterodox, the people's own beliefs and behaviour admit of much greater variety in what they regard as truly 'Islamic'. Clearly it seems to me that the Islamicists' vision has tended to obscure the inherent and underlying pluralism within Indian Islam as a practised religion.[115]

In the light of the mounting evidence to the contrary, the hoary notion of a quintessential polarity between the religious complexes of the so-called orthodoxy and heterodoxy or that of the elite and the folk does appear increasingly indefensible. Scholars of comparative religion have been long used to differentiating between the "transcendental" and "pragmatic" complexes within a single religious world, which often cut across the inner social and cultural barriers. In the words of David Mandelbaum:

> Whatever terms are chosen, the important fact is that both are used as part of the whole setting of religion in India, each is employed for generally differing (though frequently overlapping purposes) within the frame of religion and each is popularly considered to be complementary to the other.[116]

It is difficult to see that the "purist" champions in South Asian Islam are able to hold their ground much longer and continue to deny the rightful place of the regional and syncretistic developments as "a part and parcel of an integrated and unified religious system . . . in Indian Islam".[117]

In its empirical development, no system of ideology, beliefs and practices could be divorced from its spatial-social context. The social and cultural mores of the believer invest particular meanings and symbolism into those beliefs and practices as far as possible as a means of accommodating them to his *weltanschauung*, and leave the rest of his previous cultural baggage to coexist, generally harmoniously, with his new acquisitions. A student of this phenomenon is more meaningfully challenged to unravel this complex interface between the old inheritance and the new acquisition. In the context of Islam in Java and that in the Tamil-speaking region of South India Ricklefs' and Susan Bayly's efforts respectively have been directed to this approach, as noted above.[118] In his critically important study in the popular "sufi poetry" in the Sindhi language, Ali Asani emphasizes the "seminal role" of the so-called "folk, low or little tradition," in "propagating Islamic ideas within this population." He writes:

> Most studies of Indian Islam, while focussing on the elitist facet, have treated the folk tradition marginally – a treatment that is rather surprising considering the tradition's impact on a substantial proportion of the Muslim population, not to mention . . . its seminal role in propagating Islamic ideas within this population. [119]

Islam's encounter with Bengal, in the same manner, has its own specific social and cultural contexts which proved determining in recasting Islam into its distinctive regional mould. The Islamic revivalists and other observers encountered a situation in Bengal that resulted, not from a later debasement of Islam, but from the original conditions of culture-contact in the region. Nurtured and nourished by a rich combination of social, cultural and political circumstances in the history of medieval Bengal, the dominant form of Bengal's Islamic response blossomed, over a long period of time, into a rich syncretistic and acculturated tradition. The so-called degenerate and devitalised Islam in later Bengal was nothing but an embodiment of an earlier perception and formulation by Bengal Muslims of their religion in a syncretistic frame of reference. The syncretistic tradition remained the dominant form of Islamisation in Bengal for several centuries until the nineteenth century witnessed a massive and organised assault on this tradition and on the cultural values and norms necessary to sustain it. The history of Muslim Bengal had then entered its new modern phase, when Islamisation wore a new face in a new context.[120]

There is a final issue concerning the process of Islamisation. The adaptive process inhered in Islamisation is considered "not usually a conscious process," though "as in the case of personal law, it could be and was legitimised."[121] The major purpose of my own studies in the Islamic syncretistic tradition, on the other hand, has been to focus on

the making of the syncretistic tradition by the conscious efforts of the Bengali Muslim cultural mediators, with a view to disseminating Islam in a more locally familiar and meaningful form.[122]

Richard Eaton expressed reservations about "Roy's mediators" being engaged "quite self- consciously and deliberately" in "concocting their syncretic brew for the masses", and added:

Possibly much of Roy's literature reflected not so much the product of a conscious selection . . . as the survival of a purely Bengali substratum of values and ideas . . .[123]

There was of course much, coming from their long historical past, that the Bengalis, like any other people, held in common. The purpose of my study has neither been to deny such developments nor to explore them. My specific concerns have been to "find" and explain the presence of such indigenous matters in the literary efforts of the mediators which clearly evince their anxiety to foster the Islamic consciousness of the teeming masses of Bengal Muslims with attempts to win the latter's allegiance to a reconstructed Islamic tradition in the vernacular Bengali, couched in familiar and popular syncretistic forms and symbolisms. The problem set for my investigations has been as limited and specific as perhaps the objectives of "my mediators". It was precisely because of the converts continuing to be steeped in non-Islamic cultural heritage of Bengal that the Muslim *literati* were compelled to construct a tradition which Bengal Muslims could call and claim as their own. Saiyid Sultan bemoaned the fact that Bengali Muslims "in every home", denied of any comparable Islamic alternative in the

Bengali vernacular, resorted to the Hindu epics, the Mahabharata and the Ramayana.[124] This prompted him to compose his *magnum opus*, *Nabi-vamsa*, to wean Muslims away from the Hindu epics, *puranas* and *mangal-kavyas*. His subtle and purposive tampering with and construction of new myths about Krisna to vindicate the mission of Muhammad[125] provides rather clear and incontrovertible evidence of the mediators' "self-conscious and deliberate" role in constructing a popular and meaningful tradition for Bengali Muslims.[126]

The "conscious" promotion of an "Islamic purpose" in the Muslim vernacular literature in South Asia finds equal recognition in Susan Bayly's studies in the Tamil region. Despite the pervasive syncretic religious and cultural ethos of the Tamil maritime people, she rightly reminds us that they were "converts rather than Hindus." Even worshippers at "the most ecclectic of the Muslim and Christian shrines," she informs us, "preserved some sense of a distinct religious identity, however strongly this was overlaid with elements of a joint and undifferentiated religious culture." She mentions their "legends" which "employ Hindu terminology and language to describe Muslim and Christian victories over explicitly Hindu enemies." This is, she concludes, "as much a confrontation with alien religious traditions as an expression of shared values and shared ideology."[127] The adaptive process could, and did indeed become quite purposefully "conscious" rather than remain a mere survival of the cultural "substratum".

NOTES

1. William W. Roff, "Islamisation, 'communitas', symbols, and institutional structures. A Summary," in Dietmar Rothermund (ed), *Islam in Southern Asia. A Survey of Current Research* (Wiesbaden: Franz Steiner Verlag, 1975), p. 1.

2. Thomas W. Arnold, *The Preaching of Islam: A History of the Propagation of the Muslim Faith* (London: Luzac, 3rd edn, 1935).

3. For a useful introduction to such studies, see Nehemia Levtzion (ed.), *Conversion to Islam* (N.Y.: Holmes & Meier, 1979).

4. Geoff A. Oddie (ed.), *Religion in South Asia. Religious Conversion and Revival Movements in South Asia in Medieval and Modern Times* (Delhi: Manohar, 1977), p. 4, & passim.

5. Peter Hardy, *The Muslims of British India* (Cambridge: Cambridge University Press, 1972), p.8; Asim Roy, *The Islamic Syncretistic Tradition in Bengal* (Princeton: Princeton UP, 1983; or its Indian edition, New Delhi: Sterling Publishers, 1987), pp. 38-39, 252-53. [Henceforth cited as *Syncretistic Islam*.]

6. D.B. Forrester, "The depressed classes and conversion to Christianity, 1860-1960," in Oddie (ed.), *Religion in South Asia*, p. 35; also Roy, *Syncretistic Islam*, pp. 38ff.

7. Roy, *Syncretistic Islam*, pp. 39-40. Kinship ties "provided natural avenues of communication and contact which were of considerable importance in the further spread of the movement." [Geoff A. Oddie, "Christian conversion among non-Brahmans in Andhra Pradesh, with special reference to Anglican missions and the Dornakal diocese, c. 1900-1936," in Oddie (ed.), ibid., p. 83; also W. Garlington, "The Baha'i faith in Malwa," in ibid., p. 110;

J.T.F. Jordens, "Reconversion to Hinduism, the *shuddhi* of the Arya Samaj," in ibid.

8. Forrester,"Depressed classes", p. 4

9. Roy, *Syncretistic Islam*, pp. 40-41.

10. Ibid, pp. 6-7, fn. 7, 21-30, 58, 68-70.

11. E.A. Gait, Report [on Bengal], *Census of India*, 1901, vol. 6, pt 1 (Calcutta,1906), pp. 169-70; James Wise, *Notes on the Races, Castes, and Trades of Eastern Bengal* (London: Harrison & Sons, 1883), p. 6; Maulawi Muhammad M. Khan, "Social divisions in the Muhammadan community", *The Calcutta Monthly*, vi, no.1 (July, 1896), p.3; J. Talke, "Islam in Bengal", *The Muslim World*, iv (1914), p. 12; Roy, ibid.,pp. 35-38.

12. Forrester, "Depressed classes", p. 45; also J.W. Pickett, *Christian Mass Movements in India* (New York: Abingdon Press, 1933), pp. 128-29; Geoff A. Oddie, "Christian conversion in Telegu country, 1860-1900: a case study of one protestant movement in the Godavery-Krishna delta," *Indian Economic and Social History Review*, xii, no. 1 (Jan.-Mar 1975), pp. 76-77; Roy, ibid., p. 43.

13. Roy, ibid., pp. 43ff. ; Richard Eaton has recently characterised it as a "struggle against the forest" by "daring pioneers," and links the eastern delta with "an expanding economic frontier zone" of rice cultivation. [Richard M. Eaton, "Mughal religious culture and popular Islam in Bengal," (Paper presented at a Conference on "Regional Varieties of Islam in Pre-Modern India," held in Heidelberg in July 1989), pp. 1, 4.]

14. *East Pakistan: Land and People* (Karachi: Govt of Pakistan, the People of Pakistan Series, no. 2, n.d.), p. 23. Cf. also: Muslims in Bengal "appear to take less readily to a town life than the Hindus; but elsewhere the reverse is the case and in the United and Central Provinces, in Madras, and in many of the adjoining states the proportion of the Muhammadans in towns is double that of Muhammadans in the population at large." [Herbert Risley et al (eds), *The imperial Gazetteer of India* (Oxford: Clarendon Press, new rev. ed., 26 vols, 1931), vol. 1, p. 455; also Gait, ibid., p. 484.]

15. D.N. Majumdar and C.R. Rao, *Race Elements in Bengal. A Quantitative Study* (Calcutta: Statistical Publishing Society, 1960), p. 96; also Roy, *Syncretistic Islam*, pp. 26-28.

16. O.H.K. Spate and A.T.A. Learmonth, *India and Pakistan: A General and Regional Geography* (London: Methuen, 3rd edn, 1967), p. 574; also R.K. Mukerjee, *The Changing Face of Bengal – A Study in Riverine Economy* (Calcutta: Calcutta UP, 1938), pp. 4, 7-9.

17. Spate and Learmonth, ibid., p.575.

18. Krisnarama-das, *Raya-mangal*, ed. by S.N. Bhattacharya (Bardhaman, 1956); and Abdul Karim, *Kalu-Gaji (Ghazi)-Champavati* (Calcutta, n.d.); Roy, *Syncretistic Islam*, pp. 46, 53, 235-41.

19. Radha Kumud Mukerjee, ibid., pp. 27-28; Roy, ibid., pp. 49-50.

20. Roy, ibid., pp. 52-54.

21. Yogindra Singh, *Modernization of Indian Tradition* (Delhi: Thompson Press (India) Ltd, 1973), p. 73.

22. Ghaus Ansari, *Muslim Castes in Uttar Pradesh: A Study in Culture Contact* (Lucknow: Ethnographic and Folk Culture Society, UP, 1960), pp. 38, 62.

23. For such changes of names among *Atraf* Muslims in Bengal, see Roy, *Syncretistic Islam*, pp. 29-30; Rafiuddin Ahmed, *The Bengal Muslims 1871-1906. A Quest For Identity* (New Delhi: Oxford UP,1981), pp.112-13.

24. Singh, *Modernization*,p. 75.

25. Mattison Mines, "Islamization and Muslim ethnicity in South India," in Rothermund (ed.), *Islam in Sothern Asia*, pp. 55-56.

26. William W. Roff, "Islamization, 'communitas', symbols", in Rothermund, ibid., p. 2.

27. Mines, "Islamization and Muslim ethnicity", p. 56.

28. Satish C. Misra, "Indigenisation and Islamisation in Muslim society in India," in S.T. Lok-handwalla (ed.), *India and Contemporary Islam* (Simla: Indian Institute of Advanced Study, 1971), p. 366.

29. "Indigenisation in India subsumes a pull towards the Hindu system . . . it is possible to judge to some extent the degree of indigenisation suffered by the 'foreign' Muslim communities which brought them nearer their Indian coreligionists and other Indian groups." Referring to the "Indian Muslim communities", Misra writes, "the pull they had was in another direction." Ibid., p. 368.

30. Roy, *Syncretistic Islam*, pp. 250-51.

31. Louis S.S. O'Malley, *Popular Hinduism* (Cambridge UP, 1935), p.17.

32. Tarachand, *Influence of Islam on Indian Culture* (Allahabad: The Indian Press (Publications) Private Ltd, 2nd edn, 1963), Introduction, ix; see also James G. Frazer, *The Golden Bough*, pt 6: "The Scapegoat" (London, 3rd edn., 1925), pp. 89-90.

33. Ali S. Asani, "Sufi poetry in the folk tradition of Indo-Pakistan," *Religion and Literature*, xx, no.1 (Spring 1988), p. 81.

34. As early as the fourteenth century, the influential Muslim *sufi,* Makhdum-i Jahaniyan Jahangasht forbade Muslims not to use Indian equivalents for the name of Allah. [Annemarie Schimmel, "Reflections on popular Muslim poetry," *Contributions to Asian Studies*, 17 (1982), p. 18; also, ibid., p.82.]

35. Ja'far Sharif, *Qanun-i Islam*, English tr. by G. Herklot and ed. by William Crooke (Oxford, 1921).

36. Garcin de Tassy, *Memoire sur les Particularites de la Religion Musalmane dans l'Inde* (Paris, 1831).

37. (Mrs) Meer Hassan Ali, *Observations on the Musulmauns of India*, ed. by William Crooke (Oxford, 1917).

38. The Report, *Census of India*, 1901, vol. 18, pt 1, p. 152. Also Asani, "Sufi poetry in the folk tradition," p. 82; and his, "The Khojahs of Indo-Pakistan: the quest for an Islamic identity," *Journal Institute of Muslim Minority Affairs*, viii, no.1 (January 1987), p. 31.

39. This particular part of the essay relies heavily on my article (forthcoming): "The interface of Islamization, syncretization, and regionalization: the Bengal paradigm," pp. 1-3. This arose out of a paper presented at a conference in Heidelberg (July, 1989) on the "Regional Variations of Islam in Pre-modern South Asia" sponsored by the South Asia Institute, University of Heidelberg. The paper is included in a forthcoming volume to be published by the Institute. [Henceforth cited as "Interface of Islamization".]

40. *Siyar ul-Muta'akherin*, cited, Qazi Abdul/ Abd al-/ Wadud, Hindu-Musalmaner Birodh [in Bengali] (Santiniketan: Visva-Bharati, 1936), p.16.

41. Wise, *Races and Castes*, p. 6.

42. Roy, *Syncretistic Islam*, Preface, ix-x, xiii-xxi.

43. *The Moslem Chronicle* (Calcutta), 28 January 1905, p. 193.

44. Cited in Anthony Mascarenhas, *The Rape of Bangladesh* (Delhi: Vikas Publications, 1971), p. 18. Among the "major points of discontent" between the Bengalis and West Pakistanis Mascarenhas mentions "the absurd denigration of the piety of the Muslims in the east wing by those in the west". [Ibid. p. 14] He reminisces about a Punjabi military officer, placed in an East Pakistan district during the Bangladesh crisis, who grabbed a handful of the "the rich, black earth" of the place and exclaimed, "My God, what couldn't we do with such wonderful land", and then added: "But I suppose we would have become like them." [Ibid., p.11].

45. M. Ayub Khan, *Friends Not Masters* (London: Macmillan, 1967), p. 187.

46. Emphasis mine. Henceforth all empheses in quotations are mine unless otherwise indicated.

47. Aziz Ahmad, *An Intellectual History of Islam in India* (Edinburgh: Edinburgh UP, 1969), pp. 44, 46.

48. Aziz Ahmad, *Studies in Islamic Culture in the Indian Environment* (London: Oxford UP, 1964), pp. 163-64.

49. Muhammad Mujeeb, *The Indian Muslims* (London: Allen & Unwin, 1967), p. 22.

50. Hardy, *Muslims of India*, p. 27.

51. Francis Robinson (ed.), *Atlas of the Islamic World Since 1500* (Oxford UP, 1982), p. 119.

52. Eaton, "Mughal culture and Bengal, " p. 1.

53. Imtiaz Ahmad, "Unity and variety in South Asian Islam. A summary," in Rothermund (ed.), *Islam in Southern Asia*, pp.6-8.

54. Momtazur Rahman Tarafdar, *Husain Shahi Bengal, 1494-1538* (Dhaka: Asiatic S[ociety] of P[akistan], 1965), pp. 163-64.

55. R. Ahmed, *Bengal Muslims*, pp. 54-55.

56. Azizur Rahman Mallick, *British Policy and the Muslims in Bengal 1757-1856* (Dhaka: Asiatic SP, 1961), p. 3.

57. Ibid., pp. 7-8.

58. Ibid., p. 9.

59. In a study of Muslims in Bengal, Mallick seems to overlook here that while Muslims formed a minority in the Indian subcontinent, they were a majority of the Bengal population.

60. Ibid., p. 29.

61. Roy, *Syncretistic Islam*, p. 6.

62. Ibid., p. 7. See also below.

63. Mushirul Haq, "A Note for the ICSSR Workshop on Religion, Politics and Society," held on October 25, 1979, cited Imtiaz Ahmad (ed.), *Ritual and Religion among Muslims in India* (New Delhi: Manohar, 1981), p. 8.

64. Aziz Ahmad, *Intellectual History*, p. 51.

65. I. Ahmad, "Unity and variety," p. 6; also Singh, *Modernization*, p.76, which provides some ideas and expressions for Ahmad.

66. Ziaul Hasan Faruqi, "Orthodoxy and heterodoxy in Indian Islam," *Islam and the Modern Age*, 32 (1979), p. 34.

67. Ibid.

68. Reference here is to my post-graduate research work in the late 1960s, leading to my doctoral thesis in 1970 [Asim Roy, "Islam in the environment of medieval Bengal", Ph.D. thesis (Canberra: Australian National U, 1970.)] My claim in this respect is based on a rather casual survey of this particular area. I should be pleased to know the truth of this position.

69. I. Ahmad (ed.), *Ritual and Religion*, p. 12.

70. I. Ahmad, "Unity and variety," pp. 6-7.

71. Susan Bayly, "Islam in Southern India: 'purist' or 'syncretic'?," in Chris A. Bayly and D.H.A. Kolff (eds.), *Two Colonial Empires* (Dordrecht: Martinus Nijhoff Publishers, 1986), pp. 36-37.

72. Susan Bayly, "The limits of Islamic expansion in South India," (paper presented at a Conference on "Regional Varieties of Islam in Pre-Modern India," held in Heidelberg in July 1989), p. 6.

73. Bayly, "Islam in Southern India," pp. 36-37.

74. Ibid., p. 57. Cf. also "Surely what begins to emerge then is a picture of a single religious culture of great complexity and variability but with fundamental elements of belief and practice held in common among a very large part of the population." [Ibid., p. 59.]

75. Bayly, "Islamic expansion in South India," p. 3.

76. I. Ahmad, "Unity and variety," p. 6.

77. Aziz Ahmad, *Intellectual History*, p.44.

78. Ibid., p. 51.

79. Ismail A. Lambat, "Marriage among the Sunni Surati Vohras of South Gujarat," in Imtiaz Ahmad (ed.), *Family, Kinship and Marriage among Muslims in India* (Delhi: Manohar, 1976), p. 80.

80. Partap C. Aggarwal, "Changing religious practices: their relationship to secular power in a Rajasthan village," *Economic and Political Weekly*, iv, no.12 (1969), pp. 547-51.

81. Bayly, "Islam in Southern India", p. 40.

82. Mines, "Islamization and Muslim ethnicity," p. 72.

83. Ibid., p. 69.

84. Ibid., pp. 55, 76-77.

85. Singh, *Modernization*; Faruqi,"Orthodoxy and heterodoxy", pp. 9-36; Partap C. Aggarwal, "A Muslim sub-caste of north India: problems of cultural integration," *Economic and Political Weekly*, i, pp. 159-67; Satish C. Misra, *Muslim Communities in Gujarat* (Bombay: Asia Publishing House, 1964.)

86. Mines, "Islamization and Muslim ethnicity," pp. 84-85.

87. Lina M. Fruzzetti, "Muslim rituals: the household rites vs. the public festivals in rural India," in I. Ahmad (ed.), Rituals and Religion, pp. 92-93.

88. Ibid., p. 91.

89. Ibid., p. 111.

90. Jean Ellickson, "Islamic institutions: perception and practice in a village in Bangladesh," *Conributions to Indian Sociology*, vi (New Series, 1972).

91. Ibid., p. 62.

92. Ibid., p. 58.

93. Clifford Geertz, *The Religion of Java* (Glencoe, Illinois: 1960).

94. Clifford Geertz, "Modernization in a Muslim society: the Indonesian case," in Robert N. Bellah (ed.), *Religion and Progress in Modern Asia* (New York: The Free Press, 1965), pp. 96-97.

95. John D. Legge, *Indonesia* (Sydney: Prentice-Hall of Australia, 2nd edn, 1977), pp. 59-61.

96. Deliar Noer, *The Modernist Muslim Movement in Indonesia 1900-1942* (Kuala Lumpur: Oxford UP, 1973), p. 19. Noer uses the term putihan for santri.

97. M.C. Ricklefs, *Jogjakarta Under Sultan Mankubumi 1749-1792. A History of the Division of Java* (London: 1974); also his "Islamization in Java," in Levtzion (ed.), *Conversion in Islam*, pp. 100-128; Christine Dobbin, *Islamic Revivalism in a Changing Peasant Economy. Central Sumatra, 1784-1847* (London: 1983); Peter Carey, *Babad Dipanagara. An Account of the Outbreak of the Java War (1825-30)*, (Kuala Lumpur, 1981).

98. Ricklefs, "Islamization in Java", pp. 126-27.

99. Supra, p. 2, fn. 11.

100. M. Martin, *The History, Antiquities, Topography, and Statistics of Eastern India* [compiled from Buchanan MSS. (1807-1814)] (London, 1838), vol. 3, p. 150; Roy, *Syncretistic Islam*, pp. 36- 37.

101. Maulawi Muhammad M. Khan, "Social divisions in the Muhammadan community", p. 3; Roy, ibid., p. 37.

102. A. Ahmad, *Intellectual History*, p. 44.

103. Ibid., pp. 45-46.

104. Ibid., p. 48.

105. Ibid., p. 50.

106. Bayly, "Islam in Southern India", p. 44.

107. Bayly, "Islamic expansion in South India," p. 5.

108. Mirza Nathan, Baharistan-i'Ghaybi , English tr. by M.I. Borah (Gauhati: Govt of Assam, 1936.), vol.1, pp. 6, 167.

109. Ibid., p. 53.

110. Ibid., pp. 273-74.

111. Ibid., vol. 2, p. 671.

112. Shihab ud-Din Talish, Fathiya-i 'Ibriya, English tr.by J.N. Sarkar, in his *Studies in Aurangzab's Reign* (Calcutta: Calcutta UP, 1933), p.198.

113. Ibid., p. 191; also cited, Henry Blochmann, "Koch Bihar and Assam," *Journal of the Asiatic Society of Bengal*, pt 1, no. 1 (1872), p. 67.

114. Ghulam Husain Salim, *Riyaz us-Salatin*, English tr. by Maulavi Abdus Salam (Calcutta, 1902), p. 291.

115. I. Ahmad (ed.), *Ritual and Religion*, p. 18.

116. David G. Mandelbaum, "Introduction. Process and structure in South Asian Religion," in Edward B. Harper (ed.), *Religion in South Asia* (Seattle: Washington UP, 1964), p. 10.

117. I. Ahmad (ed.), *Ritual and Religion*, p. 14.

118. Supra, p. 14.

119. Asani, "Sufi poetry in the folk tradition," p. 81.

120. Roy, *Syncretistic Islam*, pp. 250-52; also his "Interface of Islamization," pp. 24-25.

121. I. Ahmad (ed.), *Ritual and Religion*.

122. Roy, *Syncretistic Islam*, p. 251.

123. R. M. Eaton, "Review" of ibid., in *Journal of Asian Studies*, xliv, no. 2 (February 1985), p. 443; cf. also ". . . the process of Islamization, understood as a tendency involving a conscious rejection of syncretic elements that persist as remnants of pre-conversion orientations and ethos. . ." [I. Ahmad (ed.), *Ritual and Rleligion*, p. 10.]

124. Roy, *Syncretistic Islam*, p. 69.

125. Ibid., pp. 96-98.

126. Roy, "Interface of Islamization," pp. 25-26.

127. Bayly, "Islam in Southern India", pp. 64-65.

3. Sexuality – An Islamic Historical Perspective with Special Reference to South Asia

SEXUALITY, or attitudes to and relationships between sexes, is a fascination as old and vital as life itself. As the most basic level of human relationship, it forms a primary concern not only of religion, philosophy, morality, and law but of art, literature, mythology, and science as well. The underpinnings of a society are often revealed by an examination of its standards and criteria for what is accepted and rejected, approved and deprecated in social behaviour. To probe the sexual mores of a society and its individuals in the light of these questions is to provide a basic and rather effective means of defining and understanding the same.

The study of sexuality in the context of Islam and Muslims by modern scholars has, however, been a desideratum. Not until the sixties of this century any serious academic undertaking in this area was to be found. Even so, this interest at its early stage was not embodied in the English language. Both the major works to appear since are in French.[1] The first substantial undertaking in English appeared in 1979, incorporating the results of the Sixth Della Vida Biennial Conference on sex and society in medieval Islam, held, in May 1977, under the auspices of the G.E. von Gruenbaum Center for Near Eastern Studies, University of California.[2] B.F. Musallam's very recent study in birth control in pre-modern Islam also offers some perspectives on eros in Islam.[3] And if, in the context of Classical Islam, the study of sexuality seems to have aroused interest rather recent and quantitatively meagre, one is only looking at a clean slate in the matter of academic interest in the erotic and sexuality in South Asian Islam.[4] We shall, however, return to this issue a little later.

This tardy response to Islamic sexuality is ironical in that there is a growing realisation of a more positive sexual attitude in Islam than in traditional Christianity. The "sexual revolution" of recent times in the West has brought about a wide dispersion and a heightened awareness of sexuality among people, urging many to try to live their own sexual lives, sacred or profane, normal or deviant. The "seminal" importance of sexuality in human affairs has forced its recognition on the West. Until then, a pervasive negative sexual attitude had been attributed to traditional Christianity. R.W. Southern, a distinguished medievalist, contrasts what he calls the "sex-negative" attitudes in Christianity with "sex-positive" religion and society of Islam.[5] Franz Rosenthal, while pointing out that modern Western scholarship "takes a generally favourable view of the Muslim system as reflected in the theoretical, ideal guidelines of religion and law," does not totally concur with Southern's positive-negative polarity, but concedes:

> Islam always took care to admit that sexuality existed as a problematic element in the relationship of individuals and society and never hesitated to leave room for the discussion of approval or disapproval. Traditional Christianity was inclined to pretend that sexuality's legitimate right of existence was limited, and further discussion was avoided as much as possible.[6]

This may create an impression that Islam has achieved an ideal fusion between sex and religion. Such a view would, however, be a gross oversimplification. Islam, like other belief-systems, reveals a significant hiatus between the ideal and the actual. This gap, in Islam, is to be understood in more than one sense. The first discrepancy concerns two aspects of the ideal itself. Islam offers a striking contrast between the sensual pleasures of Paradise and the more restrictive moral code of life on earth.[7] While some Muslims and non-Muslims had undoubtedly seen it as reinforcing the argument for sexuality in Islam, the dichotomy itself had strengthened in many believers a realisation of the disruptive potential of sexuality on earth. Moreover, Muslim society had its share of the champions of celibacy and asceticism, who regarded religion and sex incompatible. Finally, in Islam as in traditional Christianity, the ideals of sexual morality find their contrasts in real life. Subsequently, the laws in most Western countries were gradually adapted to leave most sexual matters out of their ambit. Subject to the triple principles of free consent, adulthood, and privacy, modern Western laws remain content to regard sexuality a matter of individual conscience and private morality. *Sharia*, or the Islamic Law, is based on a principle very opposite to the modern Western, and makes no distinction between law and morality. No sexual relationship among Muslims is permissible unless it is legal as well. Otherwise it constitutes a criminal offence.[8]

I

As in all other respects in Islam, attitudes to sex and sexual morality are moulded by the Qur'an and the *Sunna*, or the examples of the Prophet as recorded in the *hadith* on the basis of the testimonies of his companions. Major aspects of sexual behaviour and the most important elements in the Muslim sexual ethic are in the Qur'an, elaborated by *hadith*, or the tradition of the Prophet, and *akubra*, or later tradition of the companions of the Prophet. The keynote of this cumulative tradition, bearing on sexuality, is: "legal sex or no sex at all."

Islam clearly recognises, as noted above, the existence and importance of sexuality as a major human concern. Of the "six" categories of "pleasures" on earth such as food, drink, clothing, scent, sound, and sex, some medieval Muslim writers chose "sexual enjoyment as the greatest of human pleasures."[9] Abstinence from sex was vaguely associated with the cause of insanity. Jalal al-Din Rumi, the mystic poet, alludes to it.[10] The Prophet himself had a rather positive sexual attitude. In an oft-quoted *hadith*, the Prophet expressed his liking for women, along with perfume and prayer. According to another, he regarded every copulation "a meritorious act comparable with alms giving."[11] He was reportedly the first in Islam to use an aphrodisiac. In response to his complaint to Jibrail (Gabriel) about his "weakness of potency" the angel recommended him a special food which "would give him the power of forty men."[12] "It is this example and confession of the Prophet", says Burgel, "that made erotic pleasure if not an integral part, in any case a not unseemly aspect of a pious man's life."[13] Muslim medical and other literary sources contain references to numerous aphrodisiacs. And magic picked up where medicine stopped. Magical recipes to arouse or kill conscupience, love etc. were also quite popular.[14] In reference to conscupience (*shahwa'*) which, he thought, dominated the Arab nature, al-Ghazzali, the great medieval scholar-mystic, remarked:

> If one wife does not suffice, marry upto four times. Even if there is no content in heart, change is advisable. Ali married again seven days after Fatima's death. His son Hasan married 200 wives, four at a time. The Prophet would say to him, "you resemble my nature and my character!"[15]

Having conceded that the primary objective of coition was progeniture, al-Ghazzali was willing to recognise "a value of its own" in terms of "its unrivalled but always all too brief delight, arousing man's longing for the lasting one in the world to come."[16]

II

This positive affirmation of sexuality in Islam is, however, rigidly confined to the bound of Islamic law *(shari'a)* and morality. *Shari'a* clearly differentiates between *nikah*, or legal sex, and *zina*, or illicit sex. The legal intercourse for a woman is with her husband only, while for a man it is extended beyond his wife or wives to concubines and slave girls.

The Qur'an and *hadith* strongly enjoin marriage on the believers. Men are even urged to find spouses for the slaves. The example of the Prophet, in whom the believers are told by Allah that they "have a noble pattern" (*Sura* 33:21), had finally set the tone for marital sex in Islam. In his early life, Muhammad was engaged in a relationship of happy monogamous matrimonial love with Khadija and had four daughters out of this wedlock. Later in his life he was involved in polygamous relationships. But he strongly favoured marriage.

Despite the dominant position of marriage the issue of marriage vs celibacy remained long alive in the history of Islam. The question of asceticism and celibacy has been mentioned above.[17] Some later *Sufis*, or mystics, frankly underlined the importance of marriage for prosecuting religious activities untrammelled by sex, as Junaid frankly admitted: "I need sex the way I need food." In a rather rare *hadith* bearing on the Prophet's sexual life, we are told that his desire was once aroused by a woman, and he resorted forthwith to his wife Zainab and "satisfied himself in her". The Prophet is also said to have remarked: "when a woman approaches, she comes like a *shaitan* go to your wife, she has the same thing as the other".[18] The Prophet's uxoriousness had been a strong argument against celibacy. Despite this, there are some good evidence to suggest a strong movement in favour of celibacy in early days of Islam, and again later. Some mystics were deeply concerned about their family responsibilities interfering with their spiritual pursuits. As in many other vital areas, al-Ghazzali's reasoned and balanced analysis of the relative advantages and disadvantages of marriage and celibacy contributed largely to the resolution of the question. He summarised the advantages of marriage in the following terms: procreation, sexual gratification, housekeeping, enlargement of the kinship circle, and finally, the struggle of the soul in upholding justice and responsibility in respect of the wife or wives and children. Against these Ghazzali arrayed the disadvantages of which three were most important, namely possibilities for illegal livelihood, inability to discharge duties to the family, and distraction from Allah. It was for individuals, according to Ghazzali, to weigh up the situation for themselves, and "there is no question but that he should marry" provided one is capable of fulfilling all his obligations, familial and spiritual.[19] "The practical considerations of sexual gratification were so strong", observes James C. Bellamy, "that sex and the responsibilities of family life might endanger one's hope of salvation could deter only a very few men from following the course approved by the religious and social norm of Muslim society".[20]

The Islamic laws regarding sexual behaviour are strongly designed to preserve the institution of marriage and marital sex, subject to the recognition of concubinage in Islam. Islamic Criminal Law recognises two different categories of offences, *hadd*, or defined offences with fixed punishments, and *ta'zir*, lesser offences where the determination of punishment is a matter for the discretion of the authorities. Extra-marital sexual intercourse by persons, married or unmarried constitutes the *hadd* offence of *zina*, and punishable by 100 lashes, if unmarried, and by stoning to death, if married. The offence of *zina* is so grave that accusation without proof is itself a *hadd* offence and liable to the most serious charge of defamation with a punishment of 80 lashes.

Zina requires very strict and rigid system of proof, almost rendering an actual conviction and punishment rather impossible. Doubts have been raised about the rationale of this rigidity, and suggestion has been made that the law was not really designed to bring offender to justice in order that undesirable publicity to a violation of this central maxim of Islamic sexual morality could be avoided and that while the law was broken, it was not to be seen as broken. Noel Coulson rejects this line of reasoning as "facile and cynical". He points out that for *hadd* offence Islamic Law is against inflicting any punishment should there be a shadow of doubt as to the guilt of the accused. For *zina* the rule is obviously carried to the fullest extent. This is because Islam brought about a radical change by elevating the marital status and enhancing the position of women as wives and mothers. The pre-Islamic notion of women as child bearing chattels was replaced by a bilateral and contractual relationship in which the husband claimed exclusive right to sexual union with his wife against the dower, wife's right to maintenance and inheritance. The Islamic provisions for *zina* were clearly aimed at upholding this newly elevated marital status which was the corner stone of the Islamic Family Law.[21]

III

Islamic attitudes to sex are marked by as much directness as pudency and prudery . The opinions on the nature of pudency and prudery in early Islam, however, vary. Franz Rosenthal and James Bellamy both find prudery as a very consistent theme of Muslim behaviour ever since the time of the Prophet. The Qur'an urges "sexual modesty" (*Sura* 33: 35; 24: 30ff.) for both men and women; and the *hadith* and *akhbar* generally refrain from referring to sex in personal contexts, and their language is chaste and uniformly serious.[22] Pudency was not quite enjoined by the law and could not have been enforced. But the *hadith* and *akhbar* were rather important in fostering a strong sense of pudency and prudery. Some *hadith* clearly urged it. According to a *hadith* "the Prophet was more modest than a virgin in her private quarters; if he found something to be distasteful, we could see it in his face". Lack of modesty was often compared to disbelief. Bellamy points out:

> . . . there is good evidence that it has increased with the passage of time. It is much more difficult today to publish an obscene book in the Muslim world than in the West, and . . . Muslims sometimes show embarrassment at the frankness of the works produced by their ancestors in the Middle Ages.[23]

It is perhaps this gradual stiffening of attitude of pudency that prompted Burgel to adopt an apparently dissimilar position from Rosenthal and Bellamy. Burgel believes that the Prophet's companions and the early Muslim notables were "far from prudish in their expression about erotics." His view is based on the authority of al-Jahiz, the brilliant ninth-century Muslim writer, who ridiculed the false modesty, affectation and hypocrisy of his contemporaries opposed to outspokenness in literature. Jahiz cited an anecdote from a reputed *hadith,* which evidenced outspokenness in sexual matters in a gathering graced by the presence of the Prophet, his favourite wife A'isha and her father Abu Bakr. But the description of the incident clearly suggests that "voices were raised against this kind of candor from the very beginning".[24] Besides, that Jahiz and Ibn Qutayba, his contemporary, who also used explicit language for sexual subjects, had felt compelled to apologise for their outspokenness and caution others against excesses of literary explicitly clearly underline the persistence and dominance of this sense of prudery and pudency in Islam. By the middle of the eleventh century in the classical period the sense of prudery in sexual attitudes had strengthened so much that a merchant banker of Tunisia out of a sense of propriety, chose not to mention his wife in his many letters where his children and all others were mentioned. Another young schoolmaster wrote to his mother about his prospective bride, and, out of the same sense of decency, described her beauty in Hebrew and not in Arabic as was the case with the rest of the letter.[25] Even physicians were reluctant to speak about some topics. Many seemed apologetic about discussing "subjects which they were not sure were to be considered medical problems or moral problems to be left to society to handle".[26]

The growing strength of pudent and prudish attitudes was perhaps ultimately drawn from a situation of steady formulation and integration of the mores of Islamic sexual morality and ethic through a mass of didactic literature in the forms of *hadith*, *akhbar*, and *risala* or *kitab.* The initiative and dedication of a people to be called *Ahl al-hadith* who organised highly popular reading sessions of this didactic literature gave Islam its religiosity and moral flavour. To this was added the contributions of the *Sufi* mystics who also drew upon these prosaic material to transform them into a fine instruction in living sexual morality and ethic for Muslims.[27]

IV

Of the various problems associated with the study of sexuality in Islam, as under any other religious and moral systems, one has to contend with the most formidable one of ascertaining the nature and extent of the gulf between the norm and practice, the ideal and actual, the scriptural and the living realities. The study of a sensitive and delicate subject like sexuality cannot, by its very nature, but be limited by its rather meagre and non-empirical data. To bridge the gulf between the normative and the real existential worlds of his study has always been a despair of a historian bound almost entirely by the nature of his written sources. Nowhere else is the task more daunting than a study of the sexual attitudes and behaviour of a multitudinous community bound by a religion and divided by ethnic and cultural diversities. The theoretical or normative perspective is relatively easily derived from a perusal of the scriptural, philosophical, moral and ethical works. For an appreciation of the reality of the situation at an existential level one cannot but turn almost exclusively to the creative or fictional literature. To what extent does literature, however, reflect the societal reality and morality is a crucial question which we shall have to explore later.

Besides the basic scriptural works like the Qur'an, *hadith* and *akhbar* and their ancillary legal and juristic sequels, philosophical treatise on love like *Risala fil-'ishq* (Treatise on Love) by Ibn Sina, or on marriage like al-Ghazzali's "Book of Marriage" in "Revival of the Religious Sciences", and handbook on courtly love and wedlock like *Tauq al-Hamama* ("Necklace of the Dove") by Ibn Hazm (d.456 A.H./1046 A.D.) and on etiquette (*adab*) like Ibn Arabi's *al-Futuhat al-Makkiya* offer a broad normative perspective on sexuality in Islam. In addition there are some practical guidebooks of coition *(bah)* with occasional anecdotes. The most well-known among them is the *Perfumed Garden* by Shaikh Nafzawi (flourished in early 15th century), which gained the reputation of the Indian *Kamasutra* in Arabic. Outside the domain of these writings there is a wide range of essentially or partly secular literature shedding direct or indirect light on Islamic sexuality. Among literature of this genre, prose romances and poems are most rewarding. In prose there are epics, tales, and anecdotes. Apparently, distinction can be made between fictitious love stories such as the Persian romantic epics, *The Thousand and One Nights* and the Book of the Peacock (*Tuti Nama*), and love adventures forming part of the biographies of poets like the "Book of Songs" of Abu'l-Faraj al-Isfahani (d.356 A.H./67 A.D.). But the basis for this distinction is often rather weak. A fictitious work, as Burgel points out, may be used as a vehicle for distinct personal views on love and love morals, and the biographical materials about a celebrity, on the other hand, are not necessarily factual.[28] Finally, quite opposite from elegant and chaste love stories there is the *mujun* literature dealing with obscene erotic anecdotes and poems.

The reality and morality of the popular and entertaining literature in relation to religion and law on one hand and empirical life on the other raise significant questions. There were, as noted above, various genres of this literature in both verse and prose. The very purpose and rationale of this literature were to offer a temporary respite from the tensions of real life, and not a great deal of value was to be attached to it as a source of moral instruction. Attempts in this literature often to focus on the unusual caused distortion of the reality, and the urges of a writer for originality also encouraged artificial attempts to break away from conventionalism and traditionalism. In fictitious love stories, as in *The Thousand*

and One Nights, men and women appeared "very little restricted in their opportunities of meeting each other and making love", although gross "sexual misbehaviour is always presented as the doings of despicable characters, or as practised by lecherous fools leading to the deserved punishment . . . ."[29] Poetry raises even greater doubts, when Muslim literary critics recognised "the best poetry" as "the most deceptive one", and that "quite a few poets say things openly in their poems which are the opposite of what they leave unexpressed".[30] Further ambiguity was created by the *Sufi* mystics' metaphorical use of erotic language and symbols. All in all, most love poetry, as Rosenthal points out, was at variance with moral norms commonly accepted in Islam, and offered "some glances at a reality very different from the official ideal", providing a confirmation that "the desire for erotica expression beyond that approved by society was always alive". He argues further that imaginative literature like religion, law and philosophy developed its own standard view of what the ideal society should be like, and that standard ideal was capable of existing side by side with official Islam, for which it was "much less of a transgression to neglect a religious obligation than come out openly against its theoretical necessity". This explains why rarely the apparent discrepancy, in literature, between law and the reality was openly questioned, for it was "perfectly possible to abide by rules and at the same time believe in oneself that reality could never be in complete harmony with them and fictional longing had their own kind of legitimacy".[31] Besides, the Muslim literary critics debated the issue of poetic truth in terms of the Aristotelian concept of form and matter, and gave the verdict in favour of artistic excellence rather than truth and morality. "Form, the most powerful element in Islamic culture, won the battle over morality".[32]

V

Irrespective of the nature of reality in literature the dichotomy between the official ideal of sexual behaviour and morality and the reality emerging from the literature is often rather sharp and pronounced. Despite supreme importance being attached to marriage in Islamic law and religion, as discussed above,[33] Muslim literature reveals a contrary disposition of making differentiation between marriage and sexual pleasure (*tamattu'*). The chapters on marriage and sexual life in the *Qabus Nama,* a Persian tract, provide good illustration of this point:

> If you take a wife . . . do not choose her for her beauty. For if you want beauty you may take a sweetheart . . . a wife is taken as a housewife, not for carnal pleasure. As for this latter a slave girl may be bought from the bazaar without too much trouble and expenditure. But the wife must be perfect. . .
> .[34]

The idea of pleasure in extra-marital sex is more forcefully brought out in the anecdote about the poet Farazdaq. The poet, already married, exercised some undue pressure on a woman to make her yield to his sexual demand. The woman apprised the poet's wife of it, and the two women together worked out a situation in which the poet copulated with his wife in a dark room mistaking her for the other woman. When the truth was discovered, he exclaimed, "So, it was you! Praise be to God! How sweet you are when forbidden, and how disgusting when allowed!"[35]

Similarly, the monogamous ethos in love relationship is consistently projected in the literature. The idea of true love is based on monogamous relationship. All the great figures of love in literature are couples, and it is significant that most great couples symbolising true love are of pre-Islamic origin such as Wis and Ramin, Khusru and Shirin, Yusuf and Zulaikha, and Solomon and Bilqis, the queen of Sheba. Some famous Islamic couples like Laila and Majnun, and Jamil and Buthaina are of early Islamic origin and belong to the rather stylised tradition of 'Udhrite family of lovers.

There are stories about polygamous relationship broken eventually by jealousy, as in the story of Qamar al-Zaman in *The Thousand and One Nights*. The great poet Nizami spoke of his three successive wives, especially of the first. He writes:

To marry one wife is enough for a man, the husband of many is the husband of none.[36]

A whole range of erotic and sexual relationships and practices not in conformity with the official ideal are found in literature. These range from heterosexuality through homosexuality to auto erotism, transvestism and bestiality, in addition to other sexual matters pertaining to any one of these broad categories.

Among heterosexual relationships illicit sex in the form of flirtation, fornication and adultery, 'Udhrite love, and prostitution may be included. Reports and anecdotes about poets and writers like 'Umar ibn abi Rabi'a, Imru'l-Qais and Farazdaq, and their poems refer to illicit love affairs and adventures necessitating masquerades in order to escape the observer (*raqib*). In the love tales the most common circumstance for a young wife's involvement in an affair is the prolonged absence of her husband on a commercial voyage or pilgrimage. This is the frame of the *Tuti Nama* story as well as the background of many other stories included in it, and also of *The Thousand and One Nights*. Countless are the tales of how unloved husbands were duped by a cunning wife and her lover.[37]

'Udhrite love is a striking phenomenon of early Arab poetry and love life. The origins and nature of this concept of love are not easy to determine. It is, in essence, an a-sexual love, absolute love, love as idea, where fate or adverse social circumstances impose a tragic barrier against physical or matrimonial union, but the love remains undying till the end. Jamil and Buthaina, Majnun and Laila, Qais and Lubna, 'Urwa and 'Afra' are classical examples of Arab 'Udhrite love. In a variant of the 'Udhrite love theme, the story ends in union rather than in tragic separation. Elements of 'Udhrite love permeated love poetry of non-'Udhrite poets, and had also channelled into the Persian love poem, or *ghazal* and became an integral part of it.[38]

Islam legalises concubinage and sexual intercourse with slave girls or girls bought "from the bazaar". But there are references to sexual relationships outside this legal category and rather akin to prostitution. Al-Jahiz discusses a special sexual relationship *(marbutin)* of men with a type of singing girl, *qaina* (pl. *qiyan),* and seeks to justify it in terms of the Prophetic sanction for "the lesser offences" *(al-lamaa).* The dancing girls usually belonged to a rich owner, with access given to them for his chosen clients. Burgel considers such a house a "maison de passe" if not simply "an upper class brothel". There is of course specific reference to the presence of brothels in Muslim lands.[39]

Both religious-legal and literary sources mention homosexual relationships for both men and women. Lesbianism occurs in the story of King 'Umar bin al-Nu'man, figuring in the 390th night of *The Thousand and One Nights.* The Prophetic tradition condemns lesbianism along with sodomy.[40] In the eye of Islamic law the two cardinal sexual sins are *zina,* or fornication and adultery, and sodomy. The Qur'an mentions repeatedly the story of the people of Lot, and forbids sodomy in unequivocal terms. The Prophet curses the sodomites in several *hadith.* The vice of sodomy is so disgusting that of all the animals only pigs and asses engage in it, says one source. The Muslim juristic opinion would seem to have had "less concern about homosexual relations between adult males than they had for relations between a man and a boy", because "boys were a greater temptation". According to one source,

> I have less fear for a pious young man from a ravening beast than from a beardless boy who sits with him.[41]

Pederasty, also known as the cult of ephebes, or attractive male youths, became rather widely familiar in Muslim literature, especially Persian, since the period of the Abbasids. The princely author of *Qabus Nama* not only allowed but recommended his son not to restrict himself to either of the sexes, alluding to relationship with slave boys *(ghulam).* The poet Abu Nuwas disliked females because of their "impurity", and preferred "boys".[42] Goitein does not find any significant role of this practice or even homosexuality in pre-Islamic Arabia, and accounts for its origin as an "outcome of the superimposition of a caste of warlike conquerors over a vast defenceless population". Pointing his fingers at "the Arab, Turk or Mongol Conquerors", he writes:

After the endless supply of girls of all races, colours, shapes and personalities had been tasted, the over satisfied and refined appetites had to be satisfied elsewhere. The cult of ... attractive male youths, originally was a privilege of the men in power ... the example of the ruling classes filtered down, and became a state of life for the entire community.[43]

The early sources of Islamic law almost unanimously insist on the death penalty for the sodomites, who will suffer dreadful tortures and humiliation in the next world. He will be resurrected in the form of a pig or a monkey. He will, along with six other groups of sinners, be the first to be thrown into hell.[44]

Besides heterosexual and homosexual deviations the sources refer to sexual abnormalities not covered under these two broad categories, such as bestiality and attitudes relating to reversal or confusion of sex identity like transsexualism, transvestism and intersexualism or hermaphroditism. On bestiality the Islamic law is unequivocal. In the words of a Prophetic tradition: "Whomever you find who has had intercourse with an animal, kill him and kill the animal."[45] On the reversal of the sex or gender identity the absence of details about a few known cases render it difficult to make positive identifications of them either as transsexualism, or transvestism or hermaphroditism. It is, however, interesting to point out that Bellamy finds it "curious" that an alleged transvestite (mukhan-nath) was "not classed with the sodomites." [46] A modern sexologist is not likely to equate transvestism with "sodomy" or male homosexuality. A transvestite is perhaps more capable of a homosexual relationship than a normal male person, but is often married and has children. However, the Prophet's dislike for these deviations is expressed in a hadith in which he curses man who act like women and women who act like men.[47]

Various other ideas and practices with bearings on sexuality find mention in early Islamic literature, while many others such as sadism, masochism, necrophilia, cunnilingus, fellatio or irrumation are not mentioned. There is no word for incest in Arabic, but this is covered by the prohibited degree of consanguinity for marriage. There are depictions of incestuous situations, but in all cases the culprits suffer bad end. Masturbation is frequently mentioned particularly in the religious-legal literature, although the law is somewhat uncertain about this sexual practice, The opinions are sharply polarised on its moral and juristic defence. The Malikites forbid it completely, and the Hanbalites and a section of the Hanafis allow it to relieve the pressure of sexual desire. A hadith includes the masturbator among seven offenders first to enter the hell fire. Finally, the issue of coitus interruptus ('azi) also engages the attention as much of traditionalists and jurists as other writers of materia medica, belles letters, erotica and popular literature. B.F. Musallam's thorough study on birth control in Islam[48] clearly reveals the popularity of the issue. The Prophet did not seem to have a strong feeling against it, saying: "If God wants to create it (the fetus), this action will not prevent it". Despite some early reservations against this practice, the sheer weight of evidence clearly establishes its general acceptance in the Muslim world. One of the reasons for birth control cited by Muslim jurists was that a man might wish to divorce his wife in the foreseeable future – and divorce was fairly easy in Islam. A second argument most frequently used was the fear of begetting slave children of a concubine, legally recognised in Islam.[49]

VI

The study of sexuality in reference to Muslims in South Asia is problematical because of the nature of its sources. First, South Asia does not have the natural advantage of West Asia where the primary Arabic religious-legal tradition not only had set down the normative guidelines for sexual morality but also somewhat reflected the situation in the region. The same tradition based on the Qur'an and *Sunna* provided the theoretical framework of sexual behaviour for South Asian Muslims, but did not derive their ideas from the South Asian situation. Secondly, the South Asian question is further complicated by an almost total lack of any interest in studying Muslim sexuality in this region. It is quite commonplace that the historiography of South Asian Islam has been rather more disproportionately oriented towards either political or religious-cultural than social or societal concerns. And the study of sexuality has elicited no interest whatsoever among scholars. This apathy may well have been related to the strong sense of pudency that have steadily grown in Islam, as discussed above.[50] Finally, in the absence of any basic study in the subject, any attempt in this direction must involve an extremely painstaking and time consuming research in regional literatures of diverse genres – a task quite daunting for an individual scholar.

In the circumstances, I have chosen to offer only an impressionistic picture on a none too wide canvas, drawing upon scarce and scattered material, supplemented largely by a corpus of primary literature that belongs to a particular region of South Asia with which I am most familiar, namely Bengal.

Muslim Bengali literature, like its Hindu Bengali counterpart, is broadly divided into traditional verse and modern prose (effectively from the late 19th century for Muslims). The Muslim literary tradition in verse comprises religious manuals or books of instruction in Islamic fundamentals, religious-historical or semi-historical and legendary narrative poems, mystical *pada* (short song) compositions on the model of the Vaisnava *padas*; and finally, long narrative poems based on secular romantic themes. Sexual and erotic matters may be found to lie scattered in this literature. But the 19th century saw a new genre of didactic literature written, unlike the old tradition, not in chaste Bengali but in a mixed Bengali-Urdu diction, being churned out from the cheap presses in Calcutta and becoming rather popular with the Muslim masses. Although this literature concerned itself as the old tradition with both religious and secular matters, it brought to bear on its attitude a new missionary zeal in instructing Muslims in all aspects of life including sex and sexuality. Rooted in the classical Islamic tradition as expounded by the Muslim theologians and jurists, this literature reveals undoubted traces of local influence. One of the most popular sex manuals of this variety[51] clearly acknowledges its indebtedness to *Koka-sastra*, the famous twelfth-century Sanskrit sex manual attributed to the poet Kokkaka or Koka-pandit. The women, in this literature, are classified, as in Hindu sexology, into four groups such as *padmini, chitrani, hastini,* and *sankhini* on the basis of their physiognomical features and their corresponding sexual dispositions.[52] There are also innumerable references to indigenous medical properties and prescriptions, and other recipes for the purposes of enhancing sexual virility and conscupience, making the penis larger and stronger, facilitating the vaginal passage, enlarging or reducing the breasts, maintaining total sexual dominance over wife, bringing sexually desired women or men in possession, and so on.[53]

VII

Muslim interest in Hindu sexology was evidenced as early as the first half of the 14th century, when Ziya Nakhshabi (d.1350), "a master of simple and elegant prose", translated *Koka-sastra*.[54] This erotic interest was often expressed in the works of Muslim litterateurs. In Malik Muhammad Ja'isi's (1493-1542) *Padmavat,* a brilliant product of early Indo-Islamic literature, "there are examples of purely erotic poetry of the type called *sringar rasa* in Sanskrit . . . ." Abd al-Rahim Khan-i Khanan (the early Mughal period) and Raslin or Saiyid Ghulam Nabi Bilgrami (late Mughal period) were "regarded as having excelled in erotic poetry". The greatest value of their writings, says M. Mujeeb, "lies in their having placed the Indian concept of female beauty, which was true to nature, in opposition to the conventional Persian concept, in which the sex was disguised."[55]

Love poems in Urdu which are modelled on the Persian *ghazal* are saturated with erotic imageries and nuances. The general motif of this genre of composition in which two people are involved in a most intense love relationship without the readers being told about the legal status of the lovers is in itself a significant challenge to the law. In both Persian and Urdu *ghazals*, true love emerges as driven into illicit relationship by the force of fate *(nasib)* and circumstances. True love, inspiration, life joy and humanism are contrasted with orthodoxy and legalism, or as Burgel puts it, ". . . eros stands against ratio".[56] On the other hand there is often an undoubted element of 'Udhrite love in these compositions. There is clear recognition and acceptance of the fact of separation and its rationale. In the opinion of two scholars on the Urdu love poetry under the later Mughals:

Love was seen as a danger to ordered social life, and was persecuted accordingly . . . . the unfortunate lovers themselves shared this view of love. The character of Urdu love poetry is determined by this background.[57]

Even in the nineteenth-century Urdu novel, like *The Courtesan of Lucknow* by Ruswa[58], the lovers address the beloved in a style typical of the 'Udhrite poetry. A strain of mystical love mixed with 'Udhrite as well as sensual love often lent to Urdu poetry an element of uncertainty and oscillation between mystical and profane meanings, or between sensuality and spirituality. This art of "glittering ambiguity" or of "veiling and unveiling" in Urdu poetry is shared in common with its Persian prototype.[59] During the period of Mughal decline the provincial culture of Oudh developed a popular style of music called *thumri*, or "love music that makes a sensuous appeal through repetition of words and musical phrases". Its "theme is human love, not a symbolic representation of divine longing as in the older music".[60]

An indeterminate fusion of mystical and erotic love for South Asian Muslims was perhaps most poignantly expressed in their attachment to and pursuit of the Krishna tradition both in literature and life. The appeal of Krishna to some medieval Muslims of mystical or other persuasions has been long known, and the Qur'anic sayings such as "And every people hath its guide" (*Sura* 13:7), and "To every people we have sent an apostle" (*Sura* 16: 36) had made it easier for them to accept Krishna and Rama as prophets.[61] The devotional songs of the *Vaisnavas*, or the followers of Vishnu and Krishna, "excited more mystic ecstasy in the Sufis than other forms of Hindi and Persian poetry."[62] Some were attracted to the Krishna tradition because of its "strong element of sensuousness", while some "went further towards worship and devotion".[63] As early as the 14th century Jamshid, a disciple of a reputed orthodox *Sufi* Makhdum Jahaniyan, fell into a trance of mystic ecstasy to see a group of singing and dancing Vaishnavites and joined them dancing and roaming for three days and nights on the streets of Kanauj.[64] Saiyid Ibrahim of Pihani (b. 1573), alias Rasa Khan, was a devotee of Krishna, who "gave up everything and came and settled at Krishna's reputed birthplace, Vrindavana."[65] A Pathan was converted to the intensely devotional and emotional *Vaisnava* movement in Bengal under Chaitanya, and became popular as Haridas, the servant of Hari, or Krishna. Mirza Saleh and Mirza Haidar, two Mughal dignitaries were known to have *Vaisnava* leanings.[66] Muslim interest in *Vaisnava* love themes also found expression in music. Sultan Husain Sharqi of Jaunpur is generally credited with the foundation of the romantic school of music called *khiyal*. Based on the Hindu devotional theme of Krishna's love for the milkmaids (*gopini*), *khiyal* "transformed the devotional theme to thinly veiled invocations of human love and romance".[67]

There is a very large and rich corpus of Bengali Muslim lyrics modelling itself, in both style and content, on the Hindu Bengali *Vaisnava pada*, or short songs, on Radha-Krishna love. Elsewhere I have discussed this subject in some details.[68] Much of this literature is of Sufic or mystical nature, while there is an undoubted element of the *Vaisnava* adoration of the divine love between Krishna and Radha. Regardless of the nature and source of their poetic inspiration these Muslim compositions are replete with strong and bold erotic imageries. While Radha fills her pitcher with water Krishna "observes Radha's breasts".[69] Radha's youth is about to give away "under the weight of the fruits of her bosom". (24 : 46). A look at her face "sends waves on the ocean of desire" and with her mercy the poet is ready to "plunge into her youth". (51:53). Kanu (Krishna) is "unsettled to see Radha's brassiere (*kanchuli*)" and his "mind is arrested to see Radha's breasts" (78: 61-62). Kanu appears from nowhere throws away his flute and "embraces me" (Radha), "puts his lips on mine", "presses on the breasts and tears away my brassiere with his nails". (141: 77; also 156: 81; 158: 82). Kanai (Krishna) tells Radha, "you are the lotus and I am the bee. Let us go to the garden and satisfy". (161: 83). Radha is fast asleep "unaware of Kanu lying in her embrace". (175: 87). "My (Radha) lotus of a hundred petals is in full bloom, but my bee, Krishna, is not beside me". (275: 116). Radha and Krishna

. . . remain awake in love very late in the night . . . Binodini (Radha) lies beside him . . . loses herself in a blissful state. With Kanu in her embrace and one's lips on the other's, Radha is not awake . . . .[70]

VIII

The obvious erotic elements in the love-dalliances of Krishna and Radha, combined with the sexual ideas and practices of *Shakta*-Tantrism and of the Buddhist *Sahajiyas* gave birth later in the 17th and 18th centuries to a number of rather mixed *Vaisnava* orders at the popular level, the members of which were generally called *Vairagis*. Some of these groups were strictly esoteric in practices and were given to sexual exercises. Hindus and Muslims alike could join these fraternities as they could and did earlier with Bengal Vaisnavism of Chaitanya.[71] The activities of some of them provoked strong reactions and denunciations from both Muslim and Hindu purificatory fundamentalist and revivalist movements. Dayananda Saraswati of Arya Samaj launched a vicious attack on them, while the Bengali Muslim didactic and revivalist popular literature in the 19th and early 20th centuries contain similar fulminations against Muslim adherents of them. Some Muslims were known to have been founders themselves of fraternities of this type such as Hazrati, Gobrai, Pagal-nathi and Khusi-bishwasi.[72]

In the early part of the present century, Maulana Akram Khan, a distinguished Muslim theologian and reformer, wrote strongly against "shocking and demoniac" practices of those Muslim "*marfati, faqirs, nedas,* or mystic mendicants" or "Muslim versions of the Chaitanya sects."[73] He accuses them of practising the rituals of "five essences" (*pancha-ras*) rather similar to what was known among the Bauls as "the piercing of four moons" (*chari-chandra-bhed*), or rituals involving "four matters derived from the parent's body namely, blood (*rakta*), semen (*virya*), excreta (*mal*) and urine (*mutra*). The five essences were popularly referred to as black (liqour), white (semen), red (menstrual blood), yellow (excreta), and finally, the esoteric teaching of the *murshid, pir*, or *guru*. These rituals involved coition with the practitioner's wife or other women. They attached special meanings to the Qur'anic terms and concepts. *Hauj-i kauthar*, or the divine ambrosia, was identified with menstrual fluid (*rajas*). The ritualistic drinking of semen was based on the interpretation of the key Islamic word "bismillah" (in the name of Allah) as "bij me Allah" or "Allah is in the semen (*bij /virya*)". The women disciples were sometimes involved in a ritual with their *pir* in which the women placed in a room with the *pir* would take off their clothes, and the *pir* would put their clothes away, imitating the practice of Krishna stealing the clothes of the milkmaids. This was done to the accompaniment of song and dance, culminating in the women surrendering themselves sexually to the *pir* who invariably occupied a place of supreme importance among these Vaishnavite sects. For the sect called *Aul* or *Auliya* extra-marital coition was considered of greater merit for the attainment of their religious object. They were specially taught to conquer jealousy resulting from adulterous relations. Reference was also made to a ceremony associated with "the fulfilment of desire" (*Ichhapuran- bhajan*). Its aim was to urge every member of the group, male or female, "not to feel hesitant or shy" about letting other members fulfil their sexual desires with them. All members, for this purpose, would assemble in a."secluded spot", resort to intoxicants, and fulfil their sexual desires. Any member unwilling to cooperate was treated as a "great sinner (*maha papi*) ".[74]

Also elsewhere in the Indian subcontinent religious gatherings and festivals served to ventilate the sexual urges of individuals subjected to severe limitations on free social mixing of sexes. Muslim participation in Hindu festivals of *Holi* and *Basant*[75] partially achieved this object. Even Muslim festivals such as *Id al-Fitr* performed similar functions. On this occasion, unlike the Roman Catholic Lent "rejoicing and voluptuous excesses" followed rather than preceded the particular day of abstinence.[76]

The death anniversaries (*urs*, literally "marriage") of popular saints provided similar occasions for massive mixed gatherings. The *urs* of Salar Ma'sud Ghazi, popularly called Ghazi Miyan, at Bahraich in Oudh was resorted by many seeking marriage and fertility. At Makanpur the shrine of Shah Madar was also a popular resort especially for the blind and the lame. In such large gatherings of men, women and "beardless boys",

great liberties were taken. Even a rigid Mulla like Abdul Qadir Badauni, the historian, committed an act of impropriety at Makanpur on the occasion of a pilgrimage and was severely beaten and attacked with swords by the relatives of his beloved.[77]

Mujeeb describes the features of these festivities, consisting of "song and dance, display of charm, meeting and lovemaking", and adds:

> . . . the lustful indulged themselves without fear where there were crowds of 'boys' such as would 'break the vows of ascetics, sons of gazelles matchless in love-making', 'a world of sinners attaining their heart's desire' and 'multitudes of lechers going about their business'.[78]

The cult of ephebe, or catamites, or pederasty, or handsome boys, was as well known in South Asia as in West and Central Asia. Both Abu'l Fazl and Badayuni of Akbar's times made pointed reference to it. The former considered it "a custom of Transoxiana transported into India". It was "customary with the aristocracy to keep a large number of handsome pages in their train . . . ."[79] From Tavernier, a foreign traveller in Mughal India, we hear about a Muslim governor of Surat who "wanted to enter into [an] unnatural intercourse" with a young page, a *faqir's* son, at his employ. The incident led to a confrontation between the governor and a group of *faqirs*. Shah Quli Khan Mahram was reprimanded by Akbar for his love for a boy named Qabul Khan. Ali Quli Khan was "in love" with Shahnam Beg, the son of a camel driver to whom he gave away his own wife, a former prostitute. Shahnam, after having enjoyed her, made her over to Abd al-Rahman. The latter's refusal to return her to Shahnam led eventually to the murder of Shahnam. Khan sought revenge on Rahman for Beg's murder without success, and consecrated his love and grief for Shahnam with raising a lofty building on his minion's remains near Jaunpur.[80]

The Muslim mystics were equally, if not more attracted to *amrad*, "the beardless boys" or the divine beloved. Rasa Khan, noted before,[81] fell in love with a boy. Madho Lal Husain (1539-1594), a mystic, given to song, dance and drinking, was named Madho "out of his intense attachment to a Brahmin youth of that name".[82] The case of Sarmad, a friend of the Mughal crown prince Dara Shikoh, was very well known. A Persian Jew, Sarmad accepted Islam, and on his arrival in India he became

> infatuated with a Hindu lad, namely Abhai [Abhaya] Chand, and casting off his clothes, sat down at the door of his beloved. When Abhai Chand's father became convinced of Sarmad's purity of love, he allowed him to take away the boy into his house.[83]

IX

It has been pointed out that medieval European Christians were concerned and felt threatened by two aspects of the Muslim phenomenon : power and pleasure. If Islam's political power and might terrified them its sexual life and morality also drew a great deal of their attention.[84] The medieval European travellers to South Asia provide ample justification for this view, as they offer clear expressions to their impressions of the sexual life of South Asian Muslims, especially their upper classes. Manucci wrote : ". . . all Mohamedans are very fond of women, who are their principal relaxation and almost their only pleasure". In the words of Careri, Muslims

> spent all they have in luxury keeping a vast number of servants, but above all of concubines. These being many every one of them strives to be beloved above the rest, using all manners of allurements, perfumes and sweet ornaments. Sometimes to heighten their master's Lusts they give him . . . much wine that he may require company in Bed. Then some drive away the Flies, others rub his Hands and Feet, others Dance, others play on Music, and others do other things . . . .[85]

Manucci also pointed his finger at sections of the Muslim "holymen" who had "control of the women" resorting to them, and added :

> They know how to make use of their opportunities, sparing neither Muslim, Hindu, nor Christian women, if they are good-looking. In addition they have numerous wives and slave girls in their houses . . . .[86]

According to Yasin, "the excessive indulgence of the Muslim community, particularly of the upper classes, in sexual pleasures was encouraged by the abundant booty of captive beauty in war or easy purchase in the slave market".[87] Besides, courtesanship was a consistent feature as much of the pre-Muslim as post-Muslim phases of South Asian urban social life. They were both a caste and a profession. Ala' al-Din Khalji (1296-1316) tried to control their market, as with other commodities, by putting up a fixed schedule of remuneration for their services. In Akbar's times their number became "so scandalously large that he was obliged to segregate them in a separate quarter designated as Shaitanpur or the Devil's Quarter and have registers maintained to enter the names of those who visited their quarter." A prospective young entrant to this quarter was personally interviewed by the Emperor to ascertain if there was any undue influence and pressure on her decision. Aurangzib attempted their expulsion from the city of Delhi or getting them married.[88]

X

The popular instructive or didactic literature in mixed Bengali-Urdu diction since the nineteenth century and still available in reprints, of which we have spoken above,[89] comprises a genre of what may be called a complete sexual manual, dealing with almost all conceivable sexual concerns. The following account is based on Saiyid Shah Sa'dat Ali's popular work.[90]

In this type of writings, marital copulation is very strongly recommended and its virtues are loudly proclaimed. It is soothing for the mind and is also rewarded with progenies. A wife is a "priceless jewel" should she be a chaste woman. Excessive copulation is, however, to be avoided as being rather "damaging" for health, since a drop of semen is equal to seven drops of blood. Once a week in normal cases, and once in three days where there is greater conscupience are recommended.

The literature goes at length to list occasions and grounds for not engaging in copulation. Coition on the very first night after the marriage, or in full stomach are to be avoided. A child with no sense of shame and propriety is born consequent upon copulation in the nude condition. Coition in a standing posture gives birth to a child with bad manners. A thief is the likely issue of a coition during the dawn or the dusk, and an ill-tempered child is resulted from a sexual union in a condition of unhappiness. Other occasions to avoid sexual intercourse are storm, earthquake, eclipses of the sun and the moon, after six months of pregnancy, and the menstrual period, the latter causing insanity in the resultant child. Copulation with a woman over fifty years of age is as undesirable as that with a minor girl. The jurists also prohibit, according to the author, a sexual intercourse with a woman on the top of a man. Finally, while men should not engage in copulation before the age of twenty, they usually suffer from the lack of sexual virility after sixty.

Following the precepts of Hindu sexology the Muslim didactic literature classifies women into four classes, as noted above,[91] on the basis of their sexual dispositions determined by their physiognomical distinctions. As in the Hindu literature, the two superior types — *padmini* and *chitrani* — are placed on the highest pedestal by virtue of their physical beauty, psychological endowments and sexual richness. Likewise, the inferior types–*hastini* and *sankhini* – are thoroughly castigated.

Again, the Hindu sexological notion of the seats of conscupience in a female body on each day of the lunar month are also adopted in this literature. This information is designed to help concentrate erotic acts on the particular region in the woman's body in order that orgasm is facilitated and hastened. Similar beliefs are also attached to determining the sex of the progeny with the help of choosing the time and circumstances of copulation.

The bulk of this sexual manual concerns itself with a whole range of indigenous Bengali and general Islamic popular recipes for achieving sexual objects such as keeping as well as bringing the coveted woman or women under control, enhancing conscupience, redressing impotency, strengthening and enlarging the penis, thickening the semen, prolonging the duration of coition, enlarging or reducing the size of the breasts and ensuring pregnancy.

The literature also discusses other venereal matters like masturbation, lesbianism and anal intercourse, and these practices are all strongly condemned. The last named practice sends the culprit straight to hell.

XI

Perhaps the most seminal and relevant issue concerning sexuality has reference to the role and place of women in society. The system that governs the place of women in general in South Asia, though may have had its local labels, is generally recognised as *parda* (literally "curtain"), referring to a system of veiling and seclusion of women. There are two major facets of *parda,* namely physical or spatial segregation, and covering of the female face and body. Hanna Papanek has sought to explain the meanings of its observance in terms of the twin concepts of "separate worlds" of men and women, and the "symbolic shelter" of women for protection from their sexual vulnerability in the outside world. [92]

Despite a widely prevalent belief in the Islamic origins of *parda* in South Asia, most modern scholars are convinced of its independent inception in the Hindu society. The recognition of their independence has, in its turn, induced some to draw marked contrast between the social purposes and objectives of the apparently "common" Hindu and Muslim practices of *parda*. According to this view the aims of the Muslim *parda* is directed primarily against the "outsiders", that is, the people outside the family and kins, considered a potential threat to the sexual inviolability of women. The Hindu observance of *parda*, on the other hand, is said to be geared to preserving the unity and integrity of the family and kins by upholding the respect and avoidance relationships, maintaining the differential position between the conjugal and natal families, and generally refraining from posing a threat to the male-centred family and kin structure. The case for this differential systems of Hindu and Muslim *parda* is strengthened by relating these to the respective Hindu and Muslim social organisations and values. It is pointed out that Islamic law, unlike Hindu law, provides for close kin marriage, and the consequent existence of small and almost endogamous marriage groups obviates the necessity of a bride observing seclusion in a strange surrounding with disruptive potentialities. [93]

This notion of a total dichotomy between the Hindu and Muslim observances of *parda* appears simplistic in the light of other findings and studies. First, despite Islamic legal sanctions for close kin marriage a substantial proportion of Muslims in South Asia, especially the large number of service and artisan groups, practised lineage exogamy in the same manner as their peer Hindu groups. Among Muslims of this circle intra-family respect and avoidance relationships were very commonly observed.[94]

Secondly, Muslim veiling practices outside the family do not seem to correspond to the normative pattern of "kin-outsider" polarity. In the words of Sylvia Vatuk:

> ... in many modern Indian Muslim communities the object of the veil is not so much the total outsider or stranger as it is certain persons standing intermediate to these in one's social universe, namely members of one's wider kinship circle, neighbours of one's residential district, and other Muslim to whom one or one's family is known. In other words, one observes purdah with reference to the social approval of persons whose opinion about one's respectability matter. Beyond this group, where one is completely anonymous, the veil becomes unnecessary. [95]

Thirdly, veiling and other forms of *parda* practices were observed by Muslim women, like their Hindu counterparts, before other women, in a variety of situations, thus clearly modifying the popular concept of "symbolic shelter" from male sexual aggression. From myriad ethnographic reports on the practice of veiling, especially among urban Muslim women of the younger generation, the use of veil before strangers appears clearly on the wane even for those who continue to use it in the vicinity of home. This clearly indicates that "there is more to the issue than sheltering a woman from the unwelcome advances of outsiders."[96]

Finally, following from the doubt raised immediately above, one may postulate about a common central concern underlying the South Asian *parda* system as a whole. Undeniably, the dominant concern in South Asian social development has been the preservation of the structural unity and integrity of the kin group. Marriage, involving admission of non-kin outsiders, contained serious disruptive potentialities that needed accommodation and containment. While violation of sexual purity and modesty posed a grave threat, bringing ignominy to the family and the kin group, maintaining internal hierarchical allocation of status and authority based on sex and age was no less crucial for the structural integrity of the family and kins. Parda represented a rather complex and intricate system of social and cultural devices to ensure the place of South Asian women in the local community of interacting kin and lineage groups. To ensure sexual modesty such devices ranged from fixing standards of dress to imposing behavioural restrictions on direct eye-contact, raising the voice, uncontrolled laughter, touching and so on. Likewise, the internal structure of authority was upheld by measures ranging from standardised gestures of deference to more extreme measures of avoidance relationship including veiling and spatial segregation.

XII

In conclusion a couple of issues relating to Islamic perspectives on sexuality may be underlined. First, Islam is characterised by its positive affirmation of sexuality as a practical and necessary human concern, as we have seen before. This positive attitude was, however, squarely based on an assumption of woman's subordination to man, as characteristic of a traditional society and culture. The Islamic religious tradition, as Hanna Papanek puts it very succinctly, "stresses the equality of all believers before God but clearly puts men a step above women." [97] Islam had undeniably raised, as noted before, the marital status obtained in pre-Islamic Arabia where women were no better than child bearing chattels. The provisions for dower *(mahr)* and the right to inheritance for women were rather substantial enhancement of women's position and status. And yet the overall position of women's subordination cannot be obscured. There is monogamy for women, polygamy for men; non-marital sex totally disapproved of the former, while the latter is permitted concubines and "girls from the bazzar"; men can divorce very easily, women cannot; two women are equivalent to one man as legal witness; a very widely adopted motif in Muslim fictional literature such as *Tuti Nama* and *The Thousand and One Nights* is the wife being encouraged to have an affair with another man by the prolonged absence of her husband from home – all this clearly reflect the dominant male sexist attitudes. Much of the legal-religious underpinnings of these attitudes are, however, being gradually set aside in many Muslim countries today under pressures either of the growing forces of secularism or Islamic modernism. [98]

Secondly, it appears now in retrospect that both Islamic and Hindu laws began with an advantage on traditional Christianity in terms of bringing a much greater realism to bear on the issue of sexuality in human life. With the rapid secularisation of Western law in the recent past law and sexual morality in the Western countries have been clearly differentiated and demarcated. Subject to the three overriding principles of adulthood, consent and privacy ("consenting adults in private"), state and law have been content to leave sexual morality to the individuals concerned. Even Hindu law, in the post-colonial period, underwent significant changes amounting to virtual secularisation of sexual morality. Islam, on the other hand, still largely continues to dominate and control sexual morality of its believers, forcing even its modernisers to seek legitimisation of reforms not in secular but in religious terms, though reinterpreted and reformulated.

NOTES

1. G.H. Bousquet, *L'ethique Sexuelle de L'Islam* (Paris, 1966), and A. Bouhdiba, *La Sexualite en Islam* (Paris, 1975).

2. A.L. al-Sayyid-Marsot (ed.), *Society and the Sexes in Medieval Islam* (Malibu, California:

Undena Publications, 1979).

3. B.F. Musallam, *Sex and Society in Islam. Birth control before the nineteenth century* (Cambridge: Cambridge U[niversity] P[ress], 1984).

4. I have not been able to trace even a single article directly concerned with this problem. The *parda* system, or that of the seclusion of Muslim and non-Muslim women in South Asia, has long attracted attention of observers and scholars. There is a rich corpus of ethnographic and sociological literature available on the subject. See below for a discussion on *parda*. [*Infra*, pp. 24-27].

5. Cf. "To Western ideals essentially celibate, sacerdotal, and hierarchical, Islam opposed the outlook of a laity frankly indulgent and sensual, in principle egalitarian, enjoying a remarkable freedom of speculation, with no priests and monasteries built into the basic structure of society as they were in the West. " R.W. Southern, *Western Views of Islam in the Middle Ages* (Cambridge, Massch.: Cambridge UP, 1972), p.7.

6. F. Rosenthal, "Sources for the Role of Sex in Medieval Muslim Society" in A.L. al-Sayyid-Marsot (ed.), *Society and the Sexes in Medieval Islam* (Malibu, California: Undena Publications, 1979), p.4.

7. R. Levy, *Social Structure of Islam* (Cambridge, U.K.: Cambridge UP, 1957, being the second edition of the author's *The Sociology of Islam)*, p.195; Rosenthal, "Role of Sex", p.6.

8. N.J. Coulson, "Regulation of Sexual Behavior under Traditional Islamic Law" in al-Sayyid-Marsot (ed.), *Sexes in Islam*, p. 63.

9. Rosenthal, "Role of Sex", p. 3.

10. Some Greek physicians attributed melancholia to it, as the "putrid matter of the retained semen" was thought to rise up to the brain. See J.C. Burgel, "Love, Lust, and Longing: Eroticism in Early Islam as Reflected in Literary Sources" in al-Sayyid-Marsot (ed.), *Sexes in Islam*, p. 89.

11. Burgel, ibid., p. 86.

12. Ibid., p. 90.

13. Ibid., p. 86.

14. Ibid., pp. 90-91, also note 38, p. 90.

15 . Quoted, *ibid.* ; p. 87.

16. Ibid.

17. *Supra*, p. 3.

18. J.A Bellamy, "Sex and Society in Islamic Popular Literature" in al-Sayyid-Marsot (ed.), *Sexes in Islam*, p. 30.

19. Ibid. pp. 32-33.

20. Ibid., p. 34.

21. Coulson, "Sexual Behavior under Islamic Law", p. 66.

22. Rosenthal, "Role of Sex", pp. 18ff; Bellamy, "Sex and Society", p. 29.

23. Ibid., p. 41.

24. Burgel, "Eroticism in Early Islam", p. 82.

25. S.D. Goitein, "The Sexual Mores of the Common People" in al-Sayyid-Marsot (ed.), *Sexes in Islam*, pp. 44-45.

26. Rosenthal, "Role of Sex", p. 20.

27. Bellamy, "Sex and Society", pp. 25-27.

28. Burgel, "Eroticism in Early Islam", p. 83.

29. Rosenthal, "Role of Sex", p. 15.

30. Ibid., p. 11.

31. Ibid., pp 11, 21-22.

32., Burgel, "Eroticism in Early Islam", p. 85.

33. *Supra*, pp. 5-7.

34. Quoted, Burgel, "Eroticism in Early Islam", p. 88.

35. Cited, ibid., pp. 98-99.

36 . Quoted, ibid., p. 114; also pp. 112-13.

37. Ibid., pp. 96-99.

38. Ibid., pp. 91-96.

39. Ibid., pp. 104-105; also p. 103.

40. Bellamy, "Sex and Society", p. 37.

41. Ibid., p. 37.

42. Burgel, "Eroticism in Early Islam", pp. 88, 111.

43. Goitein, "The Sexual Mores", pp. 47-48.

44. Bellamy, "Sex and Society", p. 38.

45. Ibid., p. 35.

46. Ibid., p .36.

47. Ibid.

48. See above, p. I, note 3.

49. Ibid., p. 11.

50. *Supra*, pp. 7-8.

51. Saiyid Shah S'adat'Ali, *Sahih Elaj-i Lokmani* (Calcutta: Osmania Library, 1370BS.,reprint), p.6.

52. Ibid., pp. 8-14.

53. Ibid., pp. 17-31.

54. S.M. Ikram, *Muslim Civilisation in India,* ed. by A.T. Embree (New York: Columbia UP, 1964), p. 117.

55. M. Mujeeb, *The Indian Muslims* (London: Allen & Unwin, 1967), pp. 320, 322.

56. Burgel, "Eroticism in Early Islam", p. 99.

57. R. Russell and K. Islam, *Three Mughal Poets* (London: Allen & Unwin, 1967), pp. 2-3.

58. English tr. by K. Singh and M.A. Husain, London, 1961.

59. Russell & Islam, *Mughal Poets,* ix.

60. Ikram, *Muslim Civilisation,* p. 252.

61. Asim Roy, *The Islamic Syncretistic Tradition in Bengal* (Princeton, New Jersey: Princeton UP, 1983), pp. 95-98; also M.T. Titus, *Islam in India & Pakistan* (Calcutta: Y.M.C.A. Publishing House, revised reprint, 1959), pp. 169, 246; Mujeeb, *Indian Muslims,* pp. 321-22.

62. S.A.A. Rizvi, *Muslim Revivalist Movements in Northern India in the Sixteenth & Seventeenth Centuries* (Agra: Agra UP, 1965), p. 60.

63. Mujeeb, *Indian Muslims,* p. 322.

64. Rizvi, *Muslim Revivalist Movements,* p. 59.

65. Mujeeb, *Indian Muslims,* p. 322.

66. M. Yasin, *A Social History of Islamic India 1605-1748* (New Delhi: Munshiram Manoharlal Publishers Pvt. Ltd., 2nd rev. edn, 1974), p. 82.

67. Ikram, *Muslim Civilisation,* p. 119.

68. Roy, *Islamic Syncretistic Tradition*, pp. 187-206.

69. Song no. 20 in A. Sharif, *Muslim Kabir Pada-sahitya* [in Bengali / "The Pada-literature of the Muslim Poets"] (Dhaka: Bengali Dept., Dhaka UP., 1961), p. 45. Henceforth reference to the song no. and page no. of this book of anthology is given in the body of the essay itself, the page no. following the song number.

70. Quoted in Roy, *Islamic Syncretistic Tradition*, p. 204.

71. *Supra*, p. 18; also A.K. Datta, *Bharatvarshiya Upasak-sampraday* [in Bengali "The Religious Communities of India"], ed. by B. Ghosh, pts 1 & 2 (Calcutta: Pathabhavan, reprint, 1376 B.S./1969 A.D.), p. 103; also Yasin, *Social History*, p. 81.

72. Datta, ibid., pp. 130, 139.

73. Mohammad (Muhammad) Akram Khan, *Moslem Banger Samajik Itihas* [in Bengali/ "The Social History of Muslim Bengal"], (Dhaka: the author, 1965), pp. 117ff.

74. Ibid., pp. 117-120; also Datta, *Upasak-sampraday*, pp. 112, 129-30.

75. Mujeeb, *Indian Muslims*, p. 385.

76. Yasin, *Social History*, p. 49.

77. Ibid., p. 90.

78. Mujeeb, *Indian Muslims*, p. 384. Mujeeb, curiously enough, uses the term "boys" for young eunuchs and hermaphrodites who offered themselves to sexual perverts." *(Ibid.,* note 49.) This seems to be an uncritical assumption of a similar nature as made by Bellamy. For my comments on Bellamy, see *supra*, p. 14.

79. Yasin, *Social History*, pp. 94-95.

80. Ibid., p. 95.

81. *Supra*, p. 18.

82. Mujeeb, *Indian Muslims*, p. 384.

83. Yasin, *Social History*, p. 95, note 1.

84. B.F. Musallam, *Sex and Society in Islam*, pp. 10-11.

85. Quoted, Yasin, *Social History*, pp. 93-94, note 4.

86. Quoted, ibid., p. 96.

87. Ibid., p. 93.

88. Ibid., pp. 93-94; Mujeeb, *Indian Muslims*, p. 369.

89. *Supra*, p. 16.

90. Saiyid Shah Sadat Ali, *Sahih Elaj*, pp. 1-32.

91. S. Vatuk, "Purdah revisited: a comparison of Hindu and Muslim interpretations of the cultural meaning of purdah in South Asia" in H. Papanek and G. Minault (eds.), *Separate Worlds: Studies of Purdah in South Asia* (Columbia, Missouri: South Asia Books, 1982), p. 58.

92. H. Papanek, "Purdah: separate world and symbolic shelter" in Papanek and Minault, ibid., pp. 27-44.

93. Ibid., pp. 18ff.; also Vatuk, "Purdah re-visited", pp. 55-56, 62ff.

94. C. Vreede-De Stuers, *Purdah: A Study of Muslim Women's Life in Northern India* (New York: Humanities Press, 1968), pp. 12, 31-35; D. Jacobson, "Hidden Faces: Hindu and Muslim Purdah in a Central Indian Village" (Ph.D. dissertation, Columbia U., 1970), pp. 182, 188; S. Roy, *Status of Muslim Women in North India* (Delhi: B.R. Publishing Corporation, 1979), pp. 29, 39, 140-42; P. Jeffery, *Frogs in a Well: Indian Women in Purdah* (New Delhi: Vikas, 1979), pp. 105-107; Vatuk, "Purdah re-visited", pp. 64ff.

95. Vatuk, ibid., p. 68; also Roy, ibid., p. 39; Vreede-De Stuers, *ibid.*, p. 87; Jeffery, ibid , pp. 157-59.

96. Vatuk, ibid., pp. 69, 72-73; Jeffery, ibid., p. 102.

97. H. Papanek, "Purdah in Pakistan: seclusion and modern occupations for women", *Journal of Marriage and the Family*, vol. 33, no. 3, August 1971, p. 518.

98. F. Rahman, "Islamic modernism: its scope, method and alternatives", *International Journal of Middle Eastern Studies*, vol. 1, no. 4, pp. 317-33; also his "Muslim modernism in the Indo-Pakistan sub-continent", *Bulletin of the School of Oriental and African Studies* [London], vols 21-22, 1958-59, pp. 82-99; A. Roy, "Islam and aspects of modernity in India and Pakistan", *Journal of the Asiatic Society of Bangladesh* [Dhaka], vol. 20. no. 1, April 1975, pp. 25-45.

4. The *Pir*-Tradition: A Case Study in Islamic Syncretism in Traditional Bengal

THIS CHAPTER is a study in the problem of religion and change in broad reference to the process of diffusion of Islam in Bengal. A systematic study of the phenomenon of Islam in traditional Bengal is a striking desideratum.[1] Some general and later (nineteenth and twentieth centuries) observations available on the subject reflect a broad consensus in terms of its "deviations" or "degeneration from the norms of Islamic "orthodoxy".[2] On a close examination and analysis the theory of degeneration is found untenable. The earliest extant Bengali Muslim writings negate the view that the Bengali Muslim masses were ever more "orthodox". We, on the contrary, gather from this literature that the converts were often rather ill-grounded in the fundamentals of their adopted religion. The formulations of the Islamic tradition as embodied in this literature are characteristically syncretistic and assimilative. The social and cultural contexts of the origin and development of syncretistic traditions of Muslim Bengal provide a probing insight into the process of religious change. The Bengali Muslim syncretistic traditions are multi-faceted and multi-dimensional. The limited scope of the present chapter precludes a comprehensive analysis of the whole range of Islamic syncretistic traditions in Bengal. I have only chosen to focus on the changes in Islam with reference to the syncretistic *pir*-tradition as obtained in Bengal until the puritanical, revivalist movements in the nineteenth and twentieth centuries challenged and undermined the rationale of the syncretistic tradition. Viewed in its historical context, the syncretistic tradition was as relevant and constructive to the cause of Islam in Bengal as the later purificatory revivalist movements,[3] both responding to the pressures of particular social and cultural contexts of the religious community in Bengal.

An analysis of the *pir*-phenomenon in Bengal should begin by taking note of the pitfalls in substituting analytical cliches for precise descriptions of the phenomenon in its existential and contextual positions. Conceptualisation of this particular Bengal phenomenon in terms of "sufism" or "mysticism" or even "saint worship" is tantamount to making assumption for analysis. Respect and veneration of the Muslim "saints" (*auliya/sing. wali*) and shrines associated with their names was not an exclusively Bengal phenomenon. The *sufis* or the Muslim mystics by virtue of their personal and direct mystic communion with Allah, were venerated as elect of the Muslim, and the saints were almost worshipped as the elect of the *sufis*. *Pir,* a Persian word, and etymologically "elder", is a term denoting a spiritual director or guide among the *sufis*. The functionary (described by the title is known also under the names, *shaikh, murshid,* and *ustadh.* [4] In view of this interlinking of the saint (*wall*), the mystic (*sufi*) and the mystic spiritual guide (*pir*) it is natural to approach this subject with such conceptual "assumptions". An actual analysis of the Bengal phenomenon, however, proves these prefabricated analytical tools thoroughly inadequate. This is so for several reasons:

(a) The term *sufi* does not occur even once in our sources.[5]

(b) Sufism in its classical and what may now appear as its "idealised" version of being a mystical religious attitude and system of an individual's direct communion with Allah, [6] did only have a very limited application to the Bengal situation. Even in the sophisticated "mystical" writings of Bengali Muslim authorship such "classical" concerns were never persistent or often only existed in juxtaposition with other far less "spiritual" concern. Besides, the actual adoration and worship of *pir* as a saint and holy man or a religious guide were shared by the elites and masses.

(c) This brings us to the most significant facet of *pir*-tradition in Bengal. The total range of phenomena covered by, and associated with the nomenclature, *pir,* assumed strikingly variegated forms and expressions at different cultural levels. At the level of the Bengali Muslim folk the worship of *pir* extended far beyond the range of saints and holy men, and this amorphous label came to cover a vast motley of popular objects of worship and supplication, not all of them being saints, or *sufis,* or religious personages, or Muslims, or even human beings. In this popular pantheon we are able to identify, besides saints and other religious personalities, apotheosised soldiers, pioneering settlers on reclaimed waste lands in deltaic Bengal, metamorphosed Hindu and Buddhist divinities, and anthropomorphised animistic spirits and beliefs.

A meaningful study of the *pir*-tradition in Bengal in the light of the problems and issues raised above cannot therefore fail to recognise its dissimilar developments and articulations at the two contrasting levels of the great and little traditions of Muslim Bengal. What follows is an attempt along these lines within a historical framework. The picture emerging out of this analysis may be taken as typical of the situation that prevailed before the aforesaid puritanical revivalism in Islam and other pressures on the Bengali Muslim society since the nineteenth century gradually changed the colour and tone of the religious landscape.

Pir and the Great Tradition

The cultural tradition in pre-Islamic Bengal may be clearly conceptualised in terms of "great" and "little" traditions. "High" Hinduism or "Sanskritic" Hinduism, alongside the popular Yogico-Tantric *natha, dharma sahajiya* cults, besides hosts of other popular objects of veneration and supplication, constituted the religious scenario. The perpetual contact and the fundamental continuity between these great and little traditions, stemming from the primary and indigenous nature of the cultures, formed a marked and significant contrast with the nature of Islamic contact with Bengal. The intrusive and exogenous character of orthodox *Sunni* Islam in the cultural milieu of Bengal forced a breach in the cultural continuum of the great and the little traditions, of the gentry and the peasantry, and of the town and the village.

The Muslim conquerors, their entourage and other immigrants to Bengal – secular or religious personages – added a new dimension to the existing polarity between the great and the little traditions namely, a racial and ethnic cleavage between the Muslim elites of foreign extraction (*ashraf*) and the Muslim -masses of humble local origin (*ajlaf* or its popular corruption, *atraf*). The fact of local conversion to Islam, largely limited to the lower strata of the Bengali society, is as explicit as its explanations are diverse and speculative.[7] Whatever were the agencies and circumstances of local conversion, we gather from the early Muslim Bengali writings that the masses of the converts were ill-grounded in Islamic religious precepts, practices and traditions, and remained steeped in pre-existing non-Muslim traditions.[8] The lack of continuity between the exogenous great and endogenous little traditions, aggravated further by the contempt of *ashraf* and orthodoxy for the "vulgar" and "profane" local Bengali language as a medium of Islamic religious and cultural expressions, created an impasse that was also fraught with the danger of converts being re-absorbed into Hinduism. The situation urgently demanded and indeed led to the emergence in the sixteenth and seventeenth centuries of a new group of Bengali Muslim elite, who "by their identification with the great tradition and with the masses" were able to "mediate the one to the other."[9]

The social contexts of these "cultural mediators" provide a valuable insight into the inner dynamics of the Muslim community in Bengal and a clear perception of the direction of their cultural tradition. While some *of* them held minor or major secular or religious offices under local government, a large number of them were popular religious preceptors, introduced as *pirs* by themselves or by their disciples. At least some of these cultural mediators held foreign lineage, but they did not possibly fall under the *ashraf* category for not having the economic and material power base of the *ashraf* class, and secondly, for not subscribing to the exclusivist *ashraf* cultural outlook. What distinguished this new cultural elite were their common concerns for disseminating "Islamic" knowledge among the masses of co-religionists, and their courageous attempt to force a complete break with the dominant alien cultural orientation of the *ashraf* and its orthodoxy by having chosen to adopt the indigenous Bengali language as the cultural vehicle. These two questions were interlinked, and the new cultural mediators did not fail to detect the connection. The exogenous great tradition, locked in the "ivory tower" of Arabic, Persian and Urdu was beyond the reach of the Bengali masses. The *ashraf* cultural monopoly maintained by linguistic apartheid was the first target of the mediators. But the language alone was not enough to bring Islam closer to the masses. If the medium of cultural communication was to be intelligible, so should be its idioms and symbols. The problem was not merely confined to making renderings into Bengali of what was in Arabic and Persian – and this would have been a much simpler and easier undertaking. The more constructive, meaningful and challenging task for them was to bring the exogenous tradition down in to line with the endogenous tradition, and restore thereby broken continuity between the great and little traditions in Bengal. The results of their efforts were crystallised into a vast corpus of Muslim Bengali literature, encompassing Islamic religious, semi-religious and secular historical and semi-historical traditions – a distinct tradition that the new cultural ideologues had reconstructed for the Bengali Muslims with its roots firmly extended into the cultural milieu of Bengal. The cultural products were characteristically and predominantly syncretistic, except those concerned with liturgical matters like prayers (*namaz*), ablutions (*wazu '*), ceremonial bath (*ghusal*), fasting (*roza*) in the month of Ramazan, purification by sand (*tayammum*), funerals (*janajah*) and so on. Such liturgical matters conformed closely to standard Islamic prescriptions of the Hanafi school of law, generally followed by the *Sunni* majority in the Indian subcontinent. All other aspects of their ideas and thoughts were strikingly permeated by indigenous cultural idioms, symbols and nuances. In so far as a large proportion of these mediators were popular religious preceptors and guides, called *pirs,* an evaluation of the *pir*-tradition in Bengal needs examination of their roles in, and contributions to it.

It is beyond the scope of this present chapter to cover all facets of their syncretistic thoughts and ideas namely, mystical-esoteric, historical – legendary and cosmogonic-ontological. We propose to focus on the mystical writings, while making a few broad observations on the others.[10]

The penetration of indigenous elements is quite evident in the writings on the historical, legendary and mythical traditions of Islam. The most obvious way to reduce the polarity between the exogenous and endogenous traditions was to find parallels between the two and present Islamic situations and characters in terms known to the local people. The struggle between Islam and non-Islamic religious forces in Arabia at the beginning of the history of Islam was depicted as a struggle between Islam and Hinduism. The heroes, heroines and other figures of Islamic traditions were constantly compared, favourably or unfavourably, with their Hindu counterparts. One of the major writers, a *pir* with a considerable following, went to the extent of identifying the Islamic concept of the prophet (*nabi*) with the Hindu concept of the incarnation of God (*avatara*), and introduced the Arab prophet on the Bengali scene as the "*avatara* of *kali-yuga*".[11] The entire atmosphere of these traditions was saturated with local colour and complexion. The local landscapes, the flora and fauna, the foods, the dresses, the music and amusements, the customs and values – all conjured up the image of Bengal and breathed an air of congruity, reality and familiarity into these traditions. Similarly, the cosmogonic ideas of these writers bore unmistakable stamps of indigenous influences. The mythological rather than theological aspects of cosmogony found stress in their writings. and threw the doors wide open for Hindu creation-myths to move in.

The ideas of mystical import expounded by the *pir*-mediators, revealed a significant facet of Islamic syncretism in Bengal. Even though we are not prepared to accept the formative influence of Hindu-Buddhist mystical ideas, formulae and techniques on sufism in its growth outside India, [12] or even positive contacts and interactions between Islamic and the indigenous mystical systems on the Indian soil,[13] the Bengali Muslim mystic mediators left no doubt whatsoever about their cultural debts to the indigenous mystic tradition. The whole corpus of this mystical literature was replete with matters strikingly similar and familiar in the local context. Their efforts reveal two dimensions: (a) Local dilution, and (b) Direct appropriation.

Local Dilution

Some elements which both these mystical systems broadly held in common were often adapted and diluted enough to render their exogenous connotations redundant. The mystic path, which was variously called *darweshi, faqiri* and *ma'rifati*, was often introduced as *yoga* and *agama*. [14] The mystic preceptor and initiator called *pir* or *murshid,* was more frequently introduced in his local name, guru. It was not the name but the content of the change that seemed of greater significance. The attitude of respect due to the mystic teacher was elevated to a total veneration and worship of him. Sentiments were expressed to the extent of "taking on head dust from the lotus-feet" of the *pir*,[15] "worshipping the feet of guru", who was "faith in himself",[16] earning "greater merit than prayer *(namaz)*" by responding to the *pir's all even while engaged in prayer,*[17] and comparing him to the "supreme knowledge" incarnate, and to Isvara (Hindu God).[18]

The sufistic speculations at the general Islamic level on the relation between God as the creator (*haq*) and the world (*khalq*) in terms of His transcendence (*tanzih*) and immanence (*tashbih*), presented a spectrum of views evolved over centuries ranging from unqualified dualism to perfect monism. Muslim mysticism, particularly as an Indian phenomenon, tended to assume an intermediate position between the two extremes namely, qualified non dualism expressed in terms of pantheistic monism (*wahdat ul-wujud*).[19] The mystical concepts of these cultural mediators followed closely along the same line of progression, tending to lean towards an absolute non-dualistic model. The most usual way of bringing out the essence of this relationship between God and the world was to use metaphors and analogies, like "the formless in the form", as "heat in the fire", "hardness in clay" and "the object in the shadow".[20] The "form of Adam was made of clay" by God who lived within it "as the creative power",[21] just as *paramatma*[22] entered into the material body as *jivatma* (the individual soul).[23] Violence against all living creatures was deprecated, as all were "tokens of the greatness of God".[24] God is both "unmanifest" and "manifest", as "bird concealed in the egg", and the "tree in the seed". He unites both "faith" and "disbelief" in Himself. "He is all" and "all is He".[25] Even when distinction is made between God and man, who is but His "servant", the servant is ultimately only "one of His names". "You and I", wrote a *pir*-writer, "are but names alone, and He is all". While everybody talked at the village market creating "diverse sounds and noises", to a listener from a distance this was all "one harmonic piece". This was "the key to the truth" of one underlying many and one, who found "access to the truth" in his "mystic realisation", could not see anything but God alone.[26]

The mediators also attempted to enhance the cause of mysticism by underlining the superiority of esoteric knowledge to exoteric, scriptural and scholastic. The *Qur'an*, the *puranas* (Hindu traditions) and the *sastras* (Hindu religious law books) could not lead one to the path of *yoga*, which was the command of God. One could memorise the whole of the *sastras*, read the *Qur'an* for a hundred years, and yet he was not as purified as the leading *faqir*. The chief among the learned and scholars was not more than a servant of the *faqir*.[27] *Ma'rifat* was identified with *agama*, both being esoteric and containing the essence of the ultimate and single truth, while *sharia't* was exoteric and variegated in nature.[28]

Direct Appropriation [29]

Apart from attempts to introduce Islamic mystical concepts diluted more or less with indigenous parallels and symbols, the mystical writings of the cultural mediators also revealed a direct and outright recourse to locally known and used mystical techniques, formulae and idioms of Yogico-Tantric origin. The wide popularity of these ideas among the Bengali Muslims was evidenced not only by these writings but also by two other Muslim compositions, in which the respective authors resorted directly to Hindu religious traditions influenced by Yogico-Tantric ideas. One was Shaikh Faizullah's *Goraksa-vijaya*,[30] which was a direct contribution to the *natha* tradition. The other was Shaikh Chand's *Hara-Gauri Samvada,*[31] which made a thorough exposition of Yogico-Tantric ideas, adopting the Tantric and Nathist motif of the revelation of esoteric ideas put into the mouth of Hara or Siva in response to the inquiries of Gauri or Shakti. It is rather difficult to identify the particular channel through which these ideas influenced the minds of these writers. The history of medieval Bengal witnessed the emergence and nourishment of various cults and sects influenced by Yogico-Tantric ideas, such as the Buddhist *Sahajiyas,* the Nathists, the *Vaishnava Sahajiyas* and to some extent, the *Bauls.* Naturally enough, there was much that these cults held in common for example, the supreme importance attached to the mystic initiator (*guru*),[32] the importance of the human body as 'the microcosm of the universe (*dehatattva*) and the resultant psycho-physiological culture (*kaya-sadhana*). And yet it appears that the Yogico-Tantric ideas of the Muslim writers were largely derived through the Nathist channel, as evidenced by a large stock of Nathist terminologies in their writings, We have also noted above that one of the earliest and the most popular works on the *natha* tradition was written by a Muslim, Shaikh Faizullah.

Dominating the entire background of the esoteric disciplines in medieval Bengal was the idea of the supreme importance of the human body transformed into a microcosmos, and the consequent emphasis on the bio-mental culture. An all-embracing and elaborate structure of homologies – cosmic, theological. natural and physical – was effectively used to illustrate this subtle truth of mystico-physiology. The Bengali Muslim mystics located in the body the sun, the moon, the stars, earth, heaven, nether region, air, fire, twelve houses of the zodiac, seven days, rivers such as the Ganges, the Bhagirathi and the Indus and also those of Hindu[33] and Muslim[34] traditions.[35] Four traditional Hindu ages,[36] and the four *Vedas*[37] were identified in the human body, along with the four revealed book[38] and the four Sufic stations[39] (*muqam*).[40] In Adam's body, seen as microcosmos, was located four parts of the "moon" (*chari-chandra*) – a Nathist concept.[41]

The Yogico-Tantric concepts and formulae of mystico-physiology with esoteric significance attached to nerve-plexuses, veins, limbs, breath-control and retention of *semen virile* found great favour with the Muslim cultural mediators. The "piercing" or "penetration" (*bheda*) of the six nerve-plexuses (*chakras*), known as *shat-chakra-bheda,* was the central concept in all Yogico-Tantric systems. One of the writers chose a rather suggestive title for his mystical work, *Chari-muqam-bheda* ("the Piercing of Four Mystical Stages"), and named the entire mystical process *yoga.*[42] The twelve houses of the zodiac were traced and the four Sufic "stations" were related to the six Yogico-Tantric *chakras.*[43] There were frequent references to "sun" and "moon", and *pingala* and *ingila* or *ida* in the Yogico-Tantric mystical sense to refer generally to the two important nerves on the right and the left in the body.[44] The union of these two, meaning the union of the two currents of the vital wind, called prana (inhalation) and *apana* (exhalation), was considered a yogic ideal. The important yogic practices of retention of inhaled air (*kumbhaka*),[45] the well-known Nathist practice of "stealing the ambrosia" (*ksechari-mudra*),[46] the role of *khema* or *khemai* in the Nathist system as the vigilant sentinel of the body against all illusions and temptations, and finally, various physical postures (*asana*) and gestures (*mudra*), popular among the Yogico-Tantric groups, all found their way in the mediating efforts of the Bengali Muslim *pirs*.[47]

Pir and the Little Tradition

The *pir*-tradition as interpreted and moulded at the folk-level marked a qualitative difference from its more sophisticated formulations by the cultural mediators, as discussed above. The speculative and the "mystical" contents, even in their largely diluted forms as shaped by the latter, formed no part of the "cultural baggage" of the "little" *pir*-tradition. The Bengali Muslim folk developed almost a cult and a pantheon of *pirs* to whom they resorted in the trials and tribulations of their hard and struggling every day life.

The *pirs in Bengal were as ubiquitous as their numbers were legion. Their shrines were found in every nook and corner of Bengal – in desolate country lanes, in the fields and groves, in forests, and in the mountains. There were historical and legendary pirs,* real and fictitious *pirs,* universal and local *pirs and old and contemporary ones. The process of popular canonisation went on through the centuries. The veneration showed to them in the lifetime persisted with greater ardour after their death through visitation or pilgrimage (ziyarat)* to their shrines (called either *mazar* or *dargah*). Visitation of the shrine was, however, neither a uniquely Bengal nor even an India phenomenon. It was not also an exclusively folk monopoly. But the widely extended application of the term *pir*, as noted before, gave the little *pir*-tradition in Bengal its distinction and context. *Pir*, in this particular context, over-reached the religious categories of mystic guides, saints and holy men to accommodate disparate types of individuals, local deities and animistic spirits, all subjected to a process of folk religious transmutation that may be conceptualised as "pirification". An analysis of the religious-cultural process of pirification should enable us to comprehend better the character of the Islamic little tradition, and of Islam in relation to the Muslim masses of Bengal.

Pirification seems to provide the most significant clue to the process of Islamisation of the Bengali masses, as well as the only connecting thread linking Islam and the vast masses of rural converts. In the absence of clear and adequate evidence on the subject, the question of the local conversion of a very large section of the Bengali rural masses had long been a subject-matter of fertile historical speculations, as mentioned earlier.[48] There seems, however, a consensus among observers on the role of the "*sufi* " preachers and teachers in winning over the hearts of the Bengali masses, ground down by the social rigours and indignities of the caste system. Elsewhere,[49] I have attempted to focus on the complex nature of the problem and on the diverse agencies and circumstances underlying the process of conversion. It is in this context that the disparate elements lumped into congeries of *pirs emerge as significant.*

An analysis of the whole range of *pirs* known in Bengal down to the nineteenth century, suggests a broad division of them into one set of historical-legendary characters and another of totally fictitious and unreal elements, such as pirified animistic spirits and Hindu-Buddhist popular deities. A more careful examination of the beliefs and traditions associated with a number of historical-legendary figures demands a further sub-division of this category into those who earned popular veneration primarily as religious preachers, guides or saints, and others who seemed to receive popular canonisation for having performed for the people a necessary but rather less spiritual or religious role.

In assessing the roles particularly of the religious elements among the *pirs,* the importance of two institutional innovations in the setting of rural, Bengal, namely, the *pir's hospice (astanah or khanqah)* or his tomb *(dargah or mazar),* placed in the care of his followers, should not be overlooked. The significance of the *pir's astanah* and *dargah* in terms of catering to the material and religious-emotional needs of the people in the neighbourhood seeking such help, seemed obvious in the nature of circumstances. To the masses of the low castes and untouchables, who were denied direct access either to a temple or to its Brahman priest in a society steeped in exaggerated notions of ritual pollutions, the novelty of those twin Muslim institutions with open and total access was rather attractive. These were attracted not only towards the personal and religious charisma and thaumaturgic powers of a living *pir,* but also to such memories of a dead "saint", perpetuated in his shrine by his followers. In the case of a tomb, in particular, it is interesting to speculate on the possible psychological impact of the Muslim practice of burying the dead and erecting tombs, contrasted with the Hindu-Buddhist practice of consigning the corpse to flames. It also seems likely that the more popular anti-caste Yogico-Tantric religious groups in medieval Bengal, committed to rather esoteric psycho-physiological exercises, were unable to respond to the needs for a simpler, more emotive and personal religion. Significantly enough, it was left for the great Bengali religious leader, Chaitanya, to sound later the sweeping, levelling, intensely personal and emotional call of this Bengal Vaisnavism as an alternative. If the atmosphere of these institutions was emotionally congenial for the rural folk, no less attractive were those institutions' capacity and willingness to offer material comforts to the people. The *khanqahs* and *dargahs* were often supported by large or small land grants. An inscriptional reference to a *pir* credited him with bestowing "advantages upon the poor and the indigent."[50] A Bengali folk-ballad extolled a certain *pir* for not taking himself "even a particle of the gifts" made by people to him, and on the other hand distributing them all "among the poor and the famished." [51]

The question of providing for the material needs of the rural folk was a crucial element in the process of Islamic conversion as well as in that of pirification. Among those variegated elements pirified in Bengal, we could easily identify many who earned their canonisation by virtue of their active involvement and participation in essential but non-spiritual concerns of the rural communities, as demanded by their different socio-economic environments in deltaic Bengal. The distribution of Muslim population with large concentrations in the east, south-east and northern Bengal comprising the lower and "active" regions of the Ganges delta, the great embayment of lowland in the area east of Jamuna-Padma-Meghna line and the Meghna-Surma valley, was and still is a significant feature of the human geography of the land. The areas of deltaic Bengal were again characterised, on one hand by the clustering of dominant lower castes, like pods and *Namashudras* and caste-analogues of Muslim agriculturists, known as *Shekh* (*shaikh*), and weavers, called *Jola* (*Julaha*). [52] On the other, it was marked out by the absence of a firm and elaborate Hindu caste-structure. This is explained by the fact that the upper classes occupied the more stable and settled western part of the delta, and gradually pushed the earlier settlers and agriculturists to the more active part of the delta [53] − a process further accelerated by gradual shifts in the courses of rivers in Bengal from west to south and south-east, [54] resulting in corresponding shifts in the location of fertile soil. The rainfall in the lower delta was between sixty and ninety-five inches, while in the rest of Bengal excluding the northern submontane region it was between 50 and 60 inches: The Meghna-Surma embayment was perhaps "the most amphibious part of Bengal" during the rains. The lower tracts were flooded to a depth of 8-15 feet and the homesteads were built on earth platforms 15-20 feet high. [55] The area juxtaposed to the Bay of Bengal, including Bakharganj Barisal, Noakhali and extending round to Chittagong, were precariously open to the constant threat of cyclonic catastrophes Here, agriculturists, wood-cutters, fishermen, boatmen and the like were pitted against a Nature that was at once rich and bountiful, menacing and cruel. They had to live and fight against a mighty array of adversaries − the fierce floods, cyclonic storms, brackish waters, crocodiles, snakes and tigers.

There was also an element of a "frontier society" [56] about these areas. The history of this region was largely marked by turbulence and rioting, linked with conditions of local geography. The inundation as it built new mud banks or destroyed old homesteads, tanks, orchards and cultivated fields, was the uncertain source of riches or poverly, and in this fluctuating environment he who risked most often gained most. This made the population full of daring and adventure, while the flood waters that destroyed all marks or boundaries between the fields were indirectly a constant source of social disorder. [57] The very nature of the lower delta precluded a strong and organised administrative infrastructure. Even the British administration confronted problems of this nature. [58] In the absence of political as well as social authorities, the settlers in these areas looked, in the fluid and anarchic conditions of the delta, for some foci of order, authority and assurance, which were provided so successfully and gallantly by a number of Muslim adventurers, settlers and pioneering reclaimers of waste lands that the grateful people acknowledged their own debts by commending those benefactors for pirification.

Among *pirs* connected by tradition with comprehensive functions of this nature, the most well-known was Khan Jahan Ali, also known as Khan Jahan Khan, whose tomb at Bagerhat in Khulna was one of a few popular shrines in east Bengal.[59] At Ambarabad or Umarabad in Noakhali, there existed the shrine of Ambar of 'Umar Shah, who was believed to have lived in a boat to reclaim land north-east of Bhulua. His name came to be attached to the pargana of Ambarabad.[60] In the district of 24-Parganas Mubarak Ghazi, popular as Mobra Gaji, was a widely popular *pir*, of whom it is said, he "reclaimed the jungly tracts along the left bank of the river Hugli", and each village had "an altar dedicated to him". No one would enter the forest and no crew would sail through the district, without first of all making offerings at one of the shrines. The *faqirs* "residing in these pestilential forests, claiming to be lineally descended from the Ghazi", indicated with pieces of wood, called "sang", the exact limits within which the forest was to be cut.[61] Besides, the Bengali folk literature, both Hindu and Muslim, underlined the wide popularity of a tradition involving a Ghazi, his close associate, and some elements of Hindu opposition. The Hindu *Raya-mangala* literature depicts the conflict between Daksina-raya, a local Hindu chief and Ghazi assisted by Kalu over, the control of the active deltaic region of southern Bengal. An even battle, it was ended, we read, by a happy compromise based on territorial divisions dictated by God, appearing in a significant form, half Hindu and half Muslim.[62] The Muslim counterpart of this tradition made Ghazi and his closest associate, Kalu, arrive and land at Sundarban in south Bengal "infested by tigers, snakes and crocodiles".[63] The tradition also associated them with the local woodcutters, who owed their prosperity to the former.[64] It is significant that both Daksina-raya and Ghazi were, in their respective traditions credited with command over tigers and crocodiles. Traditions associated three hundred and thirteen disciples with Shah Jalal of Sylhet who worked and settled in widely scattered and remote parts of the region, containing shrines bearing the names of a large number among them.[65] Similar beliefs assigned twelve *pirs* to Taraf in the same region.[66] We are rather unfortunate in having no knowledge about the activities of these innumerable *pirs* who spread into the remotest corners of the new deltaic areas. It is interesting to note, however, that at the turn of this century, the wood-cutters, Hindu and Muslim, went in boats to certain localities in the forests called "gais", each of which was "presided by a fakir", who was supposed to possess "the occult power of charming away tigers", and who had undoubtedly "some knowledge of woodcraft". The wood-cutters worked "six days in each week", for one day in the week was set apart for "the worship of the sylvan deity presiding over that particular forest". The *faqir,* who was to have some "personal knowledge of this supernatural personage", acted as "high priest on these occasions".[67] Besides, if the beliefs associated with the particular *pirs* were any guide to their actual roles or to at least what was expected of them, most of these *pirs* were clearly identifiable in the social milieus of the new delta. Their names were invoked either as protective spirits against tigers, crocodiles and snakes or in connection with agricultural needs. In southern Bengal, especially in the Sundarban area, Mobra Gaji [68] and Bada-Khan Ghazi or simply Ghazi were extremely popular as possessing power over tigers. The same was believed about Sahija Badshah in the vicinity of the tiger-infested forest in the Pratapgarh Pargana in Sylhet.[69] Ghazi, mentioned earlier, his close associate Kalu and even Khan Jahan 'Ali were all believed to have controlling authority over crocodiles. Shah Kamal with his *dargah* in Sirajganj was renowned for his power over serpents.[70] At Astagram in Mymensingh, no cultivator used to yoke cows to a plough without remembering Qutb Sahib.[71] Besides, Manik-*pir* and Hajir-*pir* were also believed responsible for the protection of cattle.

There was another category of *pir,* whom we prefer to call warrior-*pir* or martyr-*pir.* As implied in the characterisation itself, tradition and other historical evidence would clearly identify them as attaining martyrdom[72] in battles against "infidel" local chiefs. An important *pir* of this category was Zafar Khan Ghazi, who found mention in three inscriptions between 1297 and 1313 AD as a mighty conqueror and a "destroyer of the obdurate among infidels". Zafar Khan lost his life in action against a Hindu *raja* of Hughly.[73] Shah Isma'il Ghazi, who was a military commander under a Bengal *sultan* (1452-74), was another pirified soldier. He was known to have been beheaded by the sultan, who acted on the advice of a Hindu commandant that Shah Isma'il was in collusion with a Hindu *raja.*[74] There were a few other martyr-*pirs* like Baba Adam Shahid of Rampal in Dacca, Shah Shafi' ud-din of Chota-Pandua and Shah Anwar Quli Halwi of Phurphura in Hughly, Taj Khan of Hijli in Midnapur, Raha-*pir* of Mangalkot in Burdwan, Turkan Shahid of Sherpur in Bagura and Makhdum Shah Daula Shahid of Shahzadpur in Pabna.

So far we have analysed diverse elements within that human category of *pirs* whose historical identities, though not always very clearly established, need not, however, be doubted. On the other hand, the processs of pirification did also draw, as noted already, upon the non-human resources of popular concern. A number of pre-existing popular beliefs and practices were sought to be "Islamised" through the protean process of pirification.

There was Athka-pir [75] resorted to by people for either quick recovery from illness or escape from trouble.[76] Hajir-pir was taken to get back lost cattle.[77] Thanka-pir was believed to possess the power of regaining lost property.[78] Norapir's favour was solicited in order to fulfil a desire or a wish.[79] The particular association of banyan tree (*Ficus bengalensis*) with this *pir's* rituals suggests a possible pirification of a tree-spirit. In another village in Midnapur a banyan tree was regarded as sacred by reason of its being the supposed abode of Nekursani-*pir*. Situated on the way to the local court of justice, it was resorted to by litigants in the belief that the *pir* would bless them with success in their lawsuits. [80]

In a few other cases certain *pirs* of dubious origin and also known outside Bengal, came to be associated with beliefs that seemed more important than the *pirs* connected with those beliefs. In north Bengal the beliefs and practices about Ghazi Miyan, also called Gajna Dulha or Salar Chinula, were closely associated with marriage and fertility. Often identified with Salar Masud Ghazi of Bahraich in northern India, it was believed that Ghazi Miyan died on the day set for his marriage.[81] Another such example was Khwaja Khizr, associated with beliefs in water-spirits. A highly controversial character and of general renown in the Muslim world, he was remembered in Bengal, particularly in the rainy season, by launching in rivers and tanks small paper boats, decorated with flowers and candles. [82] There was, however, a far more popular *pir* in Pir-Badar, widely accepted in Bengal as the guardian-spirit of waters. His name was invoked by every sailor and fisherman, starting on a cruise or overtaken by a storm.[83] The shrine associated with his name was in Chittagong and was visited regularly by the local Muslims, Hindus and Buddhist Maghs. Pir-Badar was rather doubtfully identified with Shaikh Badar ud-din Badar-i 'Alam (d. 1440), who lived in Chittagong temporarily, and was buried far away in Bihar. The rituals and beliefs connected with the *pir* [84] do not warrant this identification with an itinerant and obscure *pir*. An attempt was also made to identify the *pir* with Khwaja Khizr.[85] According to another account he was a ship-wrecked Portuguese sailor, named Pas Gual Peeris Botheilo, who reached the shore by clinging to a raft.[86] The possibility of a conversion of a pre-existing Buddhist shrine and a corresponding corruption of the Buddhist entity "Bajra" into "Badar" was suggested by D.C. Sen.[87]

In places the Bengali Muslim folk made *pirs* of local non-Muslim divinities or objects of worship. In Mymensingh district Manai-pir appeared the pirified Hindu god. Kartika, and the rites and fertility beliefs pertaining to his adoration were almost identical with those of local Kartika celebrations (*Kartika-vrata*)[88] Tinnath-pir, popular in the same region, seemed no other than the *natha* trinity,[89] called Trinatha (three *Nathas*) or its corrupted form, Tinnath, or Tinnath-thakur, as popular with the local Hindus. By far the greatest figure in this category of *pirs* was Manik-pir, whose wide recognition as the guardian-*pir* of the village folk, protecting the cattle, promoting its fertility, as well as agricultural prosperity, family health and happiness, enshrined him in the hearts of the village folk, both Muslim and Hindu. Muslim mendicants (*faqir*) and village bards sang ballads glorifying the *pir*. Manik-pir's identity does not lend itself to an easy conclusion. While in some respects he partook of the Hindu god Siva's character, he also came close to resembling Goraksanath. Indeed, one tradition connected Manik with him as being his disciple.[90] A song about him lends further support to this Saivite association, according to which Manik-pir came to the house of Kalu-ghos with the cry of "*vam vam*" a common practice among Saivite mendicants. Kalu-ghos's mother offered him five small coins in the name of Panch-pir. Manik refused to accept cash and asked for milk and curd. Kalu's mother played a trick on him, as a result of which all their cattle and even the milk-maid died. She came to realise her folly and begged for the *pir*'s mercy. Manik took pity on her, struck his staff (*asa*) on the ground, and everything came back to life again. Panch-*pir* (Five-*pirs*) presents a greater riddle. The cult was popular with both Hindus and Muslims in and out of Bengal. Popular beliefs concerning this quintet of divinities left no common list of names for them. Its wide geographical distribution and popularity in India among lower orders of both Muslim and Hindu societies tend to suggest its origin from a pre-Muslim indigenous source. Agarwala traces this cult to the worship of Pancha-bira [91] and is supported by H. P. Dwivedi and S. L. Sanghavi who recognise the possibility of *bira* being pronounced as *pira* in the Panjabi dialects. [92]

Satya-pir added a whole new dimension to the syncretistic process of pirification. Pirification in this particular instance seems to reveal a significant facet of Sanskritisation as a socio-cultural process in Hinduism, being the reverse of Islamisation which was the natural concomitant of pirification in the Bengali Muslim society. The popularity of the cult seemed to have been greater among Hindus than Muslims, for the large majority of writings on the pir were Hindu contributions.[93] As was the case with other popular *pirs* the identity of Satya-pir seemed rather obscure – indeed even more than others. Although a few shrines bearing the name could be found at places, an examination of the relevant literature and tradition on the *pir* categorically rejects the historicity of the *pir*. Some traditions quite arbitrarily linked up Husain Shah, a fifteenth century *sultan*of Bengal, with the introduction of this cult.[94] Other commentators on the subject idealised it in general terms as a symbol of Hindu-Muslim syncretism.[95] In the absence of positive historical evidences we attempt to offer a possible explanation of its origins on the basis of an internal analysis of its literature. The literary tradition on the *pir adopted either of two motifs—the Brahman or the merchant motif – both aiming at vindication of the pir* in the same way as the Hindu *mangala-kavya* literature proclaimed the glory of particular popular divinities. The first motif involved a Brahman who was advised to worship Satya-pir by God, appearing in the guise of a Muslim mendicant. The Brahman's refusal to accept a Muslim divine led to God's reappearance in the form of Hindu god, Krishna – a feat which finally convinced the Brahman. The second motif concerned a Hindu sea-merchant and his son-in-law who, despite their initial scant regard for Satya-pir, were able to save their entire voyage, thanks to the steadfast devotion of the merchant's daughter to Satya-pir, and the final submission of the whole family to the *pir*. Both these versions may be interpreted as underlining a process of upper class Hindu acceptance of the Satya-pir cult. The process was closely parallelled by the gradual recognition of the popular Hindu deities by the hieratic Brahmanical order. The growing popularity of *pir* and *pir*-cults in Bengal was at once a challenge and an opportunity for the priestly class of Brahmans. The Brahman answer, consistent with their past tradition, was to create an abstract cult of Satya(Eternity/Truth)-pir, establish the essential identity of their old faiths and the new and facilitate its final absorption. It was not without significance that there were more Hindu writers on the Satya-pir tradition than Muslim, that God appeared before the Brahman in both Hindu and Muslim guises, and finally, that there was also a clear attempt to divest the cult of its Muslim associations. Vidyapati, a Brahman writer, called Satya-pir God's incarnation in the present age (*kali-yuga*) "in a faqir's guise".[96] An old Sanskritic text, the *Skanda-purana*. was interpolated, and Satya-narayana[97] emerged to render Satyapir redundant.[98] The syncretistic objects of the Hindu authors of Satya-pir tradition were clearly achieved, but their attempts did not meet with success if they intended its total absorption into Satya-narayana. Satya-pir and Satya-narayana remained, with the masses of believers, one and the same. One Muslim writer combined them both into one "Satya-pir-narayana" or "Satya-narayana".[99] Another found "Pir-narayana" sitting in Mecca.[100] A third addressed Satya-pir as Ghazi and added:

Thou art Brahma, Vishnu and Narayana. [101]

The study of Islamic syncretism in reference to the *pir*- tradition of Bengal raises issues of both methodological and theoretical import.

(1) As already noted at the beginning of the chapter an empirical perception of the *pir* phenomenon in Bengal underlines the grave limitation of substituting analytical cliches for its precise study. An uncritical assumption of pirism in Bengal in terms of "sufism" or "mysticism" or even "saint-worship" emerges in our study as highly misleading.

(2) The classical formulations of the concepts of "great" and "little" tradition, basically enunciated in the context of a "single" primary or even secondary great tradition, seem to prove inadequate as analytical tools for the Islamic phenomenon in the Bengal context. In Bengal the secondary exogenous Muslim great tradition, unable to interact with the endogenous little tradition that was culturally continuous with the primary Hindu great tradition for millennia, created conditions for the construction of an endogenous alternative syncretistic model of a great tradition for the Bengali Muslims. Consequently, the Bengal phenomenon did provide an uncommon paradigm not only of two great traditions – one orthodox and exogenous, the other syncretistic and endogenous – within the corpus of one religion but also that of a strong and vital syncretistic tradition at the level of both little and great traditions. This brings us to the more

potent issues of syncretism and Islamisation set in their methodological and theoretical contexts.

(3) The normative and "macro" perspective of the so-called "Islamists" or "Orientalists" constructed a rather narrow, rigid and largely idealistic formulation of what is, in fact, a rather complex, dynamic and protean process of Islamisation in the specific context of a society and a culture. Its result has been to see a Muslim not so much in terms of what he considers himself as a Muslim but in terms of his degree of conformity to what is generally defined and fostered as the *Sunni* orthodox ideals and expectations of being a Muslim. Conversion is rarely a culmination, and on the contrary appears a mere beginning of a gradual process of awakening to a new experience and faith.[102] The break of continuity between the old and the new faiths and worlds is a facile assumption. The gap between the "ideal" and the "actual" resulting from this assumption is often sought to be bridged by the complementary apologetics of either religious "degeneration" or "incomplete conversion". The puritanical Islamic revivalists in the nineteenth century and their academic apologists were fortunately not called upon to defend historically their claim – motivated no less by secular concerns than religious – that the Bengali Muslim had lost his grip on his faith in the course of time. The earliest extant Bengali Muslim literature presents a flat contradiction of this claim. The so-called "corrupt", "devitalised" and "degenerate" Islam in Bengal merely typified the syncretistic symbols and meanings that the Bengalis called Muslims attached to the religion that they called their own.

(4) The Bengal phenomenon suggests a significant modification of a general assumption regarding syncretism in relation to Islamisation. Syncretistic developments are generally considered exclusive of and often antithetical to Islamisation. Viewed in its historical context, Islamic syncretism in traditional Bengal cannot be taken as running counter to the social-cultural process of Islamisation in the area. On the contrary, the syncretistic formulations of esoteric and historical-legendary Islam by the Bengali Muslim cultural mediators, aimed at promoting Islam through the restoration of continuity between the great and little traditions for the Bengali Muslims, marked an advance in the cause of Islamisation which could only be seen as a gradual process of realisation of a new religion rather than an instant illumination resulting from conversion.[103] The sharp changes in the political, economic and social-cultural milieus of Bengal under conditions of British rule, which had surfaced since the nineteenth century, generated unprecedented pressures on the formation and articulation of separate religious-cultural identities among the people. The revivalist purge of accretions to and declensions from Islam, as a means of sharpening the consciousness of separate Muslim identity, resulted in complete denigration and rejection of the syncretistic values.[104] The syncretistic virtues came to be looked upon and gradually accepted as follies. The symbiotic union of syncretism and Islamisation in the social and cultural situations of traditional Bengal increas-

ingly assumed an antithetical character in the changed situations of later times.

NOTES

1. A comprehensive treatment of the subject based on unpublished literary sources has been attempted by the present writer; see A. Roy, "Islam in the Environment of Medieval Bengal" (hereinafter mentioned as IEMB), unpublished Ph. D thesis (Canberra: Australian National University, 1970); also, by the same author, "The Social Factors in the Making of Bengali Islam" (hereafter SFMBI). South Asia (The Journal of South Asian Studies of Australia and New Zealand), no. 3 (August, 1973), pp. 23-35.

2. Cf. J. Wise, Notes on the Races, Castes and Trades of Eastern Bengal (London: Harrison and Sons, 1883. Only 12 copies printed for private circulation. The present writer consulted the copy held at the British Library), p. 6; A.R. Mallick, British Policy and the Muslims in Bengal (Dacca: Asiatic Society of Pakistan, 1961), p. 26; W.Crooke (ed.), Qanun-i Islam by Jafar Sharif, Eng. tr. by G. Herklot (London: Oxford UP, 1921), "Introduction"; M. Mujeeb, The Indian Muslims (London: Allen & Unwin, 1967), p. 22.

3. The Islamic revivalist and purificatory movements in Bengal in the nineteenth and twentieth centuries, such as Faraidi, Tariqat-i Muhammadiyah (popular as, but inappropriately called, Wahhabi), Ta'aiyuni and Ahl-i Hadith, which largely derived their inspirations from sources outside the region, launched a massive propaganda and assault on "innovations" (bi'da) in contemporary Islam with the ultimate consequence of undermining the syncretistic basis of the Bengali Muslim great and little traditions.

4. J. Hastings (ed.), Encyclopaedia of Religion and Ethics (Edinburgh: T & T Clark, 1908-26), X, p. 40.

5. Cf. In north Africa "the word sufi is not always used, and popular religious leaders possessing divine grace are known rather as saints". (N.R. Keddie (ed.), Scholars, Saints and Sufis (Berkeley: California UP, 1972, Introduction, p. 1).

6. As a result of a number of empirical researches on the so-called "sufi orders" or more appropriately, "Muslim religious brotherhoods" in the Middle Eastern countries, we are beginning to realise that a number of "disparate groups" with wide ranging and divergent beliefs and practices are "lumped together" as "sufi orders". (Ibid. pp. 4-5; also V. Crapanzano, "The Hamadsha", in Keddie, ibid., pp. 327-28; L.C. Brown, "The Religious Establishment in Husainid Tunisia" in Keddie, ibid., p. 79; C. Geertz, Islam Observed: Religious Development in Morocco and Indonesia (New Haven: Yale UP, 1968), p. 48.

7. For possible parts in the conversion played by heterogeneous elements, lumped together under the amorphous label of pir, see below. For a more detailed discussion of the question see IEMB, pp. 116-78.

8. Ibid., pp. 52-61; also, SFMBI, pp. 23, 26.

9. M. Singer, "The Cultural Patterns of Indian Civilisation", Far Eastern Quarterly, XV, (1955) p. 24. Singer mentions the "leading personalities" as performing the role of cultural, mediators between the Hindu great and little traditions. Robert Redfield, in similar contexts, refers to "cultural specialists devoted to mediating between Great Tradition and Little". ("The Social Organisation of Tradition", Far Eastern Quarterly, ibid., p. 15). Arnold Toynbee develops a similar concept of a "cultural broker" in the "intelligentsia". See, A Study of History (New York: Oxford UP, 1962), V, pp. 154-58.

10. For detailed analysis see, IEMB, pp. 179-322; also, SFMBI, pp. 30-34.

11. Kali-yuga is the fourth and the last age (yuga) in Hindu tradition.

12. Pursuing in the lines of Tholuck (1821), Von Kremer (1888), Goldziher (1910) and Max Horten (1927-8), R.C.Zaehner(*Hindu and Muslim Mysticism*, London: London UP, 1960) notes effective Indian influence on *sufism*, while following Nicholson (1914), Massignon (1922) and Moreno (1946), A.Z.Arberry (*Sufism: An Account of the Mystics of Islam*, London: Allen & Unwin, 1950) rejects this view.

13. Aziz Ahmad (*Studies in Islamic Culture in the Indian Environment*, London: Oxford UP, 1964, p. 118) writes on the"general trend of exclusiveness of Sufism in India from Hindu mystical schools, with which it had so much in common" and "the merely occasional, more negative than positive contact of the two mystical systems on the Indian soil".

14. A generally used Hindu Tantric expression for esoteric truth.

15. Zain ud-din, *Rasul-vijaya*, Dms (manuscript belonging to Munshi 'Abdul Karim Collection, held at the Dacca University Library)No. 494: sl (serial) 423, fol (folio) 29; *IEMB*, p. 218.

16. Hayat Mahmud, *Hita-jnana-vani*, (text ed. by M. Islam, *Kabi Heyat Mamud*, Rajshahi, 1961), p. 38; Muhammad Khan, *Maqtal Husain* (Dms 380: s1 353), fols 1a- b; *IEMB*, pp. 218, 221.

17. Shaikh Mansur, *Sirr-nama* (Dms 569: sl 460), fols 6b ff;*IEMB* , p. 219.

18. 'Ali' Raja, *Jnana-sagara* (Dms 146 b: sl 9), fol 1; Saiyid Sultan, *Jnana-pradipa* (Dms 365: sl 152) fol 3b; *IEMB*, pp. 219-20.

19. S.A.A. Rizvi, *Muslim Revivalist Movement in Northern India*, (Agra: Agra UP, 1965), p. 59.

20. Saiyid Sultan, *Nabi-vamsa* (uncatalogued Dms), fol 1b; *Jnana- chautisa* (Dms 366: sl 153), fols 1-2; *IEBM*, pp. 189 ff.

21. A1i Raja, *Agama* (Dms 146a: sl 9), fol 73; *IEBM* , p. 191.

22. The Vedantic concept of the supreme soul.

23. 'Ali Raja'. *Jnana-sagara op. cit.*, fol 129; Saiyid Murtaza, *Yoga-qalandar (*Dms 547: sl 394), fols 8a-9b; *IEBM*, p. 191-2.

24. Ali Raja', Ibid., fol 83.

25. Haji Muhammad, *Nur-jamal* (Dms 374: sl 260), fol 6; *IEMB*, p. 194.

26. Ibid., fol 10.

27. 'Ali Raja', *Jnana sagara, op.* cit, fols 208, 215-l8; *IEMB*, pp. 199-200.

28. 'Ali Raja', *Agama, op. cit.*, fol 27; *IEMB*, Ibid.

29. The discussion here draws largely on my article, *SFMBI*, pp. 30-31.

30. Text, ed. by Munshi A. Karim (Calcutta: Sahitya-parisat Granthavali, no 64,1324 B.S./1917 AD,).

31. Dms 559: sl 556, fol 2.

32. As noted above.

33. Iksu, Ratnakara, Nabani, Ksiroda and Dadhi.

34. Rud (Oxus), Nil (Nile), Saihun (Jaxartes), Jaihun (Bactrus) and Kulsum.

35. Shaikh Zahid, *Adya-parichaya*, (text ed. by M. M. Chaudhuri. Rajshahi, 1964), *passim;* Shaikh Mansur, *op. cit.*, fols 24a-27a.

36. *Satya, Treta, Dvapara and Kali*.

37. *The Rig, Sama, Yajur* and *Atharva*.

38. The *Psalms*, the *01d Testament*, the *New Testament* and the *Qur'an*.

39. *Nasut, Malkut, Jabrut* and *Lahut*.

40. Shaikh Zahid, loc. cit,; Shaikh Chand, *Talib-nama* (Dms 694: sl 171), fols 8b-l0a; Saiyid Sultan, *Jnana-pradipa, op.cit.*, fols 9b-10a;Saiyid Murtaza,op.*cit*. fols 1a-9b.

41. Shaikh Chand, ibid.

42. 'Abd ul-Hakim (Dms 408: sl 247), fols 2a-b.

43. Saiyid Sultan, *Jnana-pradipa*, *op cit.*, fol 10a; Saiyid Murtaza, op.cit., fols 1-8a.

44. 'Abd ul-Hakim, op.cit., fols 2a-b.

45. Ibid.

46. The Nathist practice of turning the tongue back to the root of the cerebral region, reaching the source of divine ambrosia.

47. Saiyid Sultan, *Jnana-pradipa*, fol 1 la-b.

48. See H. Beverley, *Report on the Census of Bengal, 1872* (Calcutta: Bengal Secretariat Press, 1872); E.A. Gait, *Report on Bengal, Census of India, 1901*, VI, pt. 1 (Calcutta: Bengal Secretariat Press. 1902); *The Imperial Gazetteer of India*, ed. by H. Risley et al, 26 vols. (Oxford: Clarendon Press, rev. edn., 1907-09); K. Fuzli Rubbee, *The Origin of the Musulmans of Bengal* (Calcutta: Thacker & Spink, 1895); A. Karim, *Social History of the Muslims in Bengal* (Dacca: Asiatic Society of Pakistan, 1959); M.R. Rahim, *Social and Cultural History of Bengal*, 2 vols. (Karachi: Pakistan Publishing House, 1963-67), I.

49. *IEMB*, pp. 164-78

50. A.A.Khan, Memoirs *of Gaur and Pandua*, ed. by H.E.Stapleton (Calcutta: Bengal Secretariat Book Depot, 1924), p. 115.

51. "Kanka-o-Lila" in D. C. Sen (ed.), *Purba-banga-gitika*, (Calcutta: Calcutta UP, 192S-32), I, pt 2, p. 230.

52. Strong anthropometric correspondence between the Muslim masses *and Namashudras* in these areas was found in a recent survey. See, D N. Majumdar & C.R.Rao, *Race Elements in Bengal* (Calcutta: Statistical Publishing Society, 1960)

53. This appears to have been the case with the whole of the Gangetic Doab, where the higher castes lived in contiguity throughout the Ganges Valley, while, the unprivileged *Bhars, Pasis, Chamars* and *Dosadhs* of the upper plain lived in scattered clumps of houses on the brink of marshes and swamps, just like their *Mahishya, pod, Namashudra* and the Muslim *Shekh counterparts in the lower delta. R.K. Mukherjee, The Changing Face of Bengal-a Study in Riverine Economy* (Calcutta: Calcutta UP, 1938), pp. 19-23.

54. *Ibid.*, pp. 7-9.

55. O.H.K.Spate and A.T.A. Learmonth. *India and Pakistan. A General and Regional Geography* (London: Methuen, 3rd edn., 1967), pp. 575, 583.

56. R.W.Nicholas, "Vaisnavism and Islam in Rural Bengal" in D Kopf (ed.), *Bengal Regional Identity* (Ann Arbor; Asian Studies Center, 1969), p. 44.

57. Mukerjee, op cit., pp. 27-28.

58. *The Faridpur Settlement Report* (Calcutta: Superintendent of Govt. Printing, 1914), p. 56.

59. For an inscriptional reference to him, A.H.Dani, "Bibliography of the Muslim Inscriptions of Bengal", no. 28, *Appendix, Journal of the Asiatic Society of Pakistan* (Dacca), 11 (1957).

60. J.E.Webster (ed.), *Noakhali. District Gazetteer of Eastern Bengal and Assam* (Allahabad, 1911), p. 101.

61. J. Wise, "The Muhammadans of Eastern Bengal", *Journal of the Asiatic Society of Bengal* (Calcutta), LXIII (1894), pt. iii, no. 1, p. 40.

62. Krishnarama-dasa, *Raya-mangala*, ed. by B. Mustafi, *Sahitya-parisat Patrika* (Calcutta), III, pts. iii-iv.

63. 'Abd ul-Karim, *Kalu-Gaji-Champavati* (Calcutta: Gausia Library, n.d.), p. 10.

64. Ibid., 15-17.

65. *Journal of the Asiatic Society of Pakistan* (Dacca), 11 (1957), pp. 66 ff.

66. A. C. Chaudhuri,*Srihatter Itivritta,* (Calcutta, 1324 B. S 1917 AD.), I, pt ii, pp.98-100.

67. L.S.S. O'Malley (ed.), *Khulna. Bengal District Gazetteers* (Calcutta, 1907), pp. 193-94.

68. L.S.S.O'Malley (ed.),*24-Parganas Bengal District Gazetteers* (Calcutta,1914), pp.74-76.

69. B.C. Allen (ed.), *Sylhet, Assam District Gazetteers* (Calcutta, 1905) I I, p. 83; A C Chaudhurl, *op. cit.,* I. pt. i, p. 141.

70. M. Siddiqi, *Sirajganjer Itihas* (Sirajganj, 1322 B.S. 1915 AD.), p.20.

71. F.A. Sachse (ed.), *Mymensingh. Bengal District Gazetteers* ,Calcutta, 1917), p 38.

72. The titles *ghazi or shahid,* meaning "martyr", often occurring in their names,bear this point out.

73. A.H. Dani, op. cit., inscription nos. 6, 7 & 8.

74. Pir Muhammad Shattari, *Risalat ush-Shuhda* (a biography of Shah Isma'il), Eng. tr. by G.H.Damant, *Journal of Asiatic Society of Bengal,* 1874, pp. 215 ff.

75. Significantly enough, "athka" means "all of a sudden".

76. K.K. Ray, "Maimansimher Musalman Grihastha Paribare Sinnir Pratha", *Sahitya Parisat Patrika* (Calcutta, *Bangiya Sahitya Parisat),* pp. 217-18.

77. Ibid., p. 229.

78. Ibid., p. 227.

79. Ibid.,p. 223.

80. C.Ray, "On Tree-Cults in the District of Midnapur in Southwestern Bengal", *Man in India* (Ranchi, India), II, pt. ii, p.240.

81. H.D. Kundu, "Sherpurer Itihas", *Sahitya-parisat Patrtka* (Calcutta), V (additional no., 1317 B.S. 19I0 AD.) pp. 33-34.

82. J. Wise, "The Muhammadans...", op. cit., pp. 38-39; Gait, op. cit., p. 179.

83. Ibid., p. 41; M. Th. Houtsma, et al (eds.), *Encyclopaedia of Islam* (Leiden & London, 1913-36), II, p. 559 (The latter reproduces Wise in every essential detail, without acknowledgment).

84. Gait, op. cit., p. 178.

85. Ibid.

86. It was believed about Pir-Badar that he arrived in Chittagong "floating on a rock", and the neighbourhood of Chittagong being then infested by *jinns* or evil spirits, he exterminated them and took possession of the whole country. (Wise, op. cit., p. 41).

87. Sen made similar derivation of the word "Budur" forming part of the name of the famous temple Bara Budur. He also cites the case of a Buddhist word "Bajra-yogin i " being actually pronounced as "Badar-yogini". The attachment of the Buddhist Maghs" to the shrine of Pir-Badar has been already noted.

88. K.K. Ray, op. cit., p. 212.

89. Adi-natha (Siva), Matsyendra-natha or MIna-natha and Goraksa-natha.

90. S.B. Dasgupta, *The Obscure Religious Cults,* (Calcutta: Calcutta UP, rev. edn., 1962), p. 372.

91. "Bira" or *baram or baramha* worship at the popular level was possibly a survival of very popular ancient *Yaksa* worship. (V.S. Agarwala, *Prachina Bharatiya Lokadharma* (Varanasi, 1964), pp. 2-3, 1 I8-43).

92. Ibid, pp. 135-36

93. S.Sen, Bangala *Sahityer Itihasa,* (Calcutta, latest edn., 1965). I, pt. ii, pp. 452-66.

94. D.C. Sen, *History of Bengali Language and Literature* (Calcutta: Calcutta UP, 1911), p. 797.

95. Ibid.; K.K. Datta, "Relations between the Hindus and the Muhammadans of Bengal in the Middle of the Eighteenth Century ?(174-65)", *Journal of Indian History* (Patna), VIII (1929), p. 330; A. Karim, op. cit., p. 167; M. A. Rahim, op. cit., I, p. 338.

96. Quoted, S. Sen, op. cit., I, pt. ii, p. 455.

97. Narayana is another name of Lord Krishna.

98. One edition (Bangabasi) of the text ins the name of Satya-pir, and another(Venkatesvara Press) does not. (P.V.Kane,*History of Dharma-sastras* (Poona: Bhandarkar Oriental Research Institute, 1958), V, pt. i, p. 437.

99. 'Arif, quoted, S.Sen, op. cit., I, pt. ii, pp 457-58.

100. Quoted, ibid,, p. 462.

101. Faizullah, quoted, ibid.

102. Compare Geertz's observation in the Indonesian context: "Islamic conversion is not, as a rule, a sudden, total, overwhelming illumination but a slow turning toward a new light." (C. Geertz,op. cit., p. 97).

103. Cf. "Islamisation in the past has been a gradual process, a slow accretion of minor changes rather than a series of spectacular quantum jump. . .". (ibid., p. l05).

104. Cf. "Modernisation was accompanied by movements among the religious establishment to define or purify the true religion – a definition or purification that often led to a denunciation of popular practices as superstitions." (N.R. Keddie (ed.), op. cit., p. 9.) In reference to the east Bengal district of Noakhali, which became known later "throughout East Pakistan for the pervading influence of the priestly class called the Mullahs and 'pure' Islam" (A.K.N. Karim, *Changing Society in India and Pakistan* (Dacca: Oxford UP,1956), p. 133), the District *Gazetteer* records in 1911: "Formerly, it is said, the Mohammedans kept too many of their old Hindu customs, but about the middle of last century they came under the influence of a reforming priest, Maulavi Imamuddin, and are now, almost to a man, Faraizis.They abhor all innovations . . . and the worship of saints. . ." (J E Webster (ed.), *Noakhali,* op. cit., p. 39.)

PART II

ISLAMISATION AS A SOCIAL-POLITICAL PROCESS

5 The Bengal Muslim 'Cultural Mediators' and the Bengal Muslim Identity in the Nineteenth and Early Twentieth Centuries[1]

ONE OF THE major and challenging themes of modern South Asian historiography relates to the search for identity at both individual and collective levels. A vast and heterogeneous population, traditionally compartmentalised by a complex set of economic, social and cultural criteria into small primordial groups, found themselves compelled, from the nineteenth century onwards, to respond to the growing demands and pressures on them to seek identification with much larger religious and secular formations. The steady growth of a collective self-consciousness among Muslims with all its implications for the subsequent political development of this community is a significant strand in this theme. The case of Bengal Muslims presents itself, in this context, as being somewhat unique inasmuch as it both conforms to and deviates from the general pattern of development in South Asian Islam. The emergence of a stronger and sharper sense of a collective Muslim identity, and its close and direct bearings on the growth of separatist Muslim politics are matters of common concern among students of South Asian Islam and Muslims. The Bengal phenomenon does not, however, reveal a uniform and unidirectional search for an exclusive Islamic identity. The Bengal Muslim search for a collective identity was clearly caught between the two opposite pulls of an extra-territorial 'Islamic' ideology and of a local geographical 'Bengali' culture. Most studies in the growth of Muslim separatism in South Asia, including Bengal, focus on the process of 'Islamisation' preceding the separatist political development. The Bengal Muslim participation in the separatist Muslim politics, leading to the partition of India as well as Bengal, is the determinant in this common historiographical perspective. A close investigation of the Muslim Bengali literature in the late nineteenth and early twentieth centuries reveals, however, unmistakable tensions, vacillations and even clear conflicts in Bengal Muslim's self-perceptions and self-statements-uncertainties that one may also detect in the complex and dissimilar patterns of modern Muslim politics in Bengal. Moreover, if partition of Bengal (1947) saw the vindication of the 'Islamic' identity, the emergence of Bangladesh (1971) on the ruins of the 'Islamic brotherhood' of Pakistan more than merely raises doubts about some of these 'Islamic' assumptions. The story is, however, a continuing one. The developments in Bangladesh since its inception seem to reinforce the persistent image of a people still groping for a commonly acceptable identity. In this chapter, dealing broadly with the problem of growing self-consciousness of Bengal Muslims in the nineteenth and early twentieth centuries, I have chosen, therefore, to focus on the diversities and conflicts in Bengal Muslims' search for a collective identity.

I

Some of the blatant wrongs found in South Asian historiography have been perpetrated through the indiscriminate and uncritical use of the general labels of 'Hindus' and 'Muslims'. Nowhere else the force of this observation is perhaps driven home more powerfully than in a study of changing self-perceptions of traditional groups in the Indian subcontinent, subjected to various new challenges and pressures since the late nineteenth century. A general predisposition to treat Hindu-Muslim questions on the basis of a facile assumption of their clearly differentiated identities in history, past or present, proved inhibitive of more basic inquiries about the formulation of their initial group identities. Thanks to the social science approach to the problem of nationality formation, we have now a much deeper and finer appreciation of the process by which an ethnic group, 'which is objectively distinct, but whose members do not necessarily attach subjective importance or political significance to the fact', becomes transformed first into a 'community' with 'an awareness of a common identity', and then into a 'nationality' or 'nation' when the community 'mobilises for political action and becomes politically significant, that is, when it makes political demands and achieves a significant measure of success by its own efforts'.[2]

Bengal Muslims' changing forms of group consciousness correspond rather closely to this classical process of identity building. Since the late eighteenth century, Bengal's social, economic and political circumstances began to change so rapidly as to result in a significant arousal of interest, concerns and initiatives among the elites, both religious and non-religious, vying for mass support, and seeking for group mobilisation. Among various and competing symbols of ethnic group identification, such as *jati,* kin, locality, language and religion, elites chose one or the other as the central symbol to build a 'community' around it with an increased and deeper awareness of its changed identity. In Bengal, religion rather than language proved the most potent symbol for the purposes of the elite's manipulations. The 'instrumentalist' school of ethnicity in the sense of the formation of ethnic communities and nationalities, attaches critical importance to the manipulative role of elites in the use of unifying symbols of group identification to win the allegiance of its members, and achieve their effective mobilisation. The 'primordialist-instrumentalist' debates on the role of the elite and the nature of the freedom of 'choice' open to them have, in the South Asian context, been centred round the issue of Muslim separatism in the northern India.[3] The Bengal Muslim phenomenon comes much closer to the instrumentalist's position than primordialist's. The entire process of their identity formation underlines the seminal role of the elite, spurred into action by the changed historical circumstances of their position, their inner divergences and conflicts underlying their differential responses, their manipulation of symbols of group identification for the optimal participation and mobilisation of the masses, and so on all conforming essentially to the instrumentalist's model for identity building. A brief analysis of the changing historical circumstances of Bengal Muslims in the late eighteenth and nineteenth centuries, creating conditions for elite intervention, identity reformulation, and mass mobilisation, is necessary to elucidate this matter.

The undoubted core value differences between Islam and Hinduism found little recognition, in traditional Bengal, except at the level of some section of elites. The Islam as conceived and practised traditionally by the vast mass of Bengali believers was what I have characterised in my own detailed studies on this subject as 'syncretistic'.[4] The textual or doctrinal Islam, embodied in the Arabic, Persian and Urdu languages and literatures, proved totally unable to communicate and interact with the masses of believers who spoke nothing but local Bengali. This issue was further complicated not only by the orthodox elite contempt for the 'vulgar' and 'profane' Bengali language 'of the Hindus'. There was the far more critical and daunting problem of reducing the massive polarity between the alien Islamic religious and cultural symbols and those familiar ones of local origin. A Bengali-speaking section of the Muslim literati and religious elite, conceptualised as 'cultural mediators' in my studies, emerged to take up this challenge and became the architects of a rich Islamic syncretistic tradition in Bengali language and literature in the sixteenth and seventeenth centuries.[5] The tradition, nourished since then by generations of Bengal Muslims, remained for centuries an alternative syncretistic model of great tradition for the overwhelming majority of Bengal Muslims, running parallel to the exogenous model of great tradition contained in non-Bengali languages and patronised by the non-Bengali-oriented Muslim elites.

The syncretistic tradition confronted a massive challenge and was subjected to a vigorous assault in the nineteenth century by the new awakened forces of puritanism and fundamentalism both within and without Bengal. For the origins of these movements one has to look as much into the changing social, economic and political circumstances of contemporary Bengal as into those of the larger Muslim world beyond this region. But what is of special importance for us in this particular study is a critical evaluation of the impact of those anti-syncretistic fundamentalist movements on the changing perceptions of Bengal Muslim identity as well as their bearings on the issue of elite responsibility in this matter.

II

The cultural-mediators in the traditional settings of Bengal, having constructed a syncretistic model of the Bengal Muslim identity that commanded the allegiance of the Muslim majority, resolved a potentially disruptive dualism and contradiction in the social and cultural positions of Bengal Muslims. The traditional Bengal Muslim society was sharply polarised both socially and culturally between the *ashraf* (literally, the 'high'—or 'noble-born') elites and the *ajlaf* (literally, the 'commoners'), or as more commonly known in Bengal, *Atrap/Atraf* (literally, the 'wretches') masses.[6] The division between the two was multilinear and multidimensional. The nobility by birth was by far the most crucial element, the *ashraf* claiming such nobility and a higher social status based on their non-Bengali origins, ranging from Arabian, through *Ajami* (non-Arab regions of West Asia), to even the northern Indian descent. With foreign birth went *ashraf's* alien non-Bengali cultural orientation which, in effect, underscored their identification with the ethos of the Persianised Mughal aristocratic culture dominant in the northern India. The most critical component of this extra-territorial cultural orientation of Bengal's *ashraf* was their utter contempt for the Bengali language and literature, and a corresponding leaning towards Persian and Urdu. Also from the religious point of view the *ashraf* claimed to embody the highest principles and virtues of true Islam.[7] These differences were further reinforced by a high disparity between their economic positions, the *ashraf* generally holding a monopoly of economic and political power, patronage and influence.

The acknowledged superiority of the *ashraf's* position had the most serious consequence for the Bengal Muslim identity. The cumulative result of their social, economic, cultural and political dominance was a natural elevation of this social category as 'the reference model' of the Bengal Muslim society for 'social emulation'. With supreme importance attached to the non-Indian, and even non-Bengali, extraction of the *ashraf,* there was a natural tendency, among the local born aspirants to social honour, to 'discover' for themselves a foreign ancestry. The late-nineteenth-century census records of Bengal offer a clear picture of the galloping numbers of claimants to foreign extraction.[8] This social tendency towards 'ashrafisation' followed very closely to the parallel process of 'sanskritisation' among Hindus, involving social emulation of the higher and the dominant castes by the lower. The exaggerated importance of alien origin so permeated the Bengal Muslim society that a Bengali Muslim fell a logical victim to his own myth, claiming for himself at least an alien culture, if not origin, and being so regarded by all others. In many parts of Bengal, rural and urban, a Hindu was, and perhaps, to some, even now is, a 'Bengali', and a Muslim simply a 'Musalman'. The predominantly Hindu locality was often a *Bangali-para* (the Bengali quarter), and the predominantly Muslim quarter was simply a *Musalman-para*.[9]

It is not difficult, in the circumstances, to see the sources of a dualism and conflict between the twin strands of the Bengal Muslim identity, 'Islamic' and 'Bengali', which has stalked and haunted this people and their history perennially ever since. The cultural-mediators were first to face up to the problem and offer a solution. A section of the Bengal Muslim religious elite, standing closer to the masses in their capacity as mystic religious guides, *pirs*, as well as by virtue of their acceptance of, and command over, the Bengali language, the mediators showed a phenomenal courage of their convictions and a creative dynamism through their syncretistic formulation of the Bengal Muslim identity in defiance of the dominant *ashraf* religious-cultural ethos. The role of the mediators must, however, be viewed in the context of the needs and demands for such changes growing at the grassroots level. Though rather scanty, there is direct and clear evidence that 'the pressure often built up from the bottom.'[10] Evidence of this nature should, in fact, prove quite useful in setting the elite role in perspective. It is in the nature of leadership to provide form and direction to wider social concerns and urges.[11]

The acculturative and popular syncretistic tradition seemed for centuries to have run parallel to the exclusivist elite Islamic tradition, and the followers of the latter appeared to have maintained merely a condescending, if not disdainful, detachment from the former's 'follies' and 'foibles'. There is no clear historical evidence of any elitist efforts at either suppression or reformation of the popular tradition until with the appearance, in the nineteenth century, of the Muslim 'purists', fundamentalists, and reformists on the Bengal scene.

III

The importance of the nineteenth-century Islamic revitalising movements for the history of the Bengal Muslim's identity formation cannot be exaggerated, and has, in fact, been well recognised by observers. It is neither possible nor necessary for the limited scope of this study to attempt a detailed discussion of these movements, which may, otherwise, be obtained from a few particular sources, including the latest and the best work by Rafiuddin Ahmed.[12] I should hope to remain content with an analysis of their impact with bearings on our central question of the Bengal Muslim identity. A much clearer understanding of the impact may be gained from separate examinations of the 'cultural' and the 'societal' aspects of this impact, both ultimately converging on the process of formulating and strengthening the collective Islamic consciousness of Bengal Muslims as the most vital pre-condition for the emergence of Bengal Muslims as a 'political community'.

A critical evaluation of the cultural impact of these revitalising movements is rendered difficult by an assortment of reasons and circumstances. The revitalists themselves projected, naturally, a much exaggerated view about their following as well as their success. Their traditionalist opponents tended to move in the other direction. Just as some were forced into these movements under various pressures, some others participated in them emotionally, though not actively. Nor are the official sources of greater help. The census figures on the adherents of these new reforming sects do not necessarily portray the actual situation, as the ruthless government suppression of the militant elements, followed by the Wahabi Trials of 1869-70, discouraged many followers of these new groups from revealing their true affiliations to the census officials. Similarly, British officials, like William Hunter, deeply involved, in the decades after the Mutiny, in moulding a new government policy of forging an *entente cordiale* between the British government and the upper class and the educated Muslims, were more than interested in magnifying the spectre of popular Muslim disaffection. Likewise, it is not easy to assess its total impact just on the basis of contemporary and later views. As early as 1840 an English observer, James Taylor, seemed assured of the rapid progress of the Faraizi movement in the lower Bengal districts.[13] The authorities of the census of 1881 did not, on the other hand, see much prospect of their success 'among the ignorant and apathetic Moslems of Bengal'.[14] Almost as a rejoinder to this census observation James Wise, a keen English observer of the social and cultural life of the eastern Bengal districts, stressed the significance of these movements in terms of the infusion of an 'Islamic' spirit into 'a docile flock' of Bengali Muslims who were 'without a shepherd' and steeped in 'superstitious rites of the Hindus'[15] This view is generally in accord with those of many subsequent writers, especially those who wrote on the subject of Muslim separatism in Bengal. It makes a rather large assumption of a revolutionary Islamic transformation of the religious and cultural self-image of Bengali Muslims. Based on the sporadic information derived from sundry literature, official and non-official reports and observations, regional and local histories primarily in the Bengali language, the Christian missionary sources, and some 'Islamic Bengali puthi' literature – all having direct relevance to Bengali Muslim religious and cultural life in the post-revivalist period in the present century, I became aware, rather early on, of the qualified nature of the claim for an 'Islamic revolution'.[16] In recent years Rafiuddin Ahmed's systematic research in this area has clearly revealed the magnitude and vitality of the traditionalists' opposition encountered by the revivalists.[17] Besides, the extremist character of the original reformist programme underwent considerable modifications, especially since the steady extension of the more moderate influence of the *Ta'ayuni* movement and also of those that were eventually launched by the traditionalists themselves.

Nevertheless, the cultural significance of the revivalists' mission is undeniable. As early as 1941 Qazi Abdul Wadud, a brilliant Bengali Muslim rationalist thinker and writer, believed that 'the total change in Muslim perceptions', resulting from the revitalising movements, constituted a 'greater reason' for distinguishing between Bengal Muslims' 'old and new ages' than the economic and political forces of change.[18] To him, the pre-reformistic culture represented 'an accord between Hindu and Muslim thoughts', and he pointed out, rather sarcastically, that the truth of this cultural fusion was 'generally distressing to educated Muslims today' inasmuch as 'they regard it as a testimony to the extinction of their own identity'. Wadud dubbed it as a 'Wahabi-inspired view' which, he believed, 'the Muslim society generally and many Muslim thinkers in particular still refused to accept'.[19] Wadud's observation is a clear reference to the success that the revivalists had achieved in deepening the Islamic consciousness of Bengal Muslims. And this is perhaps the most seminal result of the revitalising movements. Unlike the custodians of the 'exogenous' Islam in traditional Bengal, the new revivalist leaders launched a vicious and sustained attack on the non-Islamic accretions and excrescences of Islam, and urged Muslims to return to the pristine purity of the fundamentalist Islam. This ceaseless and relentless denigration of Islam's local roots and associations forced on Muslims, both individually and collectively as members of a primordial group, a growing awareness of what they believed and practised as Muslims. As a syncretistic Muslim's total life-style lay naked before the puritan's scanning and frowning eyes, the latter was compelled to cover himself with a feeling of 'shame' and 'guilt'. Though his total life-style was perhaps far from 'reformed', he became increasingly more conscious of his conduct and standing as a Muslim. In 1919, a Bengali Muslim lamented that 'almost a quarter' of the traditionalist *Hanafis* 'did not care much for prayers *(namaz)*', and measured their piety unfavourably against that of the revivalists.[20] A quarter of a century later, two distinguished Bengali Muslim litterateurs attributed the 'gradual waning' of 'popular' Islam to the revivalist 'missionaries' and their followers among the new *puthi* writers in 'Islamised Bengali', who urged Muslims 'to crack the heads' of deviants like the traditionalist mystic-mendicants. The two Muslims concluded:

> The peace and quiet of a Bengal village was disturbed by the acrimonies of the Wahhabis and the Hanafis. The Muslim masses felt lost in this commotion, and all their finer sentiments became almost dried up.[21]

The new and growing Islamic consciousness steadily undermined the syncretistic tradition as reflected most clearly in the progressive decline, both in quantity and quality, of the rich and time-honoured syncretistic literary output. A new variety of 'Islamic puthi', using rather contrived concoctions of Urdu-Bengali dictions, proliferated to take its place, while the more literate Bengalis increasingly turned towards a totally new variety of Islamic literature of historical, biographical and polemical nature, written not in verse, as traditional, but in the newly developed modern prose. The syncretistic performer had clearly lost both his stage and audience. [22]

The revivalist movements also brought about significant changes in the social circumstances of Muslims in rural Bengal. Traditionally compartmentalised into Hindu jati-like groups within the framework of the village system, as noted before, the rural Muslims were forced, because of the revivalist campaigns and counter-campaigns, out of their fragmented social life to become increasingly interactive with other Muslim groups and localities.[23] The central factor in this change was the powerful and priest-like figure of the village *molla / mullah.* The Muslim religious life in rural Bengal was traditionally controlled by the village *mullah* and the *pir.* While the former catered for the 'spiritual', ritualistic and liturgic needs of the believers, the latter provided for the more 'spiritual', esoteric, mystical and emotional needs. Accordingly, inasmuch as the pir, often quite heterodox and syncretistic in beliefs and practices, was closer and dearer to the hearts of the rural folks, the *mullah,* by virtue of his 'scriptural' authority which extended over the total life span and the rites of passage of the believers, exercised a position of much greater power and control over their religious life. In the final analysis the religious equilibrium in the rural Muslim society was derived from a consensus about the more complementary than competitive roles of these two segments of the religious elites in rural Bengal. Although, therefore, the revivalist challenge and intrusion into the village life threatened the positions of the *mullah* and the pir alike, it was the former who found himself as the spearhead of the response and reaction. The attacks on pirism consisted in repudiating their actual veneration and adoration, if not their theoretical position as intercessors between God and man as such, their thaumaturgic powers, and finally, the highly popular festival of urs, the death anniversary of a popular pir or a saint. The *mullah's* position was also vitally and materially affected by the revivalist condemnations of his practice of reading the *fatihah,* or reciting specific verses of the Qu'ran for a whole range of socio-religious rites and observances, as well as the practice of observing, under the *mullah's* supervision, the nativity of the Prophet Muhammad, called *milad.* Besides, the widespread belief and faith in spirits, evil eyes, omens, auspicious days, and so on provided a common ground for both mullah and *pir* to carry on a rewarding business in amulets, talismans, charms, incantations, and exorcism. Confronted with the challenge, the *mullahs* organised religious debates, *bahas,* with the revivalists, which attracted Muslim gatherings from a much wider region than the traditional area of social interaction and communication for the rural Muslims.[24] Although the mullahs failed initially to present a united front, because of their internal differences and rivalries, the polemical discussions in public, backed at a later stage by the mullah-sponsored polemical writings, infused the rural masses with an unprecedented and a socially significant sense of curiosity, interest and participation in their own affairs. Besides, the accent on sharpening the Islamic consciousness helped to achieve the double objectives – internally, of social integration of the Muslim community; and externally, greater differentiation of the Muslim community from the non-Muslim. These developments had the effect of leavening the ground for the subsequent penetration of urban religious and political influences into the rural areas, successfully trying to impose a broad frame of religious unity on the community for the ultimate objective of its political mobilisation.

IV

The historical process of the emergence of Muslims in Bengal as a 'political community' is a problem of great complexity, and demands rather careful examination. The political convergence of the disparate Bengal Muslim groups under the banner of the Islamic 'crescent' was largely achieved by the end of the third decade of this century, and involved the complementary sub-processes of integration of the diverse Muslims of Calcutta, those of the *mofussil,* and finally of all Bengal Muslims. But how was this political transformation brought about? Some major studies in this area seem inclined to view this process as a largely unidirectional movement: from the metropolis to the periphery, from the urban to the rural, from Calcutta to the *mofussil*[25] An analytical approach of this nature, without adequate explanatory safeguards, can give rise to an exaggerative and distortional perspective on the role of metropolitan Calcutta. Insofar as the politisation of the Bengal Muslim community was achieved under the central symbolism of 'Muslim solidarity', the historian of Bengal Muslim solidarity can ill afford to ignore the significant groundwork made in rural Bengal through the revivalist movements since the early nineteenth century. Besides the obvious issue of a heightened Islamic consciousness fostered by these movements as noted above, it is no less significant that the rural revivalist activists, like the Faraizi leaders Haji Shariatullah and Dudhu Miyan, voiced and also fought for the economic grievances of the Muslim peasantry against the Hindu landlords and moneylenders, long before the urban Muslim politicians discovered and exploited the great potential of this issue for the purposes of political mobilisation of the rural masses in the nineteen twenties and thirties. The Bengal civilians observed a close correspondence between the Faraizi-dominated areas and the propensity towards collective agrarian uprisings in the post-Mutiny decades.[26] The considerable network of organisational cells, built by the revivalists, provided not only a novel and valuable experience in group mobilisation for the rural masses, but also a ready base for subsequent utilisation by the religious and political leaders of the Muslim solidarity movements. Likewise, rural Muslims occasionally stole the march on their Calcutta compatriots. The 'various Urdu-speaking Muslim mercantile and artisan group [sic]' of Calcutta had not been 'stirred by the wave of Pan-Islamic, sentiment' until 'the occasion of the Balkan Wars'.[27] The *'Wahhabi'* (more appropriately, *Tariqa-i Muhammadiyah,* a militant Islamic revivalist group) trials of 1863-70, on the other hand, revealed that the Muslims of Bengal districts were 'stirred' long before by the *Wahhabi campaigns for 'holy wars' (jihad)* so much that they raised subscriptions and volunteered themselves as fighters in the north-western India.[28] The essential continuity between the revivalist and the Pan-Islamic-Khilafat movements as well as their identical impact on fostering Islamic consciousness cannot be overlooked.

The urban-rural interface of the Bengal Muslim separatist politics is indeed infinitely more involuted and intertwined than it appears on its surface. There were undoubted sources of linkage between the urban and the rural sectors of Muslim Bengal prior to the present century. The rural *mullah* was often a product of an urban *madrasah;* the revivalist preacher was most commonly of an urban origin; the rural *sharif* often straddled the two worlds by virtue of his family and social links with the urban upper-class and western-educated Muslim who was either a government servant or a professional. Similarly, the prosperous Muslim peasant (*jotedar*), who lay behind much of the political mobilisation of the rural masses, not only owed his existence to an urban-rural complex of economic and social forces, but also possessed family ties with the middle-class and urban educated Muslim. All these linkages helped eventually to bring the city and the vast countryside of Muslim Bengal together. Until such time, the Muslim life in Calcutta, very largely inhabited by the Urdu-speaking non-Bengali-oriented Muslims, and dominated by a motley group of Mughal aristocratic and wealthy *ashraf* landed, official, professional, and commercial elites,[29] seemed almost to have flowed into a separate channel from that in the vast rural districts. The populist and militant hue of the revivalist movements alarmed men of property, both urban and rural, who kept them away at arm's length. With the steadily growing collaboration between the British raj and the Muslim upper classes in the post-Mutiny decades, the anti-British stance of the revivalists appeared even more disturbing to the collaborators. This set the stage, in 1870, for the first major initiative by the upper class Muslim elites in Calcutta, which had clear implications for the eventual integration of the separate worlds of Bengal Muslims. In that year, Maulana Karamat Ali, an eminent Muslim moderate revivalist, was invited to address a gathering of Muslim elites in Calcutta in which he denounced the anti-British facet of the revivalist movements.[30] In the following years, the *Taiyuni* movement led by Karamat Ali, deeply penetrated the eastern and northern Bengal, promoting on the one hand loyalism to the British and Muslim solidarity on the other, by urging moderation and stressing the greater and more immediate needs for Islamising the syncretistic life-style of the masses of Muslim Bengalis. The gradual emasculation of the spirit of 'external' *jihad* and the exclusive preoccupations since then, with 'internal' puritanical reformation contributed much to the deepening of Islamic consciousness, quickening the pace of

Muslim unity, and a heightened perception of Muslim-Hindu differentiations.

In bringing about the political integration of the community, the above linkages remained critical indeed. The social identity and correspondence between the rural gentry and the urban Western educated officials and professionals proved as potent as the social, institutional and ideological fraternity of the rural clergy (*mullahs*) and the itinerant preachers in the towns and villages. The *mullah* emerged as the linchpin in this emerging system of political communication, just as the proliferating social-religious associations (*anjuman*), urban and rural, assumed its institutional focus.[31] The *anjumans* in the *mofussil*, which often drew together on a common platform the urban educated officials and professionals, the rural gentry, the prosperous peasants and the *mullahs* were able to carry their religious and political messages to the rural masses rather effectively via the locally influential mullahs and the *jotedars*. The *anjuman's* significant contributions, in overseeing and materially supporting the work of Islamic religious, educational and literary advancement, cannot be overrated. A spate of very low-priced religious books of an instructive and didactic nature, popular as *nasihat-nama*, written in an 'Islamised Bengali' as noted before, deluged the Muslim masses.[32] For the more educated, a sophisticated version of Islamic religious, historical and biographical compositions in chaste Bengali prose was offered. About the turn of the century a number of Muslim journals, imbued with this growing sense of Islamic cultural and political identity, appeared in the urban areas of Bengal. Urban itinerant preachers, often sponsored by the *anjumans*, penetrated in considerable numbers into the countryside and gave public sermons (*waz-mahfil*) to propagate the unity of Islam (*tauhid*) and that of the community of believers (*ummah*). The preachers and the literature contributed together not only to the dissemination of the knowledge of classical Islam, but also to the fostering of the bond of Muslim unity by underlining the differences between Islam and Hinduism. Most importantly, the *anjuman's* forum steadily transformed itself into a natural and convenient outlet for ventilating the growing economic and political concerns and aspirations of the rural *ashraf*, the *jotedars*, and the educated, all in pursuit of the common objective of undermining the economic and political dominance of the Hindu *bhadralok*. The later burgeoning of Muslim politics in rural Bengal was immeasurably advanced by the considerable spadework of the *anjumans*,[33] which in itself found the soil already leavened by the *avant-garde* revivalists.

It is neither possible nor necessary, within the limited scope and purpose of this paper, to offer even a bare outline of the historical process leading to the growth of Muslim separatist politics in Bengal. In historical retrospect, it is difficult to see how the inner dynamics of the Bengal Muslim society were powerful enough to transform it into a political community without the massive inputs resulting from the British policies as well as the intransigence and inadequacies of the Hindu *bhadralok's* positions and policies. In the growth of ethnic politics the crucial importance of the attitudes and policies of the government, with its enormous capacity for distributing economic and political favours and patronage, has been widely recognised.[34] Muslim ethnicity in Bengal, as elsewhere in India,[35] owed a great deal to the British interest in helping to forge their separatist political identity as a counterpoise to the formidable nationalist challenge at the British *raj* mounted by the Bengali *bhadralok*.

The great uprising of 1857, better known as the Mutiny, marked a very significant change in the British perceptions of Indians, and led to a sharp reappraisal of the overall British position in India in strategic and political terms. The buoyant spirit of the heady reformers, envisioning a regenerated India, in the pre-Mutiny decades, sought to hide its wounded pride as well as a lurking fear in the cold isolation of a policy of political and social conservatism. Increasingly, the safety and security of the dominion were seen to rest on recognition and balancing of the innate and primordial social divisions of a motley India held together by the power and patronage of the aristocracy and gentry 'the natural leaders' of the land. The main thrusts of British attitudes and policies towards Muslims in the post-Mutiny period fitted squarely into this broad framework of political strategy of the *Raj*. The growing government concerns and preoccupations with 'special' Muslim questions and problems, relating to education, employment, and political representation, were integral to this policy of 'balancing' the 'communities'. Later concerns, for the depressed and the deprived low-caste and outcaste Hindus also sprang from similar considerations. A few additional and more specific reasons seemed, however, to underlie the growing British interests and concerns for Muslims in this period. First, the strong revival of militant Wahhabism in the sixties, which led to the assassination of the British Chief Justice of the Calcutta High Court, and also later, of Viceroy Mayo, impressed on the *Raj* the urgency of winning over the upper classes with the hope of reconciling the disaffected Muslims through the mediation of their socially superior co-religionists. Karamat Ali's pro-British ruling, mentioned above, is particularly meaningful in this context. Secondly, with the opening of the Suez Canal, in 1869, and the steady emergence of Britain as an imperial power in the Middle East, Indian Muslims were invested with a far greater political significance than perhaps seemed otherwise possible. Finally, the newly-awakened British interests in Indian Muslims corresponded rather closely to a reciprocal interest in the British rule and English education that just began to be reflected in the attitudes of some members of the Muslim upper class, such as Nawab Abdul Latif and Syed Amir Ali in Bengal. The stage was set for a long period of 'Anglo-Muhammadan' understanding that proved crucial in the emergence and nourishment of the Muslim separatist political personality. Eager to take Muslims under the protective wing of the *Raj*, Bengal civilian William Hunter, urged by Viceroy Mayo, produced after only three weeks effort, his treatise on the 'Indian Musalmans' (June 1871) which set out the rationale, 'morality', direction and form of the 'special' and 'separate' treatment of Muslims by the government. The twin major components of the Hunter-constructed myth, one of 'Muslim backwardness', uncritically and calculatively extended to all Muslims in the subcontinent, and the other of the British assumption of direct or indirect responsibility for the Muslim retardation, not only led to the special provisions for Muslims in government legislation but also offered the growing body of Muslim aspirants for position and power a rather useful self-image of deprivation and victimisation – an image that, by virtue of Hunter's statistical half-truths and rhetorical penmanship, appeared both credible and touching. The Education Commission of 1884 painted a tragic picture of Indian Muslims as 'fallen behind in the race of life under British rule'.[36]

The cumulative effect of all these forces and pressures – social, cultural and political – set the patterns of Muslim separatist politics in Bengal, based on the central principles of loyalism to, and collaboration with, the British, as well as the corresponding indifference or opposition to the nationalist forces and aspirations. A study in Muslim separatism in Bengal reveals a process of its sustained growth through the decades since the late-nineteenth century. This is clearly evidenced, *inter alia* by the Muhammedan Literary Society (1863) and the [Central] National Muhammadan Association's (1877) antipathy to both the Indian Association and the Indian National Congress, nominations of Muslim landed and professional magnates into the Government's executive and legislative councils, the partition of Bengal (1905), the foundation of the Muslim League in Dhaka (1906), the granting of separate electorate to Muslims (1909), and the successful plots and machinations of the official and non-official members of the Montagu Reform Council, in the 1920s, to make a breach in the wall of an incipient Hindu-Muslim legislative alliance under the leadership of C.R. Das and the Swarajists.[37] Bengal politics in the mid-1920s clearly attests to the steady emergency of Muslims, despite the persistence of factionalism among them, as a single political block in the legislative council, especially since the election of 1926.[38]

Muslim political separatism in Bengal had clearly come of age and had come to stay. However, the political realisation of the separatist ideology needs, for a clearer and more balanced evaluation, to be placed in the context of two contrary trends of development, political and cultural. A detailed study of Bengal Muslim politics, with particular reference to the vernacular sources since the late nineteenth century, reveals the unmistakable presence and persistence of thoughts and aspirations among Muslims which are either inconsistent or in conflict with the separatist ideology.[39] However much limited, individualistic and inefficacious such responses were to prove, the non-separatist ethos often spilled over into actual politics to take various forms. This is evidenced by the Bengal Muslims' limited support and participation in the politics of the Provincial Congress, the Indian Association, the anti-partition (1905) agitation, and the revolutionary terrorist as well as later socialist and communist movements; by the formation of the anti-partition and pro-Congress Bengal Presidency Mahommedan Association as 'a rival political association' to the Muslim League founded about the same time; by the nationalist-oriented liberal and, progressive politics of 'the young Muhammadans', leading to the conclusion of the Lucknow Pact (1916), and by the brief, but potentially significant, convergence of Hindu and Muslim Bengal, centring round, initially, the Khilafat-Non-cooperation movement, and later on, the Hindu-Muslim Pact of the Swarajists under C.R. Das.[40] Even in the politics of two decades since the substitution of the Hindu *bhadralok* dominance in Bengal politics by that of the 'Muslims', the separatist ideology was often seen to rival or run in parallel to the notion of a territorial Bengali nationalism, as was the occasion on the eve of the partition of 1947, when a few Bengal political magnates, Hindu and Muslim, made discreet deliberations, behind the backs of their respective national high-commands, on the feasibility of 'a united and independent Bengal'.[41]

V

If Muslim separatist ideology in Bengal found its political dissenters constrained and lackadaisical, its cultural detractors appeared considerably more animated, resolute and even audacious. Politics, for the masses of Bengal Muslims, proved more amenable to change and adaptation – perhaps because of its novelty and contemporaneity – than the demands on their traditional culture of antiquity. The fabric of Muslim Bengali culture rested on the twin pillars of Islam and the local Bengali culture, as noted above. Both remained integral and inseparable in their cultural self-image. Neither the fundamentalist purists nor the ashraf cultural expatriates in Bengal, who played the most vital part in Islamising the Bengal Muslim community, were historically suited to resolve this critical ambivalence in the Bengali Muslim cultural position. The antithetical nature of the social and cultural processes of 'ashrafisation' and 'Bengalicisation', or to use an alternative set of concepts, of 'exclusivism' and 'syncretism' respectively. In a long historical perspective the two emerged as alternative models of Islamisation in Bengal. In the pre-reformist centuries, the latter remained the dominant model at least for the overwhelming majority of the believers. The post-reformist period witnessed a significant shift in the balance in favour of the former. But this is precisely the point where I seriously think that the Bengal Muslim case needs to be very carefully and critically analysed and understood. The apparent success of the former should not be taken or interpreted in terms of rejection of the latter. What followed was a long process of interaction and discourse between the two before the political elites were in a position to mobilise the whole community. The case of Bengali culturalism was vigorously fought by the new and rising Bengali Muslim intelligentsia – modern educated, Bengali-speaking, and largely of middle-class service and professional background. For the second time in Bengal Muslim history there was the occasion and call for the 'cultural mediators' to reduce the polarity between the 'alien' and the 'indigenous' in Bengali Muslim cultural perceptions. The Muslim writings in modern Bengali prose in the late nineteenth and early twentieth centuries have a large content of thoughts and ideas, hopes and dreams not only about finding a legitimate place for their Bengali self but also, in many instances, about a Bengali 'nation' transcending religious barriers.

The new mediators' attention was naturally drawn to the disruptive effect, on Muslim's Bengali identity, of the *ashraf's* social pre-eminence based on their alien ancestry and culture. Their efforts, therefore, took the form of either a strong denunciation of the *ashraf's* 'Brahmanical pride' in their birth[42] or re-defining the *ashraf* social category by divesting it of its racial and hereditary components and investing it with exclusively religious, moral and educational attributes. 'There is no greatness' in the social appellations like 'Saiyid, Qazi, khan, mullah, or Shaikh'. Greatness consisted in 'the combination of knowledge and culture with religious devotion'; the *ashraf* 'without religious faith and education' were like 'the refuse of the mankind and its disgrace'.[43] Simultaneously, the mediators tried to set their Bengali origins free from the pressure of 'secrecy' and the feeling of 'shame' and 'inferiority'. In what respects could 'the intelligent, educated, religious and cultured Muslims born in Bengal' consider themselves 'inferior to the so-called *ashraf* immigrants who are uneducated, uncultured, and bereft of intelligence?' The term *ashraf* applied only to those who were of a 'cultured' and 'religious' disposition.[44] Those 'creatures called *ashraf*' had 'degraded Islam' and 'violated the commands of God and ideals of the Prophet'.[45] Attention was also drawn to the social and political consequences of this division, which 'continues to riddle the society, through and through, like a piece of termite-ridden bamboo'.[46] The Bengali Muslim aspirants to the *ashraf's* position were subjected to sardonic comments. Many, among Bengali Muslims, 'have not recovered from their delusions. They sleep inside the thatched cottages amidst the bamboo bushes and the mango groves of Bengal, and yet dream of Bagdad/Baghdad, Bokhara/Bokhara, Kabul and Qandahar . . . a fallen people indulges in unreal fancies just as the weak persons dream of supernatural things'.[47]

With an attack on ashrafism the Bengal Muslim mediator began, in faltering steps, his search for a regional identity. His path was rendered difficult by the dominant concept of the supra-territorial 'nationalism' of Islam, as emphatically outlined by a leading Muslim theologian and scholar in Bengal:

The Muslim ideal of a 'nation' is distinctive. This distinctiveness is the distinguishing feature of Muslim nationalism as well as its safety-valve . . . Muslim nationalism is not based on race, occupation, or territory; it is totally religious. Muslims all over the world form together one and an indivisible nation.[48]

In the opinion of another Bengal Muslim writer:

> The word 'nation', in a Bengali Muslim mind, can never conjure up an image of his being an inhabitant of Bengal, nor even merely of India: he then finds himself in rapport with the whole world . . . the Qu'ran in the Arabic language is the common bond of friendship, happiness and love. We cannot rupture this bond and still hope to secure our national life.[49]

The initial thoughts of the mediators were, therefore, not quite free from doubts and apologetic diffidence. Having lived for 'five hundred years in this country', it was 'not an exaggeration to say that we now belong to this land'.[50] At least 'this much can be said with certainty' that 'not all the ancestors of Bengali Muslims came to Bengal from Arabia, Iran, Turan or Turkey'.[51] Some others wrote with greater assurance and confidence about the 'Bengaliness': Bengal Muslims, whose 'ancestors whether hailed from Arabia, Persia, Afghanistan and Turkey or belonged to the local Hindu inhabitants, are all Bengalis now'. Even those whose forefathers did 'genuinely come from abroad' should have 'no reason to call themselves' so. Nothing could be more 'strange and regrettable' than that 'we are still unable to accept as homeland the country where we have been living for the last seven centuries'.[52] The extra-territorial cultural outlook was also subjected to the biting sarcasms of these mediator-writers, as noted above. 'Nobody would ever think' that there was 'a land of one's own outside the country where people have lived for a thousand years' and in which people 'have equally shared its winter and summer, fortune and misfortune, famine and prosperity, and joy and sorrow'. Bengal Muslims had, therefore, 'the full one hundred percent right to express their opinions' on matters concerning 'the country, the language and the nation of Bengal'.[53] This newly felt sense of 'right' found at times a rather more aggressive expression: '. . . we must always keep it in our mind that we have a far greater claim on the word "Bengali" than that of our Hindu neighbours . . . we, the children of Mother Bengal, are the half of the Indian Muslim population'.[54]

A notion of territorial patriotism, pivoting round the concept of a 'motherland', seemed to have entered into some mediators' perceptions. The proposition that 'Muslims all over the world are bound in a unity' could not be taken to mean 'renouncing their attachment' to their 'own countries or birth lands'. Not caring for one's own land was an attribute of the 'gypsy'. Kindness to 'the neighbours' was a 'Qur'anic command'. To remain 'indifferent' to the welfare of the land in which 'my neighbour and I live' was comparable to apostasy'.[55] The motherland was 'as dear to the Muslims as Hindus'.[56] The veins of Bengali Muslims 'contain both foreign and indigenous blood . . . of the so-called high as well as low Hindu social orders', and Muslims were 'to take pride in all this' and think that 'we are Bengali' and that 'Bengal's wellbeing . . . is our ideal'. Hindus and Muslims of Bengal 'are nothing but a part of Bengal or of larger India', and hence, 'the way to the fulfilment of their cultural life is through a realisation of this profound link with that larger entity, just as a spring fulfils itself in the enrichment of the stream'. And as soon as this truth 'truly permeates our minds' the Hindu-Muslim conflicts should 'come to an end'.[57]

Some of these mediators very clearly identified the basic source of this inner conflict in Bengali Muslim's allegiance. Their attention was directly focussed on the 'confusions' in the Muslim minds regarding the interface of 'religion' and 'nation'. They urged Muslims to be aware of their 'mistake' in not differentiating the 'meaning and significance' of these two terms, and making instead a 'facile equation' of them. A nation 'is not a religious community irrespective of a territory – it is rather a land comprising all its inhabitants, regardless of its religious diversities'. The 'universal' aspect of the religion of Islam 'does undoubtedly transcend this nation', but this was no more than 'Muslims' universal brotherhood'.[58] Muslims 'belong to the same nation as do Hindus, Christians, Parsees, or Buddhists in India'. There 'is no nation in India called Hindu, nor one called Muslim, but we have religions there of these names'.[59] That Islam 'is a religion, and not a nation' had 'slipped' those Muslims' minds who now vociferously proclaim' that Bengal Muslims 'are a Muslim nation'. Consequently, Bengal Muslims, 'nourished for a thousand years by the water and air of Bengal', found themselves 'ostracised' in their own country. Bengal still remained with them only 'a nursing mother' and not the real one. Thus, in matters of 'nationality and origins', they tended to 'look out beyond the confines of Bengal'.[60] They were easily 'moved by the sufferings of their religious brethren in Bokhara and Samarqand', but 'the picture of sufferings and deprivations in their own country, right before their eyes, casts no shadow in their minds'. They could not also be bothered by the fact that their 'brothers in Bagdad/Baghdad do not care for them'.[61] This 'supra-national love for the religious fraternity' was considered 'positively harmful for the development and security' of the country:

> Oh, you dream-loving Muslims of India! Your nice garden has been drying up, right before you; the terrifying image of the poverty is engaged in a dance of destruction all around you. But you are all wrapped up in your dream the dream of Pan-Islamic solidarity![62]

On the question of 'patriotism' Muslims 'encounter a closed door'. They were inclined to reject patriotism, which 'is the living and universal ideal of the modern age', because they found a 'conflict between this ideal and their own social interests'.[63] All patriotic people should endeavour 'to infuse nationalistic ideal' among the masses, and there was a 'special need' for inculcating 'patriotic and nationalistic ideas among Muslims'.[64]

The concept of a state based on religion and religious ideology was disfavoured by the mediators as being 'inconsistent with the spirit of the age'. The religious state 'came to its end in Europe', and for Bengalis as well as Indians there was 'no other way of development and fulfilment except to follow in the footsteps of the time'. The religious ideology served to promote 'communal fraternalisation' among both Muslims and Hindus. But the need of the time was for a new ideology that was 'more comprehensive, stronger, more progressive and suited to the time', on the basis of which 'the different communities and classes in India may develop fraternal feelings for one another'. 'The nationalist ideology alone' could accomplish this mission well. 'The organisation of the state on the basis of a religion in this age' was likely to cause 'troubles'.[65] The religious ideology was 'defeated' by its nationalist counterpart in the task of achieving 'political unity' in history. This explained why 'secular states are being formed all around the world'. The 'major weakness' of a religious ideology consisted in 'its natural tendency towards division and separation'. Such states also 'placed sectarian interest above that of the state and nation'. Hence, 'like all other civilised countries', Bengalis and other Indians should adopt 'nationalism rather than religion as the foundation of the state'. If

> we all indeed could learn to see ourselves first as Indians and Bengalis and then as Hindus or Muslims, and also learn to work under the inspiration of this thought, then this ideology, suited to the time, should bring about, before long, the unity and fraternity in India.[66]

The sense of an indivisible Bengali identity, transcending religious barriers, found its fullest expression in an affirmation of faith in universal humanism. 'A rose plant cannot realise itself in violation of the nature of plants in general', so one would not make oneself 'a model Muslim, or Indian, or Bengali' in 'disregard of the common human nature'.[67] Similar sentiments were more forcefully expressed by Qazi Abdul Wadud, one of the most brilliant products of the Renaissance movement in Bengal, and a leading figure of a pioneering band of Bengal Muslims who became directly involved in a courageous but abortive attempt to launch a 'movement for the emancipation of intellect' (buddhi mukti andolan) in Islam and in the Muslim society in the mid-1920s in Dhaka. Addressing 'the Muslim youth of Bengal', he urged them:

> Please repeat after me . . . I, first of all, am a human being by virtue of the natural right of being born so, I am a kin to all mankind irrespective of country, time, race and religion; after this, please say, I am a son of the soil – I have reinforced myself with my love for the soil and taken my stand under the sky with my head aloft – I am an offspring of Bengal, am a Bengali; and

finally, you say, I am a Muslim – the virtue and grace of my humanity and Bengaliness . . . shall attain a supreme realisation in the eternal truth of the unity of God (*tauhid*) and of equality. . . . Instead of this true attainment, Muslims in Bengal or of India, who do not lack in intelligence, have been blind to the demands of the time and place and dedicating their lives till now to the object of becoming, before everything else, Muslims – such Muslims are as meant to carry the load of the religious laws and beliefs that are, on one hand age-old and, on the other, evolved in different environments. The inevitable results of this are discomfiture and disconcertment.[68]

VI

The cultural mediators like Wadud and Wajed Ali were swept aside by the tidal waves of Muslim separatist politics, culminating in the partition of the land, and would have remained buried deep in the sand of history but for the subsequent re-emergence of East Pakistan in Bangladesh. The antecedents of Bangladesh are not confined to about twenty-four years of unequal and exploitative relationship with West Pakistan. Their roots went deeper down into her long historical past. The history of Bengal Muslims is, in a very real sense, a history of a perennial crisis of identity. The sharp polarity between the ashraf-dominated extra-Bengal Islamic ideology and that permeated by the forces of regional Bengali culture has been a persistent and a critical factor in their history. The sixteenth and seventeenth centuries saw the emergence of Muslim cultural mediators in Bengal who performed a historic task of mediation between the conflicting cultures by reconstructing a syncretistic Islamic tradition for the masses of Bengal believers. The gulf, thus, remained bridged until, in the nineteenth century, the Islamic fundamentalists, revivalists and reformists opened up once more the hiatus with their vigorous and vituperative campaigns against indigenous traits in the Muslim Bengali culture. The economic and political needs of the *ashraf*, geared to recovering their lost ground to the British and the Western educated Hindus, combined with similar interests of the rising educated middle class Muslims, aspiring to become the '*new ashraf*' in the Bengal Muslim society, contributed further to the process of an Islamic resurgence and a corresponding denigration of the Bengali culture. The pressures on the rationale, legitimacy and continuity of the Bengali cultural ethos for Bengal Muslims is overwhelming. The demands for Islamisation of life in Muslim Bengal were pervasive and extended to cover Muslim's language, literature, dress, names, religious and social conducts, beliefs, superstitions, and so on. For the second time in the history of Bengal Muslims there was a crying need to defend and reassert the 'inalienable' Bengali attributes in the making of their own personality, and the cultural mediators emerged once more in response to this historical challenge. The challenge confronting them was even more serious and difficult than that of their medieval ancestors. The latter did certainly not have to confront such a massive alignment of forces against them, actively engaged in severing and supplanting their local roots. The modern Muslim mediators held their ground and spoke their minds with the strong courage of their convictions. They achieved perhaps mixed results. Obviously, the political facet of their work, insofar as it embraced the concept and hope of a supra-religious Bengali nationalism, remained unrealised. The reasons for this failure are, of course, varied and complex. The success of the Muslim separatist movement is part of an infinitely much larger and more complex story. Apart from the very strong opposition of a powerful combination of the Islamic forces, as mentioned above, the persisting strength of the social and cultural process of 'ashrafisation' in the Bengal Muslim society, the growing 'Hindu' assumptions of the nascent modern 'Bengali' culture, and finally, the conflict of economic and political interests between the educated Hindus and Muslims – all combined to bolster up the Islamic against the Bengali identity.

Yet, the mediators clearly succeeded in what they primarily intended to achieve as 'mediators', namely, preventing 'Bengali' from being forced out of the 'Islam-Bengali' equation. The most significant and enduring monument to their achievement has been their contributions to the retention and improvement of the place for Bengali language as the exclusive medium for the Bengali Muslim social and cultural communication. Its subsequent and continuing importance for the history of this people found its dramatic and tragic expression in the Language Riot of 21 February 1952. The importance of this event for the later emergence of Bangladesh is well known, and has been given a Bangladesh official recognition in the form of an annual national observance of the Martyrs' Day on 21 February.

NOTES

1. This chapter is a modified version of a paper presented at the sixth national conference of the Asian Studies Association of Australia, held in Sydney in May 1986.

2. Paul R. Brass, *Language, Religion and Politics in Northern India* (Cambridge, CUP, 1974), pp. 8-9; also his 'Ethnicity and nationality formation', *Ethnicity*, III (1976), pp. 225-41; 'Elite groups, symbol manipulation and ethnic identity among the Muslims of South Asia', in David Taylor and Malcolm Yapp (eds.), *Political Identity in South Asia* (London, Curzon Press, 1979), pp. 35-77; 'Ethnic groups and nationalities: the formation, persistence, and transformation of ethnic identities over time', in Paul F. Sugar (ed.), *Ethnic Diversity and Conflict in Eastern Europe* (Santa Barbara, ABC-Clio, 1980), pp. 1-68; and 'Ethnic communities in the modern state', in P. Gaeffke and D.A. Utz (eds.), *Identity and Division in Cults and Sects in South Asia* (Philadelphia, University of Pennsylvania, 1984), pp. 10-20.

3. Ibid.; Francis Robinson, 'Nation formation: the Brass thesis and Muslim separatism', *Journal of Commonwealth and Comparative Politics* [hereafter *ICCP*], XV (1977), pp. 215-30; also his 'Islam and Muslim separatism', in Taylor and Yapp (eds.), op. cit., pp. 78-112:

Paul R. Brass, 'A reply to Francis Robinson's "Nation Formation: the Brass thesis and Muslim separatism"', *JCCP, XV,* (1977), pp. 231-4.

4. Asim Roy, *The Islamic Syncretistic Tradition in Bengal* (Princeton, Princeton UP, 1983); also his 'Islam in the Environment of Medieval Bengal', unpublished Ph.D. thesis (Canberra, Australian National University, 1970); 'The social factors in the making of Bengali Islam', *South Asia,* No. 3 (August 1973), pp. 23-35; 'The Pir-Tradition: A Case Study in Islamic Syncretism in Traditional Bengal', in F.W. Clothey (ed.), *Images of Man: Religion and Historical Process in South Asia* (Madras, New Era Publications, 1982), pp. 112-41.

5. *Islamic Syncretistic Tradition,* ibid., Chapter 2.

6. Ibid., pp. 58-72; also Rafiuddin Ahmed, *The Bengal Muslims 1871-1906* (Delhi, Oxford UP, 1981), pp. 5ff.

7. Saiyid Amir Ali, a distinguished member of the Bengal *ashraf* in the late nineteenth and early twentieth centuries, compared 'the Mahomedan settlers from the West who had brought with them to India traditions of civilisation and enlightenment' to the eastern Bengali Muslims who were 'chiefly converts from Hinduism' and 'still observe[d] many Hindu customs and institutions'. *The Moslem Chronicle* (Calcutta), 28 Jan. 1905, p. 193. Referring to the 'genuine Ashraf . . . who have not hitherto contracted marriages . . . with any other class', Maulawi Abdul Wali, another contemporary Muslim scholar, remarked, 'If any ancient culture and civilisation are to be sought among the Musalmans, they should certainly be sought among the members of this class'. M.A. Wali, 'Ethnographical note on the Muhammadan castes of Bengal', *Journal of the Anthropological Society of Bombay,* VII, 2 (1904), pp. 98-113. The common man's perception of the *ashraf* as setting the religious-cultural norms of the Islamic life is attested to, in a local context in East Pakistan, by an empirical study as recently as 1968 (see Ahmad Mia, 'Influence of Urban Technological Development on Common Man's Islam in Pakistan', unpublished Ph.D. thesis (Case Western Reserve University, 1968), pp. 48-9. See also Roy, ibid., pp. 63-5.

8. Roy, ibid., pp. 61-2; also Ahmed, ibid., pp. 16-17.

9. Roy, ibid., pp. 65ff.

10. Roy, ibid., p. 76.

11. There is no basic change in the nature of leadership down to our own times, as so candidly admitted by a contemporary American politician: 'The way to get somewhere in politics is to find a crowd that is going some place, and get in front of it'. (Senator Shelton Edwards, Tennessee, quoted in *Time,* 28 Aug. 1978, p. 21.)

12. Ahmed, op.cit.; Muinuddin A. Khan (ed.), *Selection from Bengal Government Records on Wahhabi Trials, 1863-70* (Dhaka, Asiatic Soc. of Pakistan, 1961); his *History of the Faraidi Movement in Bengal, 1818-1906* (Karachi, 1965); his 'Research in Islamic revivalism of the nineteenth century and its effect on the Muslim community of Bengal', in P. Bessaignet (ed.), *Social Research in East Pakistan* (Dhaka, Asiatic Society of Pakistan, 2nd revised edn., 1974); Qiyamuddin Ahmed, *The Wahabi Movement in India* (Calcutta, Firma K.L., 1966).

13. James Taylor, *A Sketch of the Topography and Statistics of Dacca* (Calcutta, 1840), p. 248.

14. .*Census of Bengal 1881, Report,* vol. 1, p. 82.

15. James Wise, *Notes on the Races, Castes, and Trades of Eastern Bengal* (London, Harrison & Sons, 1883), p. 21.

16. As recently as 1955, an empirical survey of Muslim popular beliefs and practices in then East Pakistan reinforces these doubts even after decades of Islamisation in religious, cultural and political terms. See A.K. Najmul Karim, 'Some aspects of popular beliefs among Muslims of Bengal', *Eastern Anthropologist* (Lucknow), IX, 1 (Sept.-Nov. 1955), pp. 29-41;

also Roy, 'Islam in Medieval Bengal', thesis, p. 489; Roy, 'The making of Bengali Islam', p. 35.

17. Ahmed, op.cit., especially Chapter 3.

18. Qazi Abdul Wadud, *Ajkar Katha / Notes on Today* (Calcutta, General Printers & Publishers Ltd., 1941), pp. 8-9; see also Roy, *Islamic Syncretistic Tradition*, 'Preface', pp. xviii-xxi. [*All translations from the original Bengali, quoted in this study are mine, unless otherwise indicated.*]

19. Wadud, 'Banglar Musalmaner Katha'/ 'On the Musalmans of Bengal', in his *Shashvata Banga/The* Eternal Bengal (Calcutta: Khurshid Bakht, 1951), p. 98; Roy, ibid.

20. Manirujjaman Islamabadi, 'Anjuman-i Ulema o samaj samskar' (in Bengali/'The Association of the Ulema and social reform'), *Al-Islam*, V, 3 (1326 B.S. [Bengali calendar]/1919); Roy, ibid., pp. xvi-xvii.

21. Abdul Qadir & Rezaul Karim, *Kavya-malancha / The* Garden of Poems (Calcutta, Nur Library, 1945), p.32; Roy, ibid.

22. Roy, ibid., p. xviii.

23. Ahmed, op.cit., pp. 74ff.

24. Rafiuddin Ahmed clearly identifies the various factors in the promotion of the Muslim solidarity. See ibid., Chapter 3; also his 'Islamisation in nineteenth century Bengal' in Gopal Krishna (ed.), *Contributions to South Asian Studies*, 1 (New Delhi, Oxford UP, 1979), pp. 88-120.

25. J.H. Broomfield, *Elite Conflict in a Plural Society: twentieth-century Bengal* (Berkeley, California UP, 1968); Kenneth McPherson, *The Muslim Microcosm: Calcutta, 1918 to 1935* (Wiesbaden, Franz Steiner Verlag, 1974). Cf. 'The political and social history of the Muslims in Calcutta between 1918 and 1935 is one of an exotic urban minority group which underwent a . . . process of political awakening and growing communal self-consciousness. . . . Such sentiments spread beyond the bounds of the city to encompass the Muslims of the mofussil . . . .' (McPherson, ibid., pp. vi-vii).

26. Pradip Sinha, *Nineteenth Century Bengal. Aspects of Social History* (Calcutta, Firma K.L., 1965), p. 28.

27. McPherson, op.cit., p. iii.

28. The trials revealed that 'the *Jihad* campaign had become wide-spread throughout Bengal, especially in those districts which were traversed by the rivers Ganges and Bhagirathi. . . . In these districts a net-work of compact organisation had sprung up which recruited fighters and collected subscription for the *Jihad* in the North-West Frontier . . . the influences of the movement had also swept over Eastern Bengal'. (Khan, *Selections from Bengal Govt.*, op.cit., p. 8); also Ahmed, *Bengal Muslims*, op.cit., p. 167.

29. McPherson, op.cit., ii, pp. 9ff.

30. Peter Hardy, *The Muslims of British India* (Cambridge UP, 1972), pp. 110-11 .

31. Broomfield, op.cit., pp. 208-9; Ahmed, *Bengal Muslims*, op.cit., pp. 72. 100, 162ff; Rajat K. Ray, *Social Conflict and Political Unrest in Bengal 1875-1927* (New Delhi, Oxford UP, 1984), pp. 70ff.

32. Rafiuddin Ahmed has a mistaken assumption about a pre-modern set of Muslim Bengali didactic literature (*nasihat-nama*), aiming at reforming the religious life of Bengali Muslims. [See his *Bengal Muslims*, pp. 85-6.] In point of fact, the traditional *nasihat-namas* were nothing more than a set of standard religious or liturgic manuals written in Bengali, as these were to be found in other languages. The two are clearly separable in both quantitative and qualitative terms. The corpus of the traditional *nasihat-namas* is far smaller not only in comparison with its later counterparts, but also in relation to the total and an enormous volume of Muslim Bengali literature in traditional Bengal. Besides, the traditional literature is charac-

terised by a total absence of the puritanical spirit, zeal and urgency of the modern *nasihat-nama*, dating mostly from the nineteenth century. It may be recalled here that an early nine-teenth-century Urdu revivalist writing, *Taqwiyat-ul Iman, was* met with *a* refutation published from Chittagong in Bengal. See M.A. Khan, 'Research in Islamic revivalism', op.cit., p. 59.

33. Broomfield, op.cit., p. 279; Ahmed, op.cit., pp. 161-70; Ray, op.cit., pp. 71-4.

34. See Brass, 'Ethnicity and nationality formation', loc.cit; also his 'Ethnic communities in the modern state', loc.cit; Taylor and Yapp (eds.), op.cit., passim; see also Asim Roy, 'The politics of education: the British raj and the Bengal Muslim education, 1871-1884', (paper accepted for publication in the *History of Education Review* (Melbourne) in 1988).

35. See Brass, *Language, Religion, and Politics,* op.cit., Francis Robinson, *Separatism among Indian Muslims. The politics of the United Provinces' Muslims, 1860-1923* (Cambridge UP, 1974); Hardy, op.cit.

36. *Report of the Education Commission, 1882* (Calcutta, Govt. of India Secretariat, 1884), p. 6.; also Asim Roy, 'Politics of education', op.cit.

37. Broomfield, op.cit; McPherson, op.cit; Ahmed, *Bengal Muslims;* Ray, op. cit.

38. Broomfield, ibid., McPherson, ibid.

39. There is a real dearth of published works based on such material. For a useful measure of the nature and importance of such material, see Mustafa Nurul Islam, *Bengali Muslim Public Opinion as Reflected in the Bengali Press 1901-1930* (Dhaka, Bangla Academy, 1973); also his *Samayik Patre Jiban o Janamat 1901-1930/Life and Public Opinion in the Periodical Literature* (Dhaka, Bangla Academy, 1977); Anisuzzaman, *Muslim-manas o Bangla Sahitya 1757-1918 / The Muslim Mind and the Bengali Literature* (Dhaka, Muktadhara, 1964); also his *Muslim Banglar Samayik Patra 18311930/The* Periodical Literature of Muslim Bengal (Dhaka, Bangla Academy, 1969); Qazi Abdul Mannan, *Adhunik Bangla Sahitye Muslim Sadhana/The* Muslim Pursuits in Modern Bengali Literature (Dhaka, Student Ways, enlarged 2nd edn., 1969); Najma Jasmin Choudhry, *Bangla Upanyas o Rajniti/*Bengali Novels and Politics (Dhaka, Bangla Academy, 1980); Waqil Ahmad, *Unish Shatake Bangali Musalmaner China-chetanar Dhara/The* Trends of Bengali Muslim Thoughts in the Nineteenth Century (Dhaka, Bangla Academy, 1983).

40. Broomfield, op.cit; McPherson, op.cit.; Ray, op.cit.

41. Hardy, op.cit, p. 252.

42. Muhammad Mayjar Rahman, 'Samaj-chitra'/the portrait of the society, Al-Islam, *V, 5 (Bhadra,* 1326 BS/1919).

43. Maulawi Shafiuddin Ahmad, 'Abhijatya-gaurab – ashraf-atraf'/the pride of lineage – ashraf-atraf, *Samyabadi, 1, 1 (Magh,* 1329 BS/1922).

44. Saiyid Emdad Ali, 'Ashraf-atraf', *Saogat, VII, 5 (Paus,* 1336 BS/1929).

45. A.M. Torab Ali, 'Ashraf-atraf', ibid., *VI, 1 (Shraban,* 1335 BS/1928), pp. 28-30.

46. Ibid.

47. Hamed/Hamid Ali, 'Uttar Banger Musalman sahitya'/Muslim literature of north Bengal, *Basana,* II, 1 *(Baishakh,* 1316 BS/1909).

48. Muhammad Akram Khan, 'The presidential address: the third annual Bengali Muslim Literary Conference', *Bangiya-Musalman-Sahitya-Patrika* (henceforth *BMSP), I, 4 (Magh,* 1325 BS/1918).

49. Muhammad Wajed Ali, 'Bangla bhasa o Musalman sahitya'/the Bengali language and the Muslim literature, in *BMSP,* ibid.

50. Abdul Haq Chaudhuri, 'Musalman sampraday o tahar patan'/the Muslim community and their downfall, *Islam-pracharak,* VIII, 11 *(Magh,* 1313 BS/ 1906).

51. Saiyid Emdad Ali, 'Banga bhasa o Musalman'/the Bengali language and the Muslims, *BMSP, 1*, 2 *(Shraban,* 1325 BS/1918), pp. 79-87.

52. Hamed Ali, op.cit.

53. 'Bibad'/Disagreement, *Pracharak,* 11, 6 *(Asad,* 1307, BS/1900).

54. Bidyabinodini Nurunnesa Khatun, 'Amader kaj'/Our work, *Saogat,* VII, 1 *(Bhadra,* 1336 BS/1929).

55. Abdur Rashid, 'Amader nabajagaran o shariat'/Our reawakening and the Islamic religious laws, *Shikha,·I (Chaitra,* 1333 BS/1927), pp. 98-9.

56. Ahsanullah, *Banga Bhasa o Musalman Sahitya* /The Bengali Language and Muslim Literature (Calcutta, 1917), pp. 6-7.

57. S. Wajed Ali, 'Bangali Musalman:'/Bengali Muslims: an address, in his *Jibaner Shilpa/*The Art of Life (Calcutta, Gulistan Publishing House, 1939), p. 57.

58. 'Editorial', *BMSP, 1,* 4 *(Magh,* 1325 BS/1918), p. 368.

59. Rezaul Karim, 'Bharatiya Musalmangan kon jati?'/What nation are the Indian Muslims? in his *Pakistaner Bichar/*The Trial of Pakistan (Calcutta, Kalikata Book Co. Ltd. 1942), pp. 46-7.

60. Sadat Ali Akhand, *Saogat,* VI, 5 *(Agrahayan,* 1335 BS/1928).

61. Humayun Kabir, 'Baromasir sampadakiya'/the miscellaneous editorials, in his *Dharabahikl* In Sequence (Calcutta, D.M. Library, 1942), p. 38.

62. Rezaul Karim, 'Vishva-Moslem moha'/the illusion of pan-Islamism, in his *Jatiyatar Pathe/*On the Road to Nationalism (Calcutta, Barendra Library, 1939), pp. 144ff.

63. S. Wajed Ali, op.cit., p. 16.

64. Rezaul Karim, *Jatiyata,* op.cit., p. 1.

65. Wajed Ali, *Bhabisyater Bangali/*The Future Bengali (Calcutta, Prabartak Publishing House 1941), pp. 33,105-6. The reference to possible 'troubles' in a state based on religion seems almost a prophetic vision of the problems facing Pakistan since its creation, culminating in its dismemberment in 1971.

66. Wajed Ali, ibid., pp. 106-7.

67. Wajed Ali, *Jibaner Shilpa,* op.cit., pp. 6-7.

68. K.A. Wadud, *Naba Paryay* /The New Stage (Calcutta, Moslem Publishing House, 1936), pp. 35-6.

6. Salience of Islam in South Asian Politics: Pakistan and Bangladesh

THERE ARE some general misconceptions and wrong assumptions underlying popular non-Muslim perceptions of the Islamic world, especially in the West. First, there is a tendency to regard the real world of Islam as coextensive with the "Middle East" and almost synonymous with the Arab world. This pervasive misconception would seem extraordinarily intriguing in the light of the fact that Arab Muslims constitute no more than a quarter of the total Muslim population in the world, and nearly two-third of the world's Muslims are to be found east of the Persian Gulf. For our purposes here it is even of greater interest that out of the four countries with highest Muslim population today, namely Indonesia, Bangladesh, India, and Pakistan, the last three are located in South Asia. Secondly, there has been the most persistent stereotypification of Islam as militant, violent, puritanical and fundamentalist in inspiration as well as anti-modernistic and anti-Western in orientation. For these non-Muslim critics, Muslim opposition to separation between the church and the state as well as to the very basic political concept of sovereignty of the nation-state overridden by the primacy of the concept of the *umma* (community of believers), Islamic socio-religious practices like polygamy, seclusion of women, and harsh inhumane physical punishment under the *shari'a* (religious law) courts all testify to their "conservative anti-modernistic" minds. Examples of this nature, taken together with other expressions of their "anti-Westernism" as well as their "militant, violent, puritanical and fanatical" predispositions have been noted with some avidity by these critics in their coverage of what has been seen and interpreted as the upsurge of militant Islam particularly since the 'seventies.[1]

I

A very large part of the Muslim World appeared indeed, in the last two decades, to have been in severe ferment.[2] The South Asian world of Islam, which is our particular concern here, not only found reverberations of such well-publicised developments, but itself contributed in some important respects to the totality of the phenomena. In conformity with the global trends since 1970s, South Asian Muslim world also seemed to have been revolving a great deal around the axle of what was seen as an integral part of the global phenomenon of a resurgent Islam. We shall return to these South Asian developments later.

In the light of such pervasive developments in the Muslim world, one would be tempted, and justifiably so, to read religious meaning and significance in them, as has generally been the case with sundry observers. Islamic resurgence, to most, is what it says to be – religious in its origin, inspiration and expression. Our concern here is not so much to reject totally this popular perception of the centrality of Islam in Muslim developments as to reveal its inadequacies and simplistic nature in particular reference to the two dominant Muslim countries of South Asia – Pakistan and Bangladesh.

There are some major problems with this predominantly religious interpretation of events in the Muslim world, with special reference to South Asia. First, such a perception is necessarily grounded on both a monolithic and normative view of Islam which is found totally inadequate in any empirical or historical analysis of Islamic development in a regional-cultural setting.[3] Until fairly recently we had very little social-scientific knowledge of the regional varieties and formulations of Islam.[4] Secondly, even within this limited validity of the religious explanation, this view fails to differentiate between the "appearance" and the "reality" – the "symbol" and the "substance". Religion in South Asia, as elsewhere, is so often found to conceal secular concerns. Transcendental symbols were, in reality, nothing more than convenient covers for not so elevated mundane interests. Clever, and often cynical manipulation of religious symbols for the purposes of social mobilisation by both religious and secular elites has been a dominant feature of Muslim politics in South Asia as with other communities there or elsewhere. One could so easily be misled by the apparent "religious" symbolism of the "Islamic resurgence".

There is a further, and even more contentious problem, generally speaking, in studying politics in relation to Islam, the field being "strewn", as rather succinctly put by a commentator, "with ancient potholes and modern mines", the traditional Islamic theological orthodoxy constituting the "ancient potholes", and the western academic orthodoxy of "orientalism" forming the "modern mines".[5] Both have tended to view the relationship between Islam and politics in purely scriptural or canonical terms, in total disregard of the historical realities, and hence underlined the unique absence of separation between religion and politics in Islam. In a broad general sense of a linkage between the civil society and the institutions of power, no major religion would allow this separation. One has only to look around the contemporary developments in Judaism in West Asia, Hinduism and Sikhism in India, Buddhism in both South and Southeast Asia, and the fundamentalist Christianity in the USA, the Latin America and elsewhere. To attribute to Muslims a unique disposition towards politics of religion seems, therefore, not merely unwarranted but somewhat tendentious. Besides, the separation between Islam and politics, in the more specific sense of a hiatus between the religion and state power, has remained a dominant feature of Islamic history for nearly a millennium. The unity of the temporal and spiritual in Islam is thought, even by many pious Muslim believers, to have ended, for all effective purposes, with the advent of the dynastic rule in Islam in 661 AD.

And yet it is unquestionable that there is a remarkable nexus in Islam of the faith, community, power and history. A total identity of the faith, its social ideal and the community is a special genius of Islam. The centrality of the faith and its social ideal in Islam stems from the basic belief that man alone was given a choice and responsibility which he accepted and must act upon, both individually and collectively. There is both gravity and urgency of the Islamic mission not only in the sense that there is a day of reckoning and judgment, but also because it is God's last warning and the last chance given to the mankind, after the repeated failures of the earlier prophets, to redeem themselves not merely by individual piety but through actualisation of the Islamic social ideal in history. The intertwining of the temporal and the spiritual in Islam is also facilitated by the very nature of historical development of Islam. While the church represented the organised community in Christendom, it fought the state for religious freedom or autonomy until their domains were separated on secular lines. Islam has no "church", and in its absence the "community" came to identify itself with the "state". The religious struggle for Muslims, therefore, has not been between the church and the state, but for the state; hence this identity of faith and power, religion and state, as well as the very strong appeal of an Islamic "state" among Muslims.[6] Muslim power-mongers of both secular and religious varieties discovered in this appeal a powerful instrument for manipulation and mobilisation of the Muslim masses which is so clearly revealed in contemporary Muslim politics in South Asia, as delineated below.

II

Question about Pakistan in relation to Islam is tautological. Islam is so integral to the origins of Pakistan as well as its subsequent development. The attainment of independence left the political leaders with the remaining major task of fulfilling the Islamic aspirations of the religious leadership and the masses of Muslims.[7] At the dawn of independence religious demands and expectations of the people naturally loomed large on the Pakistan horizon. The inability or unwillingness of the Pakistani rulers to rise up to this popular expectation, and more importantly, their cynical manipulation and exploitation of religious emotions and concerns of the Muslim masses, giving rise to unending social and political confusions and uncertainties have been the source of many a human tragedy of an epic proportion. A "Muslim" state created for the Muslims was an immediate reality as early as its creation, but to call it "Islamic" involved a great deal more. The story of Pakistan politics since its inception is one of a blatant pursuit of political self-interests by Pakistani ruling elites disguised in terms of religious discourse. A probe into the changing social composition of the Pakistani ruling classes and the structure of state power in Pakistan is essential to understand the role and place of Islam in this politics of elite dominance.

The most salient and enduring feature of the political system and the power structure in Pakistan has been the dominance of the big and firmly entrenched landlord and the rising capitalist classes, buttressed by the military-bureaucratic oligarchy. Pakistan inherited a colonial state apparatus in the form of its army and bureaucracy virtually in tact, a rather weak "national" party in the Muslim League dominated by landlords, and a political culture totally inadequate to ensure the primacy of the political process and of representative government. Relative to the political institutions at the dawn of independence, the military-bureaucratic structure in Pakistan was, therefore, far more developed. This set the stage for a remarkable and almost perpetual dominance of the state apparatus and politics of Pakistan by the bureaucracy and the army. There have been some shifts, over the years, in the relative power and position of each of the partners in the military-bureaucracy entente but the complementarity between the two remained unassailed.[8] The close nexus of the military, landed and capitalist interests was reinforced by some calculated measures taken by the successive military regimes. The officer corps were generally drawn from the landowning class since the colonial times. General Ayub Khan's regime both strengthened and extended this integration of the military into the propertied class. He began to make land grants to senior army officers and thus created landed interests even among officers not belonging to landowning families. Likewise, officer corps found their ways into the commercial and industrial establishments, being offered coveted positions in the boards after retirement, often as chairpersons in public corporations in the nationalised sector. This particular trend was accelerated even further under the regime of General Zia ul-Haq.[9]

The Pakistan economy was clearly geared to this political structure. The programme of economic growth launched under the military regimes in the 'sixties was designed to concentrate incomes in the hands of the industrial and landed magnates. The investment targets were to be achieved on the basis of the doctrine of "functional inequality", involving transfer of incomes from the poorer to the high income groups. We have discussed below how General Zia's "profit and loss sharing" system, justified in terms of Islamic prohibition of *riba* (interest), made such transfer of incomes easier.[10] It is not surprising therefore that by the end of that decade, a small group of families with interlocking directorates dominated industry, banking and insurance in Pakistan. Thus forty-three families represented 76.8% of all manufacturing assets (including foreign and government assets). The major industrial families were a close-knit group. Often tied by kinship relations, they usually sat on each other's board of directors. About one-third of such seats in companies controlled by the forty-three families were occupied by members of other families within the forty-three.[11]

III

Islam was brought in to play a seminal role by the Pakistani governing elite in its politics of total dominance. This role is summed up, in broad and general terms, by a Pakistani scholar:

> Aware of the attachment of the masses to Islam, the ruling classes hope to secure a future for themselves by establishing an authoritarian and exploitative system, which they claim to be Islamic. It is with this aim in view that the so-called Islamisation of state and society has been undertaken in Pakistan.[12]

To perpetuate an inegalitarian system the strategy of the governing classes was to proclaim Pakistan an ideological state based on Islam, and not a democracy. They were also able to draw, on the basis of mutual interests, the support of the conservative *ulama* (scriptural scholars) who pressed medieval Islamic scholastic tradition to the service of the Pakistani rulers, defending the status quo and legitimising the authoritarian rule.

Islam is, however, amenable to other interpretations. The Muslim fundamentalist party, the Jama'at-i Islami under Mawlana Maududi, challenged the unholy alliance between the conservative *ulama* and the government, and projected their own model of the "Islamic state". President 'Ayub Khan banned the Jama'at-i-Islami and arrested its leaders, including Mawlana Maududi, on the ground of its carrying on "subversive activities against the state" and constituting "a danger to the public peace".[13]

The difficulties facing the Pakistani rulers stemmed from the fact that howsoever onerous was the undertaking of building an Islamic society, they could not evade it. No state can live in a vacuum. Islamic or not, some ideology was critical for Pakistan's sustenance. Compulsions of this nature forced, in the next decade, a dramatic reversal of the situation, when the Jama'at's persistent campaign and penetration of the military cadres brought about the overthrow of Zulfiqar 'Ali Bhutto's civilian government through a military coup by General Zia ul-Haq, who was a close relation to Mian Tufail, the chief of the Jama'at. By the late 1960s significant changes in the social composition of the army had been occurring. Until then, the officers were "predominantly from the landowning class" and brought up in the British military tradition. The new officer corps began to draw on the petite bourgeoisie in both the urban and rural areas. They were drawn largely from the economically depressed migrants from East Punjab – like Zia ul-Haq himself – and the unirrigated Potwar region of West Punjab. This new officer corps were "less literate and more religious", "socially more conservative", and susceptible to the Jama'at's puritanism.[14]

IV

The Zia regime unleashed, not unexpectedly, a process of unprecedented Islamisation of the country's institutions. His series of reforms, labelled *Nizam-i Mustafa* (Rule of the Prophet), professedly designed to bring the country's laws into conformity with Islamic principles and values, covered three aspects of the Pakistani life: educational, judicial-legal and economic. The educational reforms laid down Arabic as a compulsory foreign language requirement, made courses in the Qur'anic and Islamic studies obligatory throughout the educational system, and proposed segregation of sexes in educational institutions at the upper level. With the promulgation of four *hudud* (sing. *hadd*, an offence contrary to clear Qur'anic sanctions) ordinances, outlining Islamic punishments and standards of evidence for theft, adultery, consumption of alcohol, and false imputation of immodesty to women, he provided for harsh and inhumane physical punishments like the amputation of hand and stoning to death. New judicial institutions in the forms of Federal Shari'a Court (Islamic law court) and the Appellate Bench of the Supreme Court were set in place to implement the new laws. There is an obvious element of tokenism in such reforms coloured in the Islamic hues in as much as the jurisdiction of the Shari'a courts, largely stacked with "Islamic moderates", excluded constitutional principles, fiscal matters, and martial law regulations.[15]

It is the Zia regime's much-vaunted programme of Islamising Pakistan's economy that has attracted wide attention. His economic programme consisted of three major reforms, claimed to have been Islamically inspired. The first two are compulsory collection of *zakat* (a tax assessed against capital assets, popularly called "poor tax") and *ushr* (agricultural tax). Both of these taxes are traditional Islamic methods of collecting and distributing welfare. *Zakat* is assessed at 2.5% of cash value of financial assets, and *ushr* at 5% of the profits from agricultural land. The collected taxes are made available to local *Zakat* Committees for distribution to poor Muslims and to charities. The third measure, relative to the Islamic injunction against collection of *riba* (interest), is officially labelled the Profit and Loss Sharing (PLS) system, popular as interest-free banking. The measure, in essence, is one of replacement of the principle of limited liability by a system of sharing profit and loss.

If the objective of this innovative measure was to eliminate financial extortion and exploitation, it seemed to have gone just the other way. First, a fairly large proportion of deposits belonged to the lower middle class, and the system discriminated against the poorer depositors. The profit to be paid to the depositor was determined by the bank's operations, while the investor could receive loans from banks at zero interest with a nominal service charge and thus make a large profit. A number of cases were actually reported where a "large number of interest-free or low-interest loans earmarked for small farmers" had been "advanced to large and influential farmers with contacts with the ruling hierarchy."[16] Secondly, the system led to widespread fraud, resulting from the corrupt business people resorting to "multiple account books". Thirdly, the business community complained of undesirable interference by the bureaucrats of public-controlled nationalised banks with the management of individual projects, obviously prompted by the profit and loss considerations. Fourthly, leaving aside the issue of the application of the PLS system to the entire economy, a substantial proportion of the banking sector continued to operate under the interest-based system. It would appear from this that "the purpose of the government is not so much to abolish the institution of interest as to make it appear to the public that interest has been eliminated from financial transactions."[17] Finally, the exclusive concern with the elimination of interest from the organised financial sector appeared hypocritical in the light of wide prevalence in the rural sector, on one hand, of extortionate interest rates charged from small farmers and landless peasants by money-lender landlords, and on the other, of *muzara'a* (share-cropping, ground rent).

Zia's accidental death or assassination (as widely suspected) has shifted the focus of Pakistan politics away from Islamisation and the Jama'at (cited as a possible motive under the assassination theory), but one would have to add, only for a while. Because, judging by the past events, one would be disinclined to overlook Islam in relation to Pakistan as yet.

V

Almost on the same note one is inclined to conclude about Islam in relation to Bangladesh and its politics. The dramatic events there, happening at a kaleidoscopic speed in the last few decades, leave no doubt that much of Bangladesh's problems can be attributed to the pressures of a dual identity of which Islam is one and vital; the other no less seminal is the local Bengali linguistic-cultural identity. The salience of Islam in Bangladesh, in a wider historical perspective, is posited in her participation in the Pakistan movement, leading to the partition of

1947. The failures, inadequacies and insincerities of the Pakistan rulers, repeatedly demonstrated in their dealings with Islam, caused a Bengali backlash in its vigorous and chauvinistic affirmation of the Bengali self to the point of almost undermining Islamic relevance to the Bangladeshis.[18]

On the morrow of the liberation, while Shaikh Mujeeb was still in the West Pakistan jail, many enthusiastic members of the caretaker government of Bangladesh tried to prevail upon and even pressurise schools and other institutions to drop "Islam" or "Muslim" from their names. Some Dhaka University academics and other members of the Bengali intelligentsia urged substitution of readings from the Qur'an, on the National Radio and Television, by "Speaking the Truth" based on secular morality and ethics.[19] On his return Mujeeb banned all religion-based political parties and groups. The process was carried further with the promulgation of the new constitution whereby the People's Republic of Bangladesh adopted "secularism" as one of the fundamental constitutional objectives. In a series of sweeping educational reforms, history books were purged of Pakistani heroes, religious instructions for minorities were introduced in schools, and on the basis of the recommendations contained in an Interim Report of the Education Commission (May 1973), religious instructions at schools from grades 1 to 8 ceased, while it was made an elective subject from grades 9 to 12, and only for Humanities. But the yawning gap between the social reality and the political idealism of the new leaders was soon revealed, as the secular ethos of the government's education policy was rejected by 75% of the people included in a government-sponsored survey, comprising primarily educationists at the school, college and university levels. They spoke in favour of a more balanced modern religious instruction. The revised education policy retained religious instruction at all levels of schools except for grades 1 to 5.[20]

This presaged an orthodox Muslim backlash, very resentful of the secularising policies of the Mujeeb government, especially its ban on the religious parties. The religious emotion was further roused by Mujeeb's close economic and political relations with the "godless" Russians and "fanatical Hindu" Indians. Rampant smuggling across the Bangladesh-India borders gave the Islamists the opportunity of pointing their fingers at India's "evil" designs on Bangladesh and its hegemonistic ambition. The accommodation of differences with Pakistan and Pakistan's recognition of Bangladesh had also removed a major obstacle in the way of repairing the broken bridge of Muslim fraternity of the former united Pakistan. Mujeeb attempted to placate the "Islamic" elements by way of enhanced Islamisation of his speech and life style, restoring the hitherto suspended Islamic Foundation to an Islamic Academy, and attending the first Islamic Conference (1974) held in Pakistan, being escorted from Bangladesh by two Arab heads of government. But it all came too late. Such religious issues, taken together with the gigantic failure of his government to deliver the economic and political goods, brought about his downfall with a military coup (1975).

Mujeeb's overthrow marked the beginning of a long period of blatant military rule, successively under Major General Zia ur-Rahman (1976-81) and Lieutenant General Husain Muhammad Ershad (1982-91), sought to be redeemed at times by dubious attempts at civilianisation. The authoritarian nature of the government persisted until the recent stepping down of Ershad under popular pressure, and the election of a parliamentary government under the leadership of Begum Khalida Zia, the widow of Zia ur-Rahman. Following in the footsteps of their Pakistani counterparts, both these strongmen of Bangladesh saw political merits in the use of Islamic religious-cultural symbols. While Zia ur-Rahman seemed to have brought some degree of discretion and restraint to bear on his Islamising ardour, Ershad bared it all. All in all, Islam bounced back in the post-Mujeeb phase onto the Bangladesh scene. The constitution of 1973 was amended to replace "secularism" with the solemn proclamation: "Absolute trust and faith in the Almighty Allah shall be the basis of all action," as well as to declare that "solidarity with Muslim states" should become a fundamental objective of the state. Religious instructions from grade 1 to 8 were made compulsory, and new textbook writing with appropriate religious contents was authorised. Islamic broadcasts and telecasts over the government-controlled media proliferated.

From mid-1970s there had been a profusion of religious literature, polemical and didactic, published in Bangladesh at the initiatives of individuals, religious associations and the government. The government made generous financial support to such projects, primarily through the Islamic Academy. The period also coincided with a phenomenal mushrooming of Islamic religious-cultural associations, the mosque societies, the Islamic missions and so on.[21] Ershad became well-known for his public display of piety, repair and beautification works on mosques, and posters and wall-hangings of excerpts from the Qur'an in government offices and public buildings. He set up a Department of Religious Affairs to supervise, *inter alia*, matters relating to the hajj-pilgrimage. He was also credited with the establishment of the Zakat Fund, nominating himself as the chairman. Finally, the ban on political parties based on religion was removed to bring a host of small and not-so-small parties into the political arena. The strongest Islamic party and the most inveterate opponent of secularism to resurface in Bangladesh politics was Jama'at-i Islami, which had been growing steadily on a political platform of fundamentalism, the Islamic state, staunch pro-Pakistanism, and rabid anti-Indianism.

The end of the period of the strongmen and the prospect of rehabilitation of the representative government in Bangladesh should hopefully help Islam find its own rightful place in the life of the people and the country, in an open and free political environment, rather than being imposed by strong hands to suit their own selfish interests. Neither the people of Bangladesh nor that of Pakistan have had a fair chance so far to ask for what they want of their religion, and not be told of what to expect.

VI

How much of all this preoccupations with Islam in the Pakistan and Bangladesh politics that we have explored are real religious concerns? The question, to many, may seem totally unwarranted. To the extent that motivations underlying particular political behaviours and actions are inscrutable one may consider conceding the point. But no religious action in the political arena does have the passport to go unchallenged, especially in a given circumstance where such an action is amenable to secular explanations as well. Much of what we perused above as politics might well have been Islamically inspired. But unless and until we are content to conclude on the basis of mere assumptions, we are obliged to raise reasonable questions and doubts to satisfy ourselves before we arrive at our conclusions. A religious concern expressed in the contexts of politics by a Muslim elite, whether religious or non-religious, assume a deeper and more intricate meaning when placed in the contexts of possible secular explanations for the same. Much of the religious discourses among political and religious elites of Pakistan and Bangladesh may not become entirely meaningful if totally divorced from vital secular considerations such as the need for legitimising the authoritarian rule, mobilising the masses, promoting national integration or suppressing ethnic subnationalism, targeting the petro-dollar and the profitable labour market of the Middle East, and so on. The social-psychological attractions for puritanical or militant Islam for the people in times of social changes and dislocations are likewise concerns not wholly spiritual. In history and politics human motivations are largely a matter of conjecture, but it behoves us to make it a rational and an educated one.

NOTES

1. Cf. *New York Times* (18/6/78): "The Moslem world rekindles its militancy".

2. Set in the context of the historic self-assertion of the Arab oil barons, the Arab world of Saudi Arabia, Egypt, Libya, Syria, Iraq and Lebanon witnessed significant developments, widely perceived as having flowed from a resurgent, and even revolutionary Islam. The most publicised case of the revolutionary Islam in action was, however, in the non-Arab world of Iran, providing the glaring example of a clerical order under Ayatollah Khomeini successfully bringing about the downfall of the world's oldest monarchy. About the same time the news media found, thanks to Moscow's intervention in Afghanistan, a new focus in the religious war of the *Mujahidin* against the "godless communists" in that country.

3. Cf. My own research on this subject in the context of Islam in the region of Bengal: see A. Roy, *The Islamic Syncretistic Tradition of Bengal* (Princeton: Princeton University Press, 1983).

4. In July 1989, the South Asian Institute, University of Heidelberg, West Germany, organised a high-powered conference which it claimed to be the first on the "Regional Varieties of

Islam in Pre-modern South Asia". The present author was invited to offer a paper on Islam in Bengal. A volume incorporating the results of this conference is scheduled for publication. [N.B.: The volume has since been published. See, the present author's contribution in that volume incorporated into the present publication under the title "The Interface of Islamisation, Regionalisation and Syncretisation : the Bengal Paradigm".]

5. E. Ahmed, "Islam and politics", in M.A. Khan (ed.), *Islam, Politics and the State. The Pakistan Experience* (London: Zed Books Ltd, 1985), p. 13

6. W. C. Smith, *Islam in History* (Princeton: Princeton UP, 197), pp. 10ff, 211 (foot note 6)

7. Poignantly illustrative of this confusion in the popular mind is the anecdote that Jinnah, the doyen of the "Westernised" Muslims in the Indian subcontinent, was greeted by the rural folks of Sind with 'Long Live Mawlana, Muhammad 'Ali Jinnah". Jinnah is said to have taken the trouble of making them able to distinguish between political and religious leadership. (H. Bolitho,*Jinnah, Creator of Pakistan*, London, 1954, p. 213)

8. H. Alavi, "The military in the state of Pakistan", paper presented at the Institute of Development Studies and Institute of Commonwealth Studies Conference, Sussex, England; cited in M.A. Khan (ed.), op. cit., p. 210

9. A. Hussain, "Pakistan: the crisis of the state", in M.A. Khan (ed.), ibid., p. 210; also Craig Baxter et al, *Government and Politics in South Asia* (Boulder, USA: Westview Press, 2nd edn, 1991), p.215

10. See below, p. 5

11. L.J. White, *Industrial Concentration and Economic Power in Pakistan* (Princeton: Princeton U P, 1972), pp. 81-85

12. O.A. Khan, "Political and Economic Aspects of Islamisation", in M.A. Khan (ed.), op.cit., p.127

13. *Pakistan Times,* 18 June 1964

14. A. Hussain, op. cit., pp. 222-23

15. *The Major Acts* (Lahore: Khyber Law Publishers, 1984), pp. 1-30; C.H. Kennedy, "Islamisation in Pakistan: implementation of the hudood ordinances," *Asian Survey,* vol.28, no.3 (March 1988), pp.307-316

16. O.A. Khan, op. cit., p. 151

17. Ibid.

18. In the anguished words of a Bangladeshi historian: "To suppress the popular demands for basic rights and to serve the selfish individual, group, and party interests, the rulers exploited the name of Islam and the religious sentiments of the people . . . . Any demand or even a small action from East Bengal for a rightful share in the administration of the country was termed as anti-Islam and anti-Pakistan and condemned in very strong terms as spreading 'provincialism and subversion'. The demand of East Bengal to recognise Bengali as one of the state languages of Pakistan culminated in the tragic events of 21 February 1952." K.M. Mohsin, "Trends of Islam in Bangladesh," in R.Ahmed (ed), *Islam in Bangladesh. Society, Culture and Politics* (Dhaka: Bangladesh Itihas Samiti, 1983), pp.227-28

19. T. Maniruzzaman, "Bangladesh politics: secular and Islamic Trends ", in R.Ahmed (ed.), *ibid.*, p. 193

20. Ibid., pp. 194-97

21. K.M. Mohsin, op. cit., pp. 233ff

7. Islam and Aspects of Modernity in India and Pakistan

IN ITS TRANSITION to modernity the Indian subcontinent has to contend, naturally enough, with Islam and the Muslims. There is, however, a qualitative difference between the part that Islam played in the time before the partition and that following it. An adequate understanding of the problems of Islam bearing on modernity in India and Pakistan demands an appreciation of this difference.

I

Generally speaking, Islam in the subcontinent as elsewhere in the Muslim world was challenged, in its pre-partition phase, with the task of defending and sustaining the Muslim community against what the believers themselves saw as a crisis – within and without the community. In the nineteenth and twentieth centuries the Muslim world was in a ferment, agitated internally by a sense of communal deterioration attributed to religious decay and degeneration, and externally by the disruptive ideological and political challenges of the West.[1] The Muslim concern stemmed from the basic Muslim view of the relationship between the religious-social ideals of Islam and their actualisation in history. The Muslims, lacking an institutionalised church, tended to identify the community with the state as the embodiment of its ideals and aspirations. The fact that realisation of the ideal in history remained questionable did not finally matter to the believers as long as they could afford the complacency of living in a "Muslim" state in the sense of being presided by a "Muslim" ruler, who was not often quite "Islamic" in his private and public conduct and posture.[2]

The British occupation of India, as general European aggrandisement at the expense of other Muslim countries, such as Turkey, Egypt, Sudan, Morocco, Persia and Indonesia, struck at the basis of this Muslim complacency and created a disconcerting chasm between a Muslim's faith and his social ideal. The sense of desperation and crisis was deepened by more subtle and pervasive ideological forces of the west, confronting the Muslims and other traditional societies, in the forms of rationalism, positivism, liberalism, utilitarianism, evangelism and nationalism.

The Muslim response in the face of this new challenge followed two broad trends: one relatively simple, populist and collectivist, and the other more sophisticated, intellectual and individualistic, the divergent patterns stemming from their respective social compositions. As at once an explanation and an answer to the growing sense of retardation and impotency in the face of the new challenges of the time, both tho populist and the elitist Muslim responses, turning inwardly, resorted to the golden age formula, underlining thereby the notion of deviations and degenerations in historical Islam. Implicit in this idea was the concern for purification of the faith and the revival of the pristine purity of Islam. Turning outwardly, the populist responsive movements, such as the so-called Wahabbi and the Faraizi, sought abortive political-military solutions through militant resistance. The more sophisticated Muslim response in this regard took the form of intellectual defence, vindication and rehabilitation of Islam as an adequate system in the eyes of its modernist external critics and its own small potentially disruptive coterie of alienated Westernised youth. The dominant strain in this intellectual posture was apologetic. The bulk of the modern Muslim responsive writings of this nature in India is characteristically of apologist quality.

In historical retrospect the Muslim intelligentsia, unlike its Hindu counterparts, confronted with basically similar challenges, would seem to have failed to discharge a creative function in leading their community in its transition to modernity. Paradoxically enough, the bulk of the Hindu intelligentsia resorted to the golden age or classical model with a view not to reviving the past but as a rationalisation for change in social and religious reforms. The subversive role of classicism, as also illustrated in the European Reformation and Martin Luther's return to primitive Christianity,[3] is often inadequately comprehended. The use of reason by the Muslim apologists in defending revelation did not strengthen the position of liberalism in Islam as a religious system. The central and fundamental theological affirmations of Islam were not subjected to creative re-interpretations in India as elsewhere in the Muslim world.[4] Islamic liberalism at its best offered solution at the individual and not collective level, intelligible and acceptable to the community. Even the close confidants of Saiyid Ahmad Khan, while fully endorsing his educational and political concerns, disapproved of his religious ideas. As a natural consequence of this dichotomous situation the Muslim modernisers in India were unable to integrate modern non-religious education with traditional Islamic learning – the two flowing into separate and mutually exclusive channels. A student in the Aligarh College received his religious education in a traditional centre, curiously attached to the college. The progress of Islamic modernism in the subcontinent remained largely caught up in this unreconciled position between traditional Islamic religious and modern secular ethos and between its religious leadership and modernisers.

The social dichotomy between traditional Muslim religious leadership holding allegiance of the masses and the non-religious western educated Muslim elite aspiring for political leadership of the community affected the course of subsequent development involving the Muslims of the sub-continent. The Muslim League, almost totally drawn from the rank of non-religious elites found its development and expansion inhibited at two levels. First, the mass-based Muslim religious leadership (e.g. of Deobond), distrustful of the "Westernised" political elites, was opposed to the use of Islam as the focus of a political party, likely to prove detrimental to the interests of Islam as a proselytising religion in the subcontinent. Secondly, the provincial Muslim politicians in the Muslim majority provinces, especially the Punjab and Bengal, refused to share the Muslim League's staunch separatist position and preferred to maintain greater range of policy options giving high priority to political partnership and legislative coalitions as conditions for ministerial stability. In its attempt to extend the political base to the masses since 1937 and to undercut the provincial leadership, the central or "national" Muslim political leadership of the League started to make heavily growing use of religious symbols and to politicise religion. The League resorted to establishing a Masha'ikh Committee of twelve, consisting of some influential Muslim *ulama*' and *pirs*, and employed them to political objectives.[5] The creation of Pakistan is the measure of success of the political elite in directing religion into a political channel and in apparently throwing a bridge across the gulf between the political and religious segments of the Muslim leadership.

But, in the process, the creators of Pakistan generated forces and conditions, which the rulers of the newly created state found baffling, disruptive and uncontrollable. In the cry for a separate homeland for the Muslims, the political leaders had touched and roused the deepest urge in the Muslim mind – the longing for an Islamic state, the rationale of a Muslim's social existence. In Pakistan something more than a mere Muslim state had come into existence. A "Muslim" state created for the Muslims was an immediate reality as early as its creation, but to call it "Islamic" was not quite the same thing. The leaders of Pakistan were left to work out through extreme confusions and conflicts the full implications of moulding a Muslim State into an Islamic one. The Muslims in India, on the other hand, placed under a secular constitutional system, found problems of different nature and dimension to contend with.

II

The creation of Pakistan polarised further the political and religious leaders in the society. Before long the modernising elites of Pakistan were caught up in a dilemma for the creation of which a large share of responsibility rests squarely on their own shoulders. As noted above, the political pressures and circumstances jettisoning religion and politics by the Muslim League particularly since 1937, and the extensive use of religious symbols backed by no attempt to clearly define their political implications, created situations to which the rulers of Pakistan were the natural heirs. The achievement of political freedom vested the political leaders with the inescapable responsibility for the fulfilment of the Islamic aspirations of the religious leadership and the masses of the people.[6] Whereas the rulers of Pakistan found before themselves the onerous task of building up the infra-structure of a viable state – a state that, apart from being a geographical monstrosity in its two extremities, West and East, with an intervening 1000 miles of alien Indian territory, comprised peoples of distinct linguistic-cultural divisions, whose only bond of unity seemed profession of a common faith.

In the face of this dilemma Pakistani modernisers have naturally tended to vacillate and contradict. Liaqat 'Ali Khan, the first Prime Minister of Pakistan declared in the constituent Assembly of Pakistan in March 1949: "Pakistan was founded because the Muslims of the sub-continent wanted to build up their lives in accordance with the teachings and traditions of Islam."[7]

Others have revealed a tendency to play down the religious content of the Pakistan movement. Four days before the birth of Pakistan, Jinnah's presidential address to the Constituent Assembly of Pakistan could have left the champions of Islamic state in Pakistan nothing but uneasy:

> You may belong to any religion or caste or creed – that has nothing to do with the business of the State. . . . You will find that in course of time Hindus would cease to be Hindus and Muslims would cease to be Muslims, not in the religious sense, because that is the personal faith of each individual, but in the political sense as citizens of the State.[8]

The same attitude is reflected in the following remark of Muhammad Munir, a former chief justice of Pakistan:

> The present argument that Pakistan was demanded in order to enable or compel the Muslims to lead their lives in accordance with the injunctions of Islam was then [referring to 1947] in nobody's mind. The transcendental had not yet been lowered into a common place and the Holy Book; and Tradition had not been converted into a potent weapon of the politicians, though implicit in the demand had been the hope that Pakistan would provide a favourable ground for experimentation in Muslim social and political doctrines.[9]

Governor General Iskandar Mirza put it rather bluntly that religion and politics do not mix. President Ayub Khan adopted a more cautious line of harnessing those two elements to the chariot of his paternalistic rule and warned Muslims against being trapped by people who, in the garb of religion, were trying to achieve political power.[10] Two months later on 6 January 1964, he cracked down on the Jama'at-i-Islami, the orthodox fundamentalist party, declared it illegal and arrested its leaders, including Mawlana Mawdudi, on the ground of its carrying on "subversive activities against the state" and constituting "a danger to the public peace".[11] A writ petition challenging the government's action in declaring the party illegal was dismissed by the High Court. "An Islamic constitution", said Ayub on one occasion, "did not mean that the Pakistani nation should revert to backwardness. Islam is a progressive religion and a religion for all times and people".[12] On another occasion he remarked that if being a Muslim meant going back to the world of 1,300 years ago, then he was not for being a Muslim.[13]

The Muslim political leaders have evidently chosen to exercise much greater realism and circumspection in dealing with the religious forces in Pakistan than in the pre-partition India. And yet the complexities facing the Pakistani political elite stem from the fact that howsoever onerous the undertaking of building an Islamic society may prove to be, they cannot easily evade it. This is for several reasons. First, they are tied to their own commitments in the past and the inherent logic of the two-nation theory and the partition, as noted above. Secondly the recognition of inadmissibility of Islamic political ideals implies more than their own failure or the failure of the Pakistanis as a people to implement them. It may also be interpreted as Islamic ideals being "irrelevant or unequal to the task of contemporary living".[14] Thirdly, the failure of the modernisers would strengthen the position of the religious orthodoxy against the so-called "Westernisers". The spectre of the religionists acquiring political power haunted the political elite from the beginning and this has, in a very large measure, been responsible for the collapse of democratic experiments in Pakistan. Finally, Pakistan or for that matter no state, can live in a vacuum. Islamic or not, some ideology has got to be evolved to sustain Pakistan. The prospect for an ideological alternative to the Islamic has not so far appeared quite bright.

Modernisation in Pakistan has therefore tried carefully to adopt a practicable frame of reference in Islamic terms. For the modernisers did not take long to realise that the viability of Pakistan without some Islamic substance was as doubtful as that on the basis of Islam. To work out a harmonious relation between the demands of a modern state and those of a religion has been the despair of Pakistan since her emergence. The difficulty is further accentuated by a complete lack of consensus regarding the principles or ideals of the "Islamic state". There were possibly as many definitions as persons wishing to offer them. The Pakistani rulers preferred a liberal interpretation of Islam without any attempt at a clear analysis of the same. Central to this approach is the conviction that religion and science are not mutually exclusive. Opposed to the traditionalist view that it is not interpretations of Islam, but concepts of the contemporary world that must change, the modernists, believing in the innate consistency between the forces of modernity and the spirit of Islam, would like to make Islamic laws applicable to modern conditions. They urge a distinction between the "form" and "essence" of the religion to preserve the "abiding values" in Islam.[15]

This particular approach raises again more questions than it answers. How does one determine an abiding value in Islam? Who decides which are abiding values? Should it be individuals who are little learned in the Qur'an and *hadith,* or those who all their lives have been studying nothing else? Men of consequence in Pakistan have desperately and vainly sought to answer such questions since the country's inception, and in the process generated social and political tensions and turmoils of gigantic proportions to which the whole Pakistani history bears witness.

III

The early stage of Pakistan, dominated by the towering figures of Jinnah and Liaqat 'Ali Khan, witnessed great political support enjoyed by the leaders, whose primary preoccupations were to build the political and administrative framework of the new state. The question of the Islamic nature of the state could not have been brushed aside. Mawlana Shabbir Ahmad Usmani, the most distinguished of the Pakistani *ulama* and the founder of the Jam'iyat al-Ulama'-i Islam, and Mawlana Mawdudi, the fundamentalist orthodox founder of the Jama'at-i Islami pressed on the issue. Qu'aid-e-'Azam Jinnah set the general tone for the political leadership of Pakistan with the remarks: "I cannot understand why this feeling of nervousness that the future constitution of Pakistan is going to be in conflict with Shariat Law? There is one section of the people who keep on impressing everybody that the future constitution should be based on the Shariat. The other section deliberately want to create mischief and agitate that the Shariat Law must be scrapped."[16]

In March 1949 the Objective Resolution was moved in the Constituent Assembly by the Prime Minister Liaqat 'Ali Khan. It declared that "sovereignty over the entire universe belongs to God Almighty alone", but He had delegated this authority to the state of Pakistan and that this was to be exercised through its people "within the limits prescribed by Him." The resolution also stated that (a) "the state shall exercise its power and authority through the chosen representatives of the people", (b) "the principles of democracy, freedom, equality, tolerance and social justice, as enunciated by Islam, shall be fully observed" (c) "the Muslims shall be enabled to order their lives in accordance with the teachings and requirements of Islam as set out in the Holy Qur'an and the Sunnah."[17]

In February 1949 'Usmani demanded the appointment of a committee, consisting of eminent *ulama* and thinkers, to advise the Constituent Assembly on the requirements of an Islamic constitution.[18] This demand was met a few months later when the Constituent Assembly's Basic Principles Committee appointed a Board of *Talimat-i Islamiyya* (Islamic Teaching). It recommended that the Head of the State should be a Muslim, with ultimate power; that government should be run by en elite of pious Muslims chosen for their piety by the Muslim electorate; that the committee of *'ulama* should decide what legislation was repugnant to the injunctions of the Qur'an and the *Sunna* and was therefore invalid; that a Legislative Assembly, which they identified with the Islamic – in fact ancient Arabian – *shura*, or tribal consultative assembly, should be empowered to demand the resignation of the Head of the State in certain circumstances. Most of the Board's recommendations were turned down by the Basic Principles Committee of the Constituent Assembly, but they left a considerable imprint on Pakistan's first (1956) and second (1962) constitutions.

After Jinnah's death, Liaqat followed the same line under a slightly thicker Islamic veneer. This was reflected in the Interim Report of the Basic Principles Committee in 1950, which referred only nominally to the *shari'a'* provisions. A conference of the *ulama* was held in January 1951 at which they were to agree on a series of amendments to the Interim Report. At this conference the fundamentalist Mawdudi joined hands with the secretary of the Talimat Board to outline twenty-two principles which were adopted as the basis of an Islamic constitution.

The assassination of Liaqat in 1951 marked a significant alteration in the balance between political and religious forces in Pakistan. His successor, Khwaja Nazimuddin and the finance minister (later Prime minister) Chaudhri Muhammad 'Ali, both susceptible to religious influences, allowed the religionists to consolidate their position quite rapidly. Extra-religious issues like the possible form of the federal structure and the parity among the constituent state units contributed to the failure of the politicians. Muslim League was routed in the East Pakistan election of 1953. And the religious orthodoxy chose to throw its gauntlet at the government in the same year. This has reference to the fierce Punjab disturbance, in fact, a vast heresy hunt. Many thousands of citizens, with extremely wide support throughout the province, rioted murderously against the dissident sect of Ahmadis and against the government for not declaring these to be religiously and politically outside the pale. For the government the issue was more than one of law and order. It involved an interpretation of Islamic government – its attitudes towards denominational minority among Muslims. Before this the government had already betrayed its mind. Censorship, for instance, was imposed on a biography of 'Aishah, the Prophet's wife, because it was objectionable to the *Sunni*, although there was nothing in the book to which a *Shi'a* would object. Similarly, when Life magazine, in reply to a letter from a reader, published a small reproduction of a *Shi'a* painting of Muhammad, the offending picture was removed from every copy sold in Pakistan. The *Shi'as* were the minority, and where public order seemed to be threatened, were treated like a minority. The majority, now on the Ahmadi, issue, perhaps expected the same result. The government however refused to accede to their demands reiterating that the Ahmadis or any other sect could not be declared a minority community if it chose to call itself Muslim and that they could not and would not be removed from any key posts they held in the state. The ugly episode had been fully investigated and the results incorporated in an illuminating report popularly known as the Munir Report. The Report squarely faces the dilemma of the concept of an "Islamic state" in modern times. If it is an Islamic state as defined by the *ulama* or the fundamentalists, it cannot be democratic in the modern sense. Technically it cannot be sovereign either, if sovereignty is vested in God:

> Absolute restriction on the legislative power of a State is a restriction on the sovereignty of the people of that State and if the origin of this restriction lies elsewhere than in the will of the people, then to the extent of that restriction the sovereignty of the State and its people is necessarily taken away. [19]

In diagnosing the source of the malaise, the Report pointed at the Pakistani Muslim who found himself

> standing on the crossroads, wrapped in the mantle of the past and with the dead weight of centuries on his back, frustrated and bewildered and hesitant to turn one corner or the other. . . . It is this lack of bold and clear thinking, the inability to understand and take decisions which has brought about in Pakistan a confusion which will persist and repeatedly create situations of the kind we have been inquiring into until our leaders have a clear conception of the goal and of the means to reach it. [20]

The Report concludes:

> Opposing principles, if left to themselves, can only produce confusion and disorder, and the application of a neutralising agency to them can only produce a dead result. And as long as we rely on the hammer when a file is needed and press Islam into service to solve situations it was never intended to solve, frustration and disappointment must dog our steps. The sublime faith called Islam will live even if our leaders are not there to enforce it. It lives in the individual, in his soul and outlook, in all his relations with God and men, from the cradle to the grave, and our politicians should understand that if Divine commands cannot make or keep man a Musalman, their statutes will not. [21]

The second Constituent Assembly passed the first constitution of Pakistan in 1956. Except of some interesting verbal changes the Objective Resolution is repeated, substantially intact, as the preamble to the constitution of the Islamic Republic of Pakistan. There were two clauses containing Islamic provisions. Clause 204 envisaged the formation of an Institute of Islamic Research to "assist in the reconstruction of Muslim society on a truly Islamic basis", and the right of parliament to legislate for the collection of *zakat* (poor-tax) from Muslims. Clause 205 made the greatest concession, not only to the traditionalists but to the Mawdudi group as well, in reiterating that a commission would be appointed to see not merely that no legislation was passed which would be repugnant to the Qur'an and the *Sunna,* but also that all existing laws should be revised in their light. It is not surprising that this constitution received the qualified approval of Mawdudi. It, however, firmly held to the principle of complete equality between Muslims and non-Muslims, the only disqualification for the latter being that only a Muslim could be appointed Head of State.

The second Constituent Assembly and the First Constitution were swept away by the political anarchy, and the martial law was proclaimed. President Iskandar Mirza changed the name of the state by ordinance to the Republic of Pakistan, dropping the Islamic epithet. A few months later Mirza himself was replaced by General Ayub Khan whose attitudes towards the question of Islamic state have already been noted above.

Following a cautious policy with regard to modernity and Islam, the military regime of Ayub Khan addressed itself to a few significant undertakings including the usual one of a constitution. In its Preamble the new constitution retained the formula of the old, in acknowledging the sovereignty of Allah over the entire universe, but changed the rest of the formula to "the authority exercisable by the people . . . is a sacred trust". This subtle change was based on the implication that man in general, and not the Pakistani Muslim in particular, is God's vicegerent on earth. The new constitution also retained the name of the state as the "Republic of Pakistan", dropping the adjective "Islamic".

As a principle of legislation it laid down that "no law should be repugnant to Islam". The Part X of the constitution provided for two basic Islamic institutions to advise Islamic orientations in governmental law and policy. The first of these was an Advisory Council of Islamic Ideology, "to make recommendations to the Central Government and the Provincial Governments as to means of enabling and encouraging the Muslims of Pakistan to order their lives in all respects in accordance with the principles and concepts of Islam". The Islamic Research Institute was established in Karachi to assist "in the reconstruction of Muslim society on a truly Islamic basis" [Art.207 (2)]. By far the most significant clause affecting future legislation was the provision that the Advisory Council of Islamic Ideology would examine all laws in force immediately "with a view to bringing them into conformity with the teachings and requirements of Islam as set out in the Holy Qur'an and Sunnah". The capital of the Republic is stipulated as being

Islamabad, and a large mosque is to occupy the centre of the city. The President must always be a Muslim. Other provisions relate to the elimination of usury (*riba*), and discouragement of the consumption of alcohol.

The most forthright and enduring achievement of the Ayub regime is to reform the Muslim Family Law. The Muslim Family Laws Ordinance promulgated by him on 2 March 1961 was based upon the report of a seven-member commission created in August 1955 to consider whether the existing laws relating to marriage, divorce, and family maintenance were in keeping with Islamic injunctions concerning the status of women. The commission was composed of six individuals of definitely modernist views, and one religious scholar who published a lengthy dissent. In brief, the commission recommended that polygamy be thoroughly discouraged; that divorce procedures be tightened up and that the wife's right of divorce also be acknowledged; that all marriages and divorces should be registered; that adequate maintenance be assured for all wives; and that the legal age at which girls could be married be raised to sixteen years.

These recommendations were urged, according to the majority of the commission, because they were in the true spirit of Islam; most of them were incorporated in the Muslim Family Laws Ordinance. That law has, of course, been attacked by many of the *ulama* as thoroughly un-Islamic. The government prohibited the distribution of a pamphlet containing the *ulama's* views, and slowly began to enforce the law. After martial law was lifted early in 1963, a bill to repeal the Muslim Family Laws Ordinance was introduced in the national assembly – the orthodox elements had chosen this measure as one with which they could fight Ayub Khan. A standing committee of the National Assembly considered the bill to repeal the Family Laws and recommended that it not be passed. President Ayub Khan referred the matter to the Islamic Advisory Council. In the West Pakistan provincial assembly a resolution in favour of the repeal of the Muslim Family Laws Ordinance was easily passed; it was easier to vote for the resolution and please one's rural constituents, than to vote against it and risk one's political position, regardless of personal conviction, especially as it was only a resolution. The repeal bill came to a vote in the National Assembly on 26 November 1963, and, after twenty hours of debate, was defeated 56-28 – an emphatic declaration that whoever was controlling opinion in the legislature, it was not the *ulama*'. A month later the Fundamental Rights Bill, the first amendment to the 1962 Constitution, extending somewhat the role of the courts by making all of the Constitution's Principles of Law-making defensible in court, specifically excluded the Muslim Family Laws Ordinance from review – it thus remains the law of the land and cannot be challenged in any court.

The growing strength of political opposition against Ayub's government saw the reassertion of religious forces and slow tactical retreat of modernism in Pakistan. The allied opposition parties joined hands with the orthodox religionists like Mawdudi' and his Jama'at, while Ayub himself accepted the leadership of the Muslim League. The religious pressures within the Muslim League were reflected in the Constitution First Amendment Act (24 December 1963) that changed the name of the state back to the "Islamic Republic of Pakistan", and also in the declaration that not only all future legislation but also all existing laws should be brought in conformity with the Qur'an and the *Sunna*. The Advisory Council of Islamic Ideology recommended the revision of Anglo-Muhammadan Penal Code that whipping might be added to six types of punishments already prescribed. It also recommended the President to establish a Religious Affairs Authority to organise Islamic institutions, rituals and practices.

All this, however, could not stem the tide of political upsurge against Ayub. The replacement of Ayub by another militarist General Yahya and the kaleido-scopic developments since then, climaxed by the secession and independence of East Pakistan, renamed Bangladesh, served only to keep the fundamental issues involving Islam in the modernisation of Pakistan in a state of suspended anima-tion. For the time being the reality of Bangladesh and its political and economic repercussions on truncated Pakistan loomed large on Pakistan's horizon. In a state of political uncertainty the religious issue was only driven underground. It is just a question of time when Pakistan will again have to face this question with the renewed urgency and application, but surely with greater vision and clarity than so far revealed.

IV

With the creation of Pakistan the Pakistani Muslims could at least look forward to the fruits of their struggle. For the Indian Muslims, i.e. the Muslims of the non-Muslim majority areas in India whose massive adhesion to the Pakistan idea in the election of 1946 helped in no small measure bring Pakistan to existence, the very success of the Pakistan idea constituted a serious crisis of identity, emo-tional, intellectual and spiritual. This does not of course apply to the nationalist Muslims, who opposed to or held aloof from the Pakistan movement. But even those Muslims, who are broadly covered by the term "nationalist", do not make a homogeneous entity. Leaving aside the secular modernist elements, a significant proportion of them may be called nationalists only by default. The *ulama'* of Deoband were opposed not to the idea of an Islamic state in principle, but to the "Westernised" champions of Pakistan of whom they were totally distrustful. Be-sides, the separated Pakistan was, for them, a disavowal of their Islamic religious mission in India – a negation of their proselytising call.

The crisis in the Indian Muslim's position stems from the basic reality that a large number of them did not really make a political choice between India and Pakistan: compulsions of geography and socio-economic realities had forced the issue. The Indian Muslim was required to make emotional adjustments at rather sensitive levels. He was to learn to regard as foreigners those with whom he had deep emotional enmeshment, and live as a fellow-citizen with those for whom he had ever felt a social and emotional distance. It is the idea of Pakistan and the emotional participation of the Indian Muslim in that idea that largely contributed to the potentially disruptive ambivalences of the Muslim position in India.

Pakistani attitudes did everything to stimulate these tendencies. Formally, its official policy was forced by realities to recognise through the Delhi Pact or the Liaqat-Nehru Pact that Pakistan had no extra-territorial claim on the Muslims of India. Emotionally the claim persisted. Central to Pakistani attitude was non-recognition of the non-communal character of India. Pakistan tended not only to deride secularism [22] but also presumed and encouraged disloyalty in Indian Muslims. They derived occasionally a morbid psychological advantage from imagined repression of Muslims or other adverse news about them in India.[23] The cumulative result of the Indian Muslim ambivalence and the Pakistani presumption and encouragement was a persistent efflux of Indian Muslim leaders actual or potential to Pakistan. Numerous young Muslims graduating from the Indian universities continued to seek jobs in Pakistan rather than in India. Several prominent Muslim political leaders, in many cases even after having taken their oath of allegiance to the new country and having accepted positions of trust, later sought and found – or were offered and accepted – opportunities to cross over to Pakistan. Literary and even religious leaders, courted by the government, transferred themselves and their loyalty to Pakistan when more highly-paid prospects were proffered by that State. Perhaps the most damaging incident occurred when a Muslim brigadier in the Indian army, with access to secret information, in 1955 voluntarily retired and at once settled down in Pakistan, accepting a Pakistan-government post.[24] This tendency had not only created a feeling of desertion among the masses of the Indian Muslims, it continued also to falsify the position of those who remained, casting serious doubt on their reliability and loyalty. It undermined eventually the cause of Indian secularism by undoing the works of the Indian secularists, Hindu and Muslim, and strengthening the case of the Hindu communalists. The inability and/or reluctance of the Muslims in India to think of themselves as Indians and not as Pakistani expatriates had created a vicious circle of maladjustment and insecurity for the community, incapacitating them from making a creative response to the dynamics of a nascent secular state.

But the problems for the Indian Muslims of coming to grips with secularism are of a deeper and more complex nature. Between two alternative means of safeguarding minority interests, namely, protection of individual rights on the basis of common citizenship, or insulation of the whole group against all other, India adopted the individual approach by the rejection of the principle of communal representation in the legislatures in the form both of separate electorates and of reserved seats. Central to Islam, as noted in the beginning of this chapter, is the conviction that its purpose includes the structuring of a social community, the organisation of the Muslim group into a closed body based on Islamic Law

(*Sharia*). It is this central conception of Islam that is being finally challenged by Indian secularism. The Muslim mind in history operated only within the traditional categories of ruling or being ruled: in post-1947 India they confronted a radically new situation of living as equals with others in a country where the majority community also had much to learn about tolerance and equality. It raised the deepest issues of the significance of revelation, truth and interaction with the faith of other peoples which the Indian Muslims needed to reach out to need religious interpretations.

In the face of the demands of the situation confronting them, the Indian Muslim response shows two contrasting uneven trends: the one orthodox, revivalist and even obscurantist and the other secular modernist. The former was more persistent, popular and articulate than the latter. The orthodox approach in Islam in the Indian setting was mainly shaped by the *ulama*, belonging to various schools – the Indian branch of Mawdudi's Jama'at, Nadwat of Lucknow, Deoband, Jam'iyat al-'Ulama-i Hind and many other minor ones, such as Tabligh Jama'at, and Tamir-i Millat.

The problem of secularism occupies considerable space in the publications of these schools and associations. There is an early attempt to misrepresent secularism through mistranslation of the word to *ghayr mazhabi* or *la dini,* the first meaning anything contrary to religious commandments, the second irreligion or atheism. Secularism as such, as a western concept and also in its Indian context, came under fire. Javid Hasan[25] argues that the concept of separation of the state and religion is "foreign to Islamic ideology", while V.S. Ahmad Basha[26] considers that it undermines values which are considered basic elements in the social personality of a Muslim. According to S. Abdul Ghaffar,[27] it is "an irony of fate" that "the country which believes in spiritual values of life and the maintenance of her spiritual and cultural heritage should have chosen to call herself secular."

Nationalism also was subjected to scathing criticism. S.M. Yusuf[28] maintains that "never in the past was the ideal of Islamic Unity confronted with such a formidable ouster as nationalism." *Radiance*[29] urges Muslims not to consider themselves a minority but an "International Party charged with the responsibility of reforming mankind." In its anxiety to drive home the point, *Radiance* misquotes Dr. Johnson, "Patriotism is the last refuge of a scoundrel". "The dream of national integration could never be achieved in India," writes *Margdeep*,[30] "unless the whole country accepted the Islamic way of life...."

The reform of Muslim Family Laws proved to be the most explosive and intricate issue involving Islam and modernity in India as in Pakistan. The traditional Muslim Law highly discriminates against the Muslim woman in favour of the male in the matter of marriage and divorce. Art. 44 of the Indian Constitution vests the Indian Parliament with the responsibility of legislating a uniform civil code. In 1948 the Constituent Assembly rejected amendments proposed by Muslim members to exempt Muslim Personal Law from the operation of Article 44.

The task of codifying Hindu Personal Law was already achieved, but the Indian Government remained very cautious in approaching the question of Muslim Personal Law. In 1963 the matter was discussed in the Parliament, when the Muslim representatives raised a storm of protests. They took the position that the Muslim religious spokesmen would themselves take initiative in this matter. The then Law Minister, A. K. Sen, agreed not to take any government initiative and welcomed that from the 'ulama. A meeting of the Nadwat-al-'Ulama was called at Lucknow, and a general body was formed along with a sub-committee to submit recommendations to the general body. The sub-committee never did meet and the matter lay in cold storage. The Muslim reformist M.C. Chagla pointed out that the delay amounts to the withholding of part of Article 15 which seeks to abolish, amongst many other grounds, sex discrimination. The Parliament is also empowered to intervene and amend the law by virtue of Article 25. The government of India cannot force this reform down unwilling throats. The initiative must come from within the community itself. Until such time the Personal Law of the Indian Muslims will lag far behind their co-religionists elsewhere, not only in Turkey and Egypt, but in Pakistan as well.[31]

Sections of the Indian Muslim intelligentsia have been trying to weaken the stranglehold of the 'ulama and the obscurantists in the society by focussing on the liberal and secular tendencies in Islamic developments. Professor Habib, Prof. Mujeeb, Dr. Fyzee and S. Abid Husain are a few noted among them. In the seminar on secularism held at the Indian Law Institute, New Delhi, and those on Islamic Tradition and Modernity at Hyderabad and Bombay organised by the Indian Committee for Cultural Freedom in 1966 and 1967, wide range of modernist views concerning Indian Islam were propounded by Justice Beg, Dr. Jeb Rahman, Laeeq Futehally, Moin Shakir, S. E. Hassnain, Anwar Mowazzam, Alam Khundmiri, and Rashiduddin Khan. At the operative level Mr M.C. Chagla, Dr S. Jeelany and Hamid Dalwai rendered distinguished service. Dalwai spearheaded a campaign to raise the Muslim women to their constitutional position as equal citizens in the teeth of orthodox persecution and harassment. In 1964, he started with a tiny delegation of seven women. In 1966 the number reached thirty. The movement then gathered momentum. In April 1968, there were 300 women in Poona itself taking active part. In June 1967, 600 Muslim women of Ahmedabad held a meeting. "It is an unfortunate irony of fate," says Karandikar, "that in secular India headed by a lady Prime Minister, the Muslim women have to launch an agitation for securing the right of equality and protection against discrimination and oppression."[32]

V

Islam has, therefore, remained a seminal factor in the process of both Pakistan and India's coming to grips with modernity. In distinguishing between the pre-independence/partition phase of the Islamic encounter with modernity and its subsequent independent Pakistani phase and the Indian one is able to perceive not only the contrasting calls of Islam but their uneven achievements as well. In relative terms, Islam in the earlier phase appeared more effective and dynamic in terms of realising the avowed objectives of the community vis-a-vis the problems of the time. In the face of external threats – actual, potential and fictional – Islam was able to provide a focus and almost a consensus, however undefined or ill-defined, for the aroused community. The historical present seen as adverse and hostile to the realisation of communal ideals, was made to change and conform to the needs of the ideal. Having recast history, and secured themselves against external threats, the Muslims came to discover a total lack of a collective self-image. If history was viewed earlier as inimical to the ideal, now the ideal itself was found, in the experiences of Muslim modernisers, wanting. The orthodox and fundamentalist leaders had already had a new version of "inimical history", dominated by the secular ("irreligious"?) and Westernised modernists. History has almost come to a full cycle since the first contact of the subcontinent Muslims with modernity.

NOTES

1. Smith, W. Cantwell. *Islam in Modern History,* Princeton, 1957, p. 47

2. The history of the subcontinent throws up at least two clear instances of direct intervention by Muslim religious leaders to smother prospects of non-Muslim political hegemony. Cf. the rise of Raja Ganesh during the Ilyas Shahi period in Bengal in the 14th century and the role of the *Sufi* Shaikh Nur Qutb 'Alam in supplanting him; also, the great Muslim religious leader, Shah Wali Allah's letters, seeking outside intervention of the Afghan ruler against the steadily mounting threat of Maratha supremacy in Delhi in mid-18th century (Third Battle of Panipat, 1761).

3. Caudwell, C. *Studies in a Dying Culture,* London, 1938, pp. 27-8; also R. Pascal, *The Social Basis of German Reformation,* London, 1933, v.

4. See D. S. Franck, ed., *Islam in the Modern World,* Washington, 1951, *passim;* N. Richard Frye, ed., *Islam and the West,* 's-Gravenhage, 1957, *passim;* also Smith, op. cit., Ch. 2.

5. Sayeed, K. B. "Islam and National Integration of Pakistan" in D. E. Smith, *South Asian Politics and Religion,* Princeton, 1969, p. 405.

6. Poignantly illustrative of this confusion in the popular mind is the anecdote that Jinnah, the doyen of the "Westernised" Muslims in the Indian subcontinent, was greeted by the rural folks of Sind with "Long Live Mawlana Muhammad 'Ali Jinnah". Jinnah is said to have taken the trouble of making them able to distinguish between political and religious leadership. (H. Bolitho, *Jinnah, Creator of Pakistan,* London, 1954, p. 213)

7. *Constituent Assembly of Pakistan Debates,* Vol. V, no. 1, 7 March 1949, p. 2.

8. Ibid., Vol. 1, no. 2, 11 August 1947, p. 20.

9. "Days to Remember", *Pakistan Times,* 23 June 1964,

10. *Muslim News International,* Karachi, November 1963, p. 8.

11. *Pakistan Times*, 18 June 1964.

12. *Pakistan Observer,* 26 January 1960.

13. Abbott, F. *Islam and Pakistan,* New York, 1968, p. 197.

14. Smith, W.C. op. cit., p. 297.

15. Zahid Hussain, President of the Pakistan Economic Association, and Chairman of the Government Planning Board, maintained in an address to the Economic Association that the belief that Islam provided a complete code of conduct must rest on our ability to distinguish clearly between beliefs, traditions and institutions which are of abiding value from age to age and those that serve only ephemeral purposes and must change to meet changing conditions . . . Islamic institutions and traditions of abiding value must be preserved.' (Association meeting at Peshwar, 11 January1955; *Pakistan Standard,* 16 January 1955). Fazlur Rahman, the well-known Director of the Central Institute of Islamic Research established under the Constitution of 1962, noted: "The Muslim liberals on whose shoulders fell the main burden of framing an Islamic Constitution, rightly felt that Islam possessed an inherent ability to express itself in fresh forms consonant with the needs of the age. Islam, thus possesses inherently the capacity to reformulate its ideas in new forms." (Fazlur Rahman "An Islamic State", *Times*, London, 14 August 1963).

16 Dawn, Karachi, 26 January 1948.

17 *Constituent Assembly of Pakistan Debates,* 1949, Vol. V. op. cit.

18. Presidential Address at Dacca Conference, 1949, p. 52.

19. *Report of the Court of Inquiry constituted under Punjab Act 11 of 1954 to enquire into the Punjab Disturbances of 1953* (Munir report), Lahore, 1954, p. 210.

20. Ibid., p. 232.

21. Ibid.

22. It is a fairly standard sarcasm to use quotation marks in referring to 'secular' India. (Smith,W.C.. op. cit., pp. 270-71).

23. "In addition to genuine sympathy, there is a strand in Pakistan psychology not very far below the surface that does not want to hear well of Indo-Muslims."(Ibid., p.273.)

24. Ibid., p. 276.

25. *Radiance,* Delhi, 5 December 1965.

26. Ibid., 31 January 1965.

27. Ibid., 28 December 1965.

28. Ibid., 13 December 1964.

29. Ibid., July 1961.

30. Ibid., October 1962.

31. Smith, D.E. *India as a Secular State,* Princeton ,1963, pp. 422-3.

32. Karandikar, M.A. *Islam in India's Transition to Modernity,* Connecticut, 1969, pp. 381-2.

8. The Politics of Education
The British Raj and Bengal
Muslim Education, 1871–1884

IF EDUCATON IS, by its very nature, relevant to politics, education in British India was integral to the political development of the region. The impact of western education on the emergence and growth of nationalism in India had long been recognised.[1] Likewise, education proved a crucial factor in the formation and nourishment of the Indian Muslim ethnicity and eventual political separatism. And this, in general terms, is the subject of the present discourse in the context of Bengal[2] with particular reference to the bearings of the educational policies of the British Raj (Government) on the growth of Muslim separatist politics. Studies in the theory and practice of ethnicity, or the building of ethnic identity and nationalism, underline the potent role not only of elites as manipulators of cultural symbols in forging and fostering group consciousness but also of government with its immense power of political and economic patronage as determining the form and pace of politicisation of ethnic consciousness.[3] British policies vis-a-vis Muslim education and Muslim responses to them bear closely on these seminal issues concerning the growth of Bengal Muslim collective identity. This, however, is not to argue that Muslim separatism in Bengal owed its inception to these factors alone. These must be seen as forming a very substantial component of a complex of multi-causal explanations.

Bengal is a critical region for the purposes of this study. At about the beginning of this century, it comprised the largest number, nearly a half, of the Muslim population of undivided India.[4] More importantly, Bengal Muslims, the overwhelming majority of whom were local converts, belonging to the lower social strata of agricultural affiliations, developed a highly unorthodox tradition of syncretistic Islam which they adhered to for centuries until challenged by the Muslim fundamentalist and reformist movements in the nineteenth century.[5] It is important for the purpose of the central argument of this chapter to point out that the Muslim fundamentalist and reformist purificatory movements had much less effect on the actual beliefs and practices of the masses of Bengal Muslims than did the urban educated Muslim campaigns for political solidarity of the Muslim community. And in this political success of the Muslim educated class the issue of British attitudes and policies towards Muslim education figures prominently.

The close and long contact of the British with Bengal is the other dimension of the importance of this region. Although the British established commercial contacts with India at the beginning of the seventeenth century and set up strong commercial bases in Madras in 1640, Bombay in 1668, and Calcutta in 1690, their steady rise to political importance began in the wake of their victory against the ruler of Bengal at the battle of Plassey in 1757. By the Regulating Act of 1773 the presidencies of Madras and Bombay under their respective governors were brought under the control of the Bengal Presidency, the position of the governor of Bengal being elevated to that of a governor-general. Even after the delegation of the specific charge of the Bengal Presidency to a newly created position of lieutenant-governor of Bengal in 1854, Calcutta remained, until 1911, the metropolis of the British Government in India under the governor-general or the viceroy since 1858 when, after the suppression of the Mutiny, the British Crown assumed direct control of the Indian Government from the East India Company. Until the shifting of the British Indian capital to Delhi (1911), Calcutta remained the hub of British Indian Government and the nucleus for the formulation and execution of governmental policies in respect of all vital matters, including education.

It is not, therefore, difficult to see why the issue of the education of Bengal Muslims in the period of British rule should have drawn much contemporary attention and generated later academic interest. Since partition of 1947 no less than five Bengali Muslim scholars chose to devote attention to this issue. There are of course others, besides the Bengali Muslims who have inquired into this question.[6] In a subject riddled with controversy, the central issue relates to one of the most explosive myths in South Asian history, namely the alleged "Muslim backwardness" in education in consequence of their loss of political and economic power and patronage due to the British take-over and victimising policies. There is some truth and much untruth in arguments of this nature as well as in the assumptions underlying these arguments. But even more critical than the question of the historical validity of these contentions is the historical genesis of the theory of "Muslim backwardness"; for there is strong evidence to affirm that this particular theory was the product of a particular historical situation in the post-Mutiny (1857) period, in the formulation and articulation of which the British Raj seemed to have taken direct initiatives. More significantly, the assumptions underlying the theory were carefully deployed to devise and execute new British policies concerning Muslim education and other relevant matters with incalculable political consequences tor the future. The political impact of these new policies was further reinforced by a steady process of Muslim elite acceptance of and identification with the newly projected official image of Muslim economic and educational retardation. The emergence and the calculated assumption of the new "cinderella image" for the Indian Muslims provided their elites with, on one hand, a convenient political defence of their own "special" demands and of the treatment offered them by the British, and, on the other, a battle-cry for the political mobilisation of the Muslim masses. A closer examination of the origins and nature of the theory of Muslim economic and educational backwardness, the eager and calculated response of the British Government based on this assumption of backwardness, and the effects of the governmental measures on the nourishment of Muslim separatist forces should enable us to unravel the politics underlying the education of Bengal Muslims in the period chosen for this study.

The choice of the two dates defining the period under study needs some explanation. The year 1871 marks the symbiotic beginning of what seemed a significant reorientation of British policy in relation to Indian Muslims. The year saw a semi-official study in the problems of Indian Muslims by a leading British Indian civilian which seemed critically important in the context of the newly growing concerns of the British government with "Muslim backwardness". Those concerns, primarily relating to Muslim education and employment, found their first official formulation in the Viceroy Lord Mayo's Government of India Resolution of August 1871. The year 1884 saw the culmination of this formative and critical stage in the development of the new British policy on Muslim education and employment in that the Government of India pledged itself firmly to this new policy by accepting, in that year, the recommendations of the Education Commission of 1882 and by setting up the Public Service Commission.

The great uprising of 1857, better known as the Mutiny, marked a very significant change in British perceptions of the Indians and led to an understandable revaluation of the overall British position in India in strategic and political terms. For a while at least the political edifice of the Raj was shaken. The ground was recovered but complacency and confidence were irreparably damaged. The buoyant reformers, who had envisioned a regenerated India, sought to hide their wounded pride in the cold isolation of a policy of political and social conservatism. More than ever, India seemed a leviathan of confusing and irredeemable congeries of "caste, community and class". The safety and security of the Dominion were thought to depend very largely on recognising and balancing these innate and primordial social divisions held together by the power and patronage of the aristocracy and gentry – 'the natural leaders' of the land. After the dusts of the Mutiny settled and passions died down the British rulers moved quickly to restore and placate the landed gentry – the *taluqdars and zamindars* – so successfully that by the end of the century they became, in the words of Viceroy Lord Curzon, "the camp-followers of the British Raj".

The main thrusts of British attitudes and policies towards Muslims in the post-Mutiny period fitted into this broad political strategy of the Raj. The pronounced government concerns and preoccupations with "special" Muslim questions and problems was related to the policy of "balancing" the "communities". On the other hand, support and encouragement of Muslims in education and employment initially directed at their upper classes and elites, stemmed from the policy of cultivating the natural leaders.

In addition. more specific reasons might have contributed to these growing British concerns for Muslims. First, the Raj was becoming increasingly wary of the revival of the militant Islamic fundamentalist movement (the *Wahhabis*) in the late 1860s. This mass-based movement under the leadership of the Muslim theologians (ulama), which began in the 1820s and merged into the Mutiny, had declared India under the British an enemy territory (*dar-ul harb*) . The suppression of the Mutiny gave rise to an expectation among the rulers about the termination of the *Wahhabi* movement as well. To their great consternation the officials uncovered a widespread *Wahhabi conspiracy in the late sixties which led to the assassination of the British Chief Justice of the Calcutta High Court. Later, Viceroy Mayo was struck down by the dagger of an assassin who was suspected of Wahhabi* leanings. Large scale arrests were followed by protracted trials which clearly brought home to the Raj the uncomfortable truth that their policy in relation to a very large section of the Muslim community had proved counterproductive. The situation impressed on the government the urgency of looking for an alternative which, in the seventies took the form of winning over the upper classes with the hope of reconciling the disaffected Muslims to British rule through the mediation of their socially superior co-religionists. Secondly, Britain was fast emerging as an imperial power in the Middle East in the late nineteenth century. The steadily growing British involvement in the affairs of the Ottoman Empire of Turkey, the rising British power and influence in Cyprus, Egypt, Sudan and Aden, and the opening of the Suez Canal in 1869 created an enormous political and economic stake for the British Empire in the heartlands of Islam. The Indian Muslims, in the context of these extra Indian developments, came to acquire a far greater political significance than would have otherwise been possible. Finally, the newly awakened British interest in Indian Muslims corresponded closely to similar interest in British rule and English education which began to be reflected in the attitudes of a section of the upper class Indian Muslims. Nawab Abdul Latif and Syed Amir Ali in Bengal and Syed Ahmad Khan in the United Provinces became the Muslim high priests of this marriage between the upper class Muslims, anxious variously to recover or sustain or improve their dominant position, and their British rulers more than willing to win their support.

While the Viceroy Lord Mayo (1869-72) remained the primary agent for this new British policy, Sir William Hunter, a leading Bengal civilian with a great flair for writing, was to provide its form and rationale. At Mayo's instance

Hunter produced in June 1871, after only three weeks' effort, a treatise, originally given the clumsy but suggestive title *The Indian Musalmans. Are They Bound in Conscience to Rebel Against the Queen*?[7] This title was subsequently changed to *The Indian Musalmans*.[8] In a nutshell, Hunter made out a case for preferential treatment of Indian Muslims by the government inasmuch as he apportioned a very large share of responsibility for the Muslim economic and educational 'backwardness' on the transfer of power to the British and the results of subsequent British policies and measures. For the more specific question of educational backwardness Hunter found explanations partly in the economic impoverishment of the Muslim upper classes, resulting from the British rule, and partly in the government's careless introduction of an educational system which proved unsuited to the "special" requirements of Muslim education.

The Muslim upper classes, according to Hunter, were hit more directly and heavily by the imposition of British rule, especially by the policy of the anglicisation of the higher administrative services launched vigorously by the Governor-General Lord Cornwallis (1786-95) . Muslims, until then, held a virtual monopoly of the higher executive, judicial and revenue positions. British experiments with the land revenue administration such as the introduction of the system of Permanent Settlement in Bengal (1793), favoured the *nouveau riche* – the compradorial traders and merchants – who were mostly Hindus. The old landlords, both Muslim and Hindu, were gradually replaced by the new who were almost exclusively Hindu. Likewise, the British land resumption proceedings in the 1820s, whereby many landholders lost their lands to the government because of their failure to produce on demand valid documents and title deeds to their respective lands, deprived many Muslims of lands, previously granted by Muslim rulers and nobility or private. religious, or charitable purposes.

As a direct consequence of this "reversal" of the economic position of Muslims, and especially because of the upper classes' loss of political and economic power and patronage, the traditional system of Muslim education based on the financial support of these classes was gravely undermined. For the same reason of economic impoverishment, Muslims were unable to take advantage of the new education system based on payment of fees; they were also unable to raise sufficient funds to establish new schools on their own initiative, as Hindus had done on a significant scale under the grants-in-aid system adopted by the government on the 1854 recommendation of the Secretary of State Sir Charles Wood. Economics were not, however, the only determinant in Muslim educational retardation. The prevailing system of education under British rule, Hunter pointed out, was regrettably unsuited and insensitive to the special needs and ethos of Muslims. In particular Muslims were worried by the secular content of the English education and the Hindu stranglehold on the education system because of the predominance of Hindu teachers and Hindu personnel in the Education Department. Finally, the prevailing education arrangements disregarded the special linguistic needs of Muslim students who were under social and religious pressure to possess some knowledge of English, Arabic, Persian and Urdu, apart from their own vernacular, if it were not Urdu.

Hunter's thesis was, therefore, a strong plea for the assumption of responsibility on the part of the British government for the arrested economic and educational growth of Muslims which rendered them unable to avail themselves of the new opportunities of British rule, flowing from the acquisition of an English education. It was a natural extension of the logic of British responsibility for Hunter to urge the government to amend the wrongs done to Muslims. In effect, Hunter's recommendation was for the British to take Muslims under their protective wing, and offer them special considerations and facilities in the field of education and employment. In this, Hunter's objective was to see the development of

a rising generation of Muhammadans, no longer learned in their own narrow learning . . . but tinctured with the sober and genial knowledge of the West. At the same time they would have a sufficient acquaintance with their religious code to command the respect of their own community, while an English training would secure them an entry into the lucrative walks of life.[9]

The most significant aspect of Hunter's analysis is the importance he attached to the new "generation" of western-educated Muslims having "sufficient acquaintance" with their own religious tradition and, correspondingly, "the respect of their own community". The political calculations underlying this anxiety about a mixture of English and traditional Islamic learning are clear. The leaders of the new "generation" of western-educated Muslims, who were rooted in their own religious tradition and drawn from the propertied upper classes, were likely to be able to "segregate" the disaffected *Wahhabis*, largely drawn from the lower classes. Besides, the Islamic blend in their education and their social respectability should enable them to communicate in Islamic idioms with their wider community with a view to drawing them into a broad frame of collective Islamic identity and Muslim political community. Finally, these comfortable classes of western-educated Muslim leaders, with considerable standing in their own community and a stake in the British rule, were expected to be useful allies against any political challenge, such as the rapidly growing and politicised Western-educated Hindus.

With these serious pressures on British imperial policy, the policy of the British Raj in relation to Muslims took an astonishingly short time to crystallise and receive official investiture. On 30 May 1871, Hunter was asked by Viceroy Mayo to write the book; the completed manuscript was submitted on 29 June. On 26 June, three days before its submission, Mayo had already prepared a note, expressing concern about and interest in greater Muslim participation in government schools and colleges. He declared:

> there is no doubt that as regards the Mahomedan population, our present system of education is, to a great extent, a failure. We have not only failed to attract or attach the sympathies and confidence of a large and important section of the community, but we may even fear that we have caused positive disaffection.

He stressed the need to make government schools attractive to the Muslim upper classes and also to reform the Calcutta Madrasah, one of the major centres of traditional Islamic learning.[10] If Mayo, therefore, seemed familiar with Hunter's recommendations in the making, Hunter betrayed a prior knowledge of the official policy in incubation, for he curiously mentioned that "the Government has awakened to the necessity of really educating the Musalmans."[11] Before long, Mayo's note and Hunter's thesis received the highest and clearest official recognition under the Government of India Resolution of 7 August 1871. The Resolution touched on some of the basic aspects of the new policies on Muslim education. While urging attention to the "special" problems of Muslim education, it suggested an increase in the proportion of Muslims teachers and some means of adapting government schools and colleges to specific Muslim purposes, such as the introduction of classical and vernacular Muslim languages.[12] Mayo's successor, Lord Northbrook (1872-76), continued the policy of special provisions for Muslim education. The government of Bengal, in 1873, took measures to reform the Calcutta Madrasah and make financial arrangements for the foundation of three more madrasahs in the three Muslim majority districts in Bengal, namely, Rajshahi, Dacca and Chittagong. The special cause of Muslim education and employment received a strong stimulus in the 1880s from the setting up of the Education Commission (1882), the Public Service Commission (1884), and the Government of India Resolutions of 23 October 1884 and 15 July 1885. All of them unequivocally upheld the principle and policy of special provisions for the amelioration of Muslim position in education and government services. The Education Commission itself (significantly enough, chaired by William Hunter) confessed that its treatment of Muslims was marked 'not merely with a regard to justice but with a leaning towards generosity', while the Resolution of October 1884 spoke of the need for 'in some respects exceptional assistance' to Muslims. Among various measures the Education Commission recommended: the acceptance of Urdu in the primary and middle schools as the Muslim vernacular, though this was not the case with many Muslims beyond some parts of northern India; introduction of Persian in middle and high schools; special standards in Muslim primary schools; special incentives for higher education for Muslims through scholarships and other means; greater infusion of Muslims as inspector of schools and in other branches of the Education Department; and a special section on Muslim education in the annual reports of the Directorate of Public Instruction.[13]

The cumulative effect of the government policies and special measures relating to Muslims, based on the assumption of Muslim backwardness, was to deepen Muslim consciousness as a social and political community. In the later political integration of the heterogeneous and disparate Muslim social groups in the subcontinent, leading to the birth of separatist politics, Muslim elites found it critically important to project a self-image of destitution, deprivation and victimisation – an image that by virtue of Hunter's statistical half-truths and rhetorical penmanship appeared strikingly credible and touching. The Education Commission of 1884 had painted Muslims tragically as "fallen behind in the race of life under British rule."[14] It is of more than ordinary interest that the National Muhammadan Association of Calcutta, founded by Amir Ali in 1878 and the first major overtly political Muslim association in India, adopted, in its submission to the Education Commission, the Muslim image of Hunter's construction and practically reproduced the main arguments of his book. Since then Hunter's thesis has remained at the core of Muslim political discourses and dialogues and, more significantly, of a whole range of academic studies in the Muslim problems of modern South Asia undertaken mainly by Pakistani and Bangladeshi scholars. The determining influence of this all-pervasive view of "Muslim backwardness" on the formation of Muslim political personality calls for a critical examination of its historical validity in the light of recent investigations.

The theory of Muslim backwardness is part of a larger myth that until recently dominated perceptions of the community. Modern research has thoroughly disproved and demolished an uncritical assumption of homogeneity and evenness of development of the community throughout India.[15] This research has only confirmed the opposition voiced by some contemporary local British officials to the general assumption of Muslim backwardness. Economic, social and cultural divisions ran as deep among Muslims as among other religious communities in India, and consequently, the impact of the British rule was not as uniform on the various social groups which formed part of the Muslim community even within one region. "To state that Muslims were backward throughout India", says Seal, "is meaningless."[16] Most of Hunter's statistical material applied, in his own words, "only to Lower Bengal, the Provinces with which I am best acquainted" and in which "the Muhammadans have suffered most severely under British Rule".[17] The upper-class Muslims had indeed suffered more in Bengal than elsewhere because of the complete take-over of the higher echelons of government services, the land revenue arrangements and the replacement of Persian as the official language by English and vernacular Bengali.[18] On the other hand, comfortable Muslims of the Upper or North-Western Provinces (NWP), Awadh and Punjab, continued to hold social dominance throughout the nineteenth century. Despite being some 13 per cent of the North-Western Provinces and Awadh (later United Provinces or UP), Muslims formed about 25 per cent of the landholders and, despite rising Hindu competition, held 45 per cent of all the uncovenanted executive and judicial posts even in the 1880s. Except for some Hindu Bengali outsiders, most lawyers in Allahabad and Awadh were Muslims. In upper India the revenue settlements, the general overhaul of the administration, and the educational requirements for government office had been far less drastic; Urdu, their vernacular and medium of instruction, remained long in use for official purposes. [19]

Muslims throughout India obviously had not been engaged in rear-guard actions nor had they been trying to recover from the wounds of a lost battle. As with the other communities, some losses were suffered by some sections of the community in some regions, others continued to maintain their social pre-eminence, while still others turned British rule to their advantage – for example, the shipping magnates and business people of the coastal regions, especially of the western coasts, or the landed gentry (*taluqdars*) and government office-holders in the UP and Punjab. Throughout India however, education, along with land-control and patronage, formed a powerful determinant of social standing. Here again, and naturally, the upper Indian situation offers a stark contradiction to the theory of a pervasive backwardness of Indian Muslims in education. In upper India, the Muslim share in education was significantly larger, though there was far less western schooling than in the advanced coastal presidencies. Though Muslims were about 13 per cent of the population in NWP and Awadh, 18 per cent of those under instruction were Muslims in 1871, and Muslims made up 20 per cent of high and middle school students in 1881. In the growing competition for English education they proved themselves 'as alert as the Hindus', and there was no question of their being "prejudiced against State education". One Director of Public Instruction in Awadh found "Muslims were more ready to avail themselves of its benefits than the Hindus were", and as for Muslims being averse to English education, "whatever may be the case in Bengal or elsewhere. it is not so in Oudh". English schools there "flourished more easily in Muslim towns", and in Awadh itself "the political danger, if there is one, lies in there being too many educated Mahomedans to find employment in the public service".[20] Likewise, in 1881-82, Muslims in Madras and Bombay Presidencies, with 6.1 per cent and 10.9 per cent of the population respectively, formed 6.5 per cent and 1.7 per cent of the pupils in schools and colleges respectively. In the Bengal Presidency which comprised areas in addition to Bengal proper and contained 24 per cent of Muslims in its population, 28.6 per cent of its school and college pupils in 1881-82 were Muslims.[21] In absolute terms and in relation to their proportion of the population in those provinces Muslims did not display greater backwardness than many other communities. However, at the higher levels of English education the Muslim proportion seemed to fall off markedly almost everywhere. Only 5.5 per cent and 12.6 per cent of such pupils in Awadh and Punjab respectively were Muslims; though 45.1 per cent and 58.1 per cent respectively of those in the oriental colleges were Muslim. Between 1876 and 1886 there were altogether 3,219 Hindu B.A.s and M.A.s as against only 98 Muslim.[22] Even then, the Muslim proportion in Arts colleges went up from 9.3 per cent to 13.6 per cent between 1881-82 and 1885-86. The Education Commission was forced to concede that Muslim educational retardation, save in higher education, was exaggerated.[23] The governments of the NWP, Punjab, Central Provinces, Berar, Madras and Assam had already reported to the Government of India, recommending against 'special' measures to help Muslim education.[24]

Bengal, however, provided the historical kernel of the very potent and powerful myth of Muslim backwardness in India. It was not only in administration and the professions that Bengal Muslims found themselves squeezed out in the latter half of the nineteenth century. The cumulative effects of the Permanent Settlement and the Land Resumption Proceedings had already begun to edge them out of land as well, as Hunter so graphically detailed. By the later nineteenth century, the dissociation of Muslims with land was glaring, particularly in the preponderantly Muslim areas of the eastern districts. In Bakharganj, Muslims, about 65 per cent of the population, held a mere 10 per cent of the land and paid about 9 per cent of the land revenue. In Mymensingh, though they were 71 per cent of the population, Muslims were only 16 per cent of the landowners and paid 10 per cent of the land revenue.[25]

Land was not the only area of Muslim tribulations in Bengal. In the latter half of the nineteenth century, the Muslim share in the government services and in professions was not only highly disproportionate to their share in the population, but also showed a declining trend. The Muslim proportion in the whole range of government services in the Bengal Presidency was reduced from 11.7 per cent in 1867 to 6.8 per cent in 1887. Likewise their proportion decreased in the gazetted positions from 12 per cent in 1871 to 8 per cent in 1881. In 1886-87, there were only fifty-three Muslims, about one-twelfth of all Indians employed in the uncovenanted executive and judicial services.[26] Muslims remained underrepresented there, even in the Statutory Civil Service, recruitments to which were based on the principle of nomination rather than public examination. Eight years after its introduction in 1879, there were only 2 Muslims out of 11 appointees, while in the UP region the Muslim number was 5 out of 11. As against 46 Hindu, Bengal had only one Muslim subordinate judge in 1887.[27] The Muslim proportion of government servants was also rather low in Bombay and Madras, but Muslims in those regions were too few to have similar impact as in Bengal or in upper India. As in government services, so in professions, the Bengal Muslim position in the latter half of the nineteenth century registered a decline. Around the middle of the century, Bengal saw more Muslims in the legal profession than all others put together. Between 1852 and 1888 no Muslim was admitted to the rolls of the Calcutta High Court. Similarly, in 1869 no Muslim was to be found among the attorneys and solicitors in Calcutta. Bengal Muslim aspirants to administrative and professional positions were an endangered species. But why?

Neither the lack of Muslims in the administration and professions nor the explanations for this lack is a matter of historical dispute. The poor representation of Muslims in those fields was a mirror-image of their meagre share in higher English education in Bengal. An analysis of the educational background of government employees in the uncovenanted judicial and executive services in Bengal, in 1886-87, reveals that almost all of them went through some university examination, one-third of them having degrees.[28] The Muslim upper classes managed to withstand Cornwallis's policy of anglicising the higher administrative positions, because Persian continued to be used, particularly in the judicial and legal spheres. Muslims continued to dominate these areas, until, from the middle of the nineteenth century, English replaced Persian as the court language, and a knowledge of English became increasingly inseparable from administrative office. In 1837, Persian was replaced in Bengal by English and the vernacular Bengali for administrative purposes. The Council of Education introduced in 1844 a system of examination for government employment. From 1859 a sizeable proportion of uncovenanted executive and judicial positions was reserved for the English-educated. All law examinations from 1864 were to be conducted in English, and in 1866, it was decided that the holder of the degree of Bachelor of Law would alone be eligible for the position of a judge in the lowest court.[29]

Even in Bengal, Hunter's view of Muslim backwardness in education requires significant modification, inasmuch as the Muslim proportion in primary education was reasonably adequate. Of the primary students in the Muslim majority districts of northern and eastern Bengal, Rajshahi had 64 per cent Muslims, Dinajpur 63 per cent, Rangpur 63 per cent, Bogra 50 per cent and Pabna 44 per cent.[30]

The Muslim deficiency in English education in the latter half of the nineteenth century was revealing, especially as their proportion became less and less the higher up the education ladder they went. In the 1870s the proportion of Muslim pupils in government schools in the various districts of Bengal ranged between 6 and 12 per cent.[31] *The Report of the Director of Public Instruction (Bengal) for 1883-4* put Muslims as "barely 10 per cent" of college and "barely 5 per cent" of high school pupils.[32] The figures for the whole of Bengal Presidency confirmed the same trends in the higher education of Muslims. The middle vernacular schools had 13.2 per cent Muslim; middle English schools 12.3 per cent; high English schools 9.6 per cent, and arts colleges 4.6 per cent.[33] In 1870, of the two Muslim candidates for the B.A. examination in Calcutta neither passed, while of 151 Hindu candidates 56 passed. In the period between 1876-77 and 1885-86 only 51 Muslims and 1,338 Hindus were awarded the B.A. degree by the Calcutta University.[34]

Thus our evidence leaves no room for doubt about the three major developments in the latter half of the nineteenth century: (a) weak Muslim representation in administration and the professions, (b) the paucity of Muslims in higher English education, and (c) the causal connection between these two developments. However, it is not clear why Bengal Muslims did not resort to English education. In fact, there is a wide range of divergent and even contradictory opinions – both present and contemporary, Muslim and non Muslim – which are often no more than speculations born of ignorance or assumptions born of prejudice and preconceived notions. Rev. J. Long, for example, seriously doubted the "aptitude" of Bengal Muslims for such education, and urged special help for them.[35] On the other hand Phillip Hartog, the first Vice-Chancellor of the Dacca University founded in 1920, took care to differentiate between the "educational" backwardness and "intellectual" competence of the same people.[36] The Education Commission of 1882, which received representations from various groups and individuals, including Muslims, mentioned Muslims having "debated even among themselves" to "account for the scant appreciation which an English education has received at their hands". The Commission itself had indulged in its own speculation or prejudice: "a candid Muhammadan would probably admit that the most powerful factors are to be found in pride of race, a memory of bygone superiority, religious fears, and a not unnatural attachment to the learning of Islam".[37]

Hunter, as we have already noted, had set the lines of subsequent inquiries, both polemical and academic, in terms of Muslim economic destitution, their special religious-cultural demands on education, and the insensitivity of the British education system, which was dominated by Hindus, to the Muslim problems. Hunter's approach was a complex of religious and secular explanations. Later writers tended to offer a mixture of the religious and the secular, or to reject one in favour of the other. Those who followed the latter course often made themselves vulnerable to self-contradictions. The Education Committee under the chairmanship of Phillip Hartog, for instance, sought to shift emphasis totally from religious to secular reasons. It attached decisive influence to secular factors such as the "sudden suppression of Persian in 1837" and "the rapid development of English education in the earlier years of the nineteenth century", when Muslims were neither prepared for nor in need of English education. However, the Committee compromised its secular stance with remarks of the following nature: "For many years the Mahomedans were suspicious of purely secular and English education, and in consequence, were very slow to make use of the new system of higher education."[38] In a very similar fashion M. Fazlur Rahman, in his study of Bengal Muslim education, rejects the notion of "Muslim hostility or prejudice against English education as such", but supports the view that "the Muslim in Bengal, as in other parts of India, could not easily co-operate with a system which was secular, as the new English education professed to be".[39]

How is one to resolve this problem? To begin with, it is necessary to be aware of serious methodological shortcomings shared by most of these writers and observers. A source of much confusion, misconception and inaccuracy is their tendency to seek answers in terms of highly abstract and normative religious categories, regardless of the socially meaningful and functional units constituting each of these categories. It is both futile and meaningless to search for clear cut Hindu or Muslim attitudes or responses to education – cliches such as the "Hindu acceptance" and the "Muslim rejection" of English education are inadequate for academic purposes. There is no dearth of evidence in Bengal and Bihar, as elsewhere, that sections of Hindus, including Brahmans, rejected and opposed English education.[40] Also, the yawning gulf between the English-educated Hindus and Muslims was not really a Hindu-Muslim issue. The English education among Hindu Bengalis was a virtual monopoly of the *bhadralok* , a small socially comfortable, respectable and dominant elite, drawn primarily from government servants, professionals and rent-receivers, and belonging to the three uppermost Bengali castes – Brahmans, Baidyas and Kayasthas. In 1883-84, a mere 9.4 per cent of the Bengali Hindus, the *bhadralok* , formed 34.5 per cent of the pupils in the lower primary schools in the Bengal Presidency, 42.2 per cent of the upper primary schools, 56.8 per cent of the middle Bengali schools, 67.3 per cent of the middle English schools, 73.4 per cent of the higher English schools, and 84.7 per cent of the colleges. Only 7 per cent of the college students and 13 per cent of high school boys had a background of trade, while 1 per cent of the college and 6 per cent of the high school pupils came from the peasantry.[41] These statistics, when related to another crucial demographic feature of Bengal Muslim life – the large proportion of Muslims who subsisted on agriculture and the paucity of occupations not connected with agriculture[42] – emphasise the fallacy of generalisations under religious labels.

The social configurations of the land had significant bearing on education. Bengal Muslims were broadly divided into a relatively small number of *ashraf* (literally, "high-born") upper class and the vast masses of *atraf* (literally, "commoners" or "rabbles"). The educational conditions and problems for these two distinct social orders were different. For the vast masses of indigent Muslim agriculturists in Bengal, the demands and conditions for education could not have been any different from those of their non-Muslim counterparts. The small share in education of members of this social class, Muslim or Hindu or whatever, was symbiotically related to their depressed social conditions. This was clearly revealed in the observation made by River Thomson, the Lieutenant-Governor of Bengal, on the report of the Director of Public Instruction in Bengal, 1883-84:

a low educational percentage of the Muhammadans is confined to those districts where they occupy a low place in the social scale, and the conditions are reversed in those parts of the country where they are comparatively well off, the facts seem to support the condition that the traditional explanation is incorrect and that it is the comparative poverty of Muhammadans rather than any special prejudices of theirs which accounts for their apparent neglect of the facilities for higher education which the existing system offers.[43]

The question was more complex than simple poverty. William Adam, in his valuable survey of the state of education in some Bengal districts in the 18308, noted that most Muslims belonged to "the humblest grade of the native society . . . who were regarded by Hindus as well as by others, both in respect of condition and capacity as quite beyond the reach of the simplest forms of literary attainments".[44]

On the other hand, the *ashraf*, by virtue of their foreign Middle Eastern ancestry, either real or fictitious, as well as their control of land and administration in the pre-British period, were socially dominant and culturally differentiated from the masses of Bengal Muslims – they spoke Persian and Urdu and held in utter contempt the vernacular Bengali of the *atraf converted masses and of the local Hindus. The lack of a substantial middle class among Bengal Muslims till the end of the nineteenth century has been a historically significant feature of their social composition. The Hindu bhadralok resembled the Muslim ashraf in* many important respects, and even shared with them the control of land and administration in pre-British times. While discussing the ruinous effects of the British rule and policies on the *ashraf,* one must not lose sight of the fact that the Hindu upper class enjoyed a fair share of the land and the administration, especially in the areas of revenue and finance, even under the Muslim rulers in Bengal. In the first half of the eighteenth century, two Muslim rulers, Nawab Murshid Quli Khan (1700-27) and Nawab Alivardi Khan (1740-56), were known to have preferred Hindus as revenue officials (amins and qanungos) and landholders (zamindars). Nine-tenths of the landholders were known to have been Hindus in this period and of the fifteen largest estates only two were held by Muslims. In the positions pertaining to the management of estates in the Muslim-majority areas of eastern Bengal, the Muslim share was calculated to be no more than 10 per cent. As late as 1774 the land revenue department in the Muslim majority district of Chittagong had only ten Muslim out of a total of thirty-nine officials.[45] The British rule did indeed strengthen and enlarge *bhadralok* holds in the land and administration, but did not originate them. The Bengal *ashraf* control in the administration and the professions undoubtedly suffered because of the British decision to dispense with Persian.

The *bhadralok* were also likely to have been caught in the same situation, for the seekers of the administrative positions among them attended Persian schools in large numbers during the Muslim rule.[46] That the same fate did not overtake them was because of the two advantages they possessed over their *ashraf* counterparts. First, the *bhadralok*, not having the *ashraf*'s large religious-cultural stake in the Persian language and literature, switched over to English far more easily. Second, not having the ashraf's contempt for the Bengali language, they were in a better position to take advantage of the growing importance of the Bengali vernacular in the changing educational and administrative arrangements. Thus their vernacular Urdu enabled the Upper-Indian ashraf to maintain their position in administration and education for much longer.

In Bengal, the *ashraf concerns with English education largely coincided with the elimination of Persian from the middle of the nineteenth century. Until then their* adherence to traditional education ensured their livelihood and saved their spirits and souls. There had been two distinct expectations of traditional education for Muslims, and two corresponding educated classes. Abdul Latif, an English-educated Bengal *ashraf,* called one of them "the learned class" and the other "the worldly class".[47] The former sought only religious vocations and traditional learning with an emphasis on Arabic knowledge; the latter, in traditional settings, needed more Persian for secular offices. For the learned class, English was as useless as Arabic and Persian for aspirants to secular offices under the British. While religious concerns are significant for the "learned class", they were less likely to motivate the "worldly class". This might perhaps explain the trickle of Bengal Muslims to English schools, even those run by the Christian missionaries, in the earlier years of the nineteenth century.[48] And it might also explain why the introduction of optional English for the Arabic students in the Calcutta Madrasah, in 1829, proved abortive, whereas the Anglo-Persian Department, established in the Madrasah in 1854, became a great success.

According to the *Report of the Council of Education, 1852-55,* there was "a growing desire for sound English education" among "the higher and more respectable classes of the Muhammedan community in Bengal".[49] Also, in the opinion of W.N. Lees, Principal of the Calcutta Madrasah, "the English language is plainly seen to be slowly but surely extending its inevitable sway over an increasing number of Mahommedan minds".[50] By 1874-5, the urge for English education had penetrated students of the *madrasahs.* Some students of the Calcutta, Rajshahi and Dacca Madrasahs were inclined towards the English language.[51] In 1881, Syed Amir Hossein, Member of the Bengal Legislative Council, went to the extent of urging the government to close the district *madrasahs except the two in Calcutta and Dacca, and advocated the pruning of the Arabic syllabi in those two institutions to accommodate English. A. Croft, the Director of Public Instruction, rejected his proposals on the ground that he "underrates the desire of Muhammedans, especially in the Eastern districts, for a purely oriental education".*[52] Demands for reorganisation of the *madrasah* system, particularly by converting the Calcutta Madrasah into a college, had been steadily growing. In 1868, Abdul Latif suggested the elevation of the Anglo-Persian Department of the Madrasah to the status of a college.[53] Amir Hossein's set of proposals also incorporated the demand for a Muslim college. Syed Ahmad

Khan, as a Muslim member of the Education Commission of 1882, strongly argued that "the Arabic Department should be abolished" and "the system of English education should be continued".[54] His recommendation was not upheld by the Commission, and the subsequent Government of India Resolution went no further than to raise the Madrasah to the level of a second grade college, offering only a First Arts degree.[55]

The gradual erosion of demands for Persian education among Bengal Muslims, seeking opportunities in the administration and professions, marked the beginning of a steadily growing demand for English education among them. Yet the British Raj was slow to make a response and seemed to show greater concern than did many Muslims to cater for the religious content in the Bengal Muslim's modern education. The political exigencies of late nineteenth-century India led the Raj to prefer an English-educated Muslim, who could be politically mobilised through a collective Islamic identity, to a secularised modern-educated individual who was unresponsive to political calls gilded with religious and cultural symbols. It was mutually beneficial for most of the English-educated Muslims convinced themselves of their need and right for "special" treatment and facilities and for the government which was willing to provide them.

NOTES

1. B .T. McCully, *English Education and the Origins of Indian Nationalism*, New York, 1940, throughout.

2. 'Bengal' here has reference to what, in official parlance, was Bengal Proper, the Bengali-speaking region of the much larger administrative entity of the Bengal Presidency. The area covered in this study generally corresponds to present Bangladesh and the Indian state of West Bengal.

3. See Paul R Brass, 'Ethnicity and nationality formation', *Ethnicity*, vol.3, 1976, pp 225-41; also his 'Ethnic communities in the modern state' in P Gaeffke and D A Utz (eds), *Identity and Divisions in Cults and Sects in South Asia*, Philadelphia, 1984, pp 10-20; D Taylor and M. Yapp (eds), *Political Identity in South Asia*, London, 1979.

4. On the eve of the Partition of India there were 35 million Muslims in Bengal as against 95 million in the whole of India. Currently, the Bengali-speaking Muslims, numbering well over 100 million distributed over Bangladesh and India, constitute the largest ethnic Muslim community in the world after Indonesia.

5. For the background and the contents of the Islamic syncretistic tradition in Bengal, see Asim Roy, *The Islamic Syncretistic Tradition in Bengal*, Princeton, 1983; also his 'The social factors in the making of Bengali Islam', *South Asia*, no. 3, 1973, pp.23-35. For the Islamic revivalist movements in Bengal and their effects upon the Muslim society and politics, see Rafiuddin Ahmed, *The Bengal Muslims 1871-1906*, Delhi, 1981; and his 'Islamisation in nineteenth century Bengal' in Gopal Krishna (ed.), *Contributions to South Asian Studies 1*, Delhi, 1979, pp.88 120. Also, Muinuddin A. Khan, *History of the Faraidi Movement in Bengal, 1818-1906*, Karachi, 1965; and his 'Research in the Islamic revivalism of the nineteenth century and its effects on the Muslim community of Bengal' in Pierre Bessaignet (ed.), *Social Research in East Pakistan*, Dacca, 1964, pp.38 65.

6. M. Fazlur Rahman, *The Bengali Muslims* and *English Education (1 765-1835)*, Dacca, 1973; Azizur Rahman Mallick, *British Policy and Muslims* in *Bengal 1757-1856*, Dacca, 1977; Lateefa Khatun, Some aspects of the social history of Bengal with special reference to the Muslims, 1854-1884, M.A. thesis, University of London, 1955; Sufia Ahmed, *Muslim Community in Bengal 1884-1912*, Dacca, 1974. A major study in some relevant problems is Aparna Basu, *The Growth of Education and Political Development in India, 1898-1920*, Delhi, 1974.

7. London, 1871.

8. Second edn, London, 1872. See F.H. Skrine, *Life of Sir William Wilson Hunter*, London, 1901, p.I99; Anil Seal, *The Emergence of Indian Nationalism*, Cambridge, 1968, pp. 306-7; Peter Hardy, *The Muslims of British India*, Cambridge, 1972, pp. 85ff.

9. Hunter, p. 209.

10 . Note by Lord Mayo dated 26 June 1871, Mayo papers, Education 12/V; Hardy, pp. 85, 90.

11. Hunter, p.204.

12. Correspondence on the subject of the education of the Muhammadan community in British India and their employment in the public service generally, *Selections from the Records of the Government of India*, no. 205, Home Department serial no.2, Calcutta, 1886, part 3, p.I52 (*Education Selections (1886)*).

13. *Report of the Education Commission (1882) (REC)*, Government of India Secretariat (G.L Secretariat), Calcutta, 1884, pp.505-7.

14. *REC*, p.6.

15. Seal, pp.300ff; Hardy, pp.117ff; Francis Robinson, *Separatism among Indian Muslims: the Politics of the United Provinces' Muslims 1860-1923*, Cambridge, I974, throughout.

16. Seal, p.300. Also, 'the Muslims were by no means a subordinate community everywhere in India . . . their status in a locality depended on the land, patronage and education they continued to enjoy. In some places they enjoyed a good deal . . . indeed, over the whole country, it would be as hard to find a generally accepted ranking of religious communities as it would be to find a generally accepted ranking of Hindu castes'.

17. Hunter, p.I49.

18. Seal, pp.302-3.

19. Cf. 'In the North-Western Provinces we have a complete reversal of the state of things in Bengal . There the Muhammadans are vastly outnumbered by the Hindus; but, inasmuch the unlettered multitudes are mainly Hindu, while the Muhammadans as a class belong to the middle and higher strata, the latter possess much more than the share of Government employment which their numbers would give them, and are comparatively a thriving a energetic element in society.' C.J.Lyall, Note, 24 September 1882, *Education* Selection (1886), p. 337.

20. *Report of the Director of Public Instruction*, Oudh, I875, pp. 7-10, quoted in Seal, p.306.

21. REC, p.484.

22. *Report of the Public Service Commission 1886-87 (RPSC)*, Calcutta, 1888, appendix M, pp.78-9.

23. REC, pp. 494ff.

24. A. Croft, *Review of Education* in *India* in *1886, with special reference to the Report of the Education Commission*, Calcutta, 1888, pp. 318,322.

25. Hunter, p. I77; also William Hunter, *A Statistical Account of Bengal*, London, 1875-57, vol.5, pp.I94,214,226,458,465.

26. *Proceedings*, A, Home Department (Establishment), Government of India, June 1904,

no.103, pp.l31-2; Hunter, p.l61; *Education Selections (1886)*, p.240.

27. RPSC, 1888, p.38; *Proceedings of the Public Service Commission*, Calcutta, 1887, vol.6, p.43.

28. RPSC, pp.34-41; see Seal, table 38, p.118.

29. Khatoon, pp. 180-201; Seal, p.302.

30. *General Report on Public Instruction in Bengal (GRPIB), (1874-5)*, Calcutta, 1876, p.100.

31. GRPIB(1872-3), p.219, 228-29; GRPIB(1873-4), pp.32,63,65-6; *Education Selections (I886)*, p.l80.

32. GRPIB (1883-4), p.l45.

33. GRPIB (1883-4), p.l49.

34 RPSC, appendix M, pp.78-79.

35. Rev. J. Long, 'The social condition of the Muhammedans of Bengal and the remedies', *Transactions of the Bengal Social Science Association*, nos 1-2,1868, p.62.

36. Phillip Hartog, *Some Aspects of Indian Education Past and Present*, London, pp.51-52.

37. REC, p.483.

38. *Interim Report of the Indian Statutory Commission (Hartog Report)*, London, 1929, p.209.

39. Fazlur Rahman, pp.ii and 10.

40. Mallick, pp.310-11; Pradip Sinha, *Nineteenth Century Bengal: Aspects of social history*, Calcutta, 1965, pp.37ff.

41. GRPIB (1883-4), pp.10-11 and General Statistics, p.xii; also J.A. Bourdillon, *Report of the Census of Bengal, 1881*, Calcutta, 1883, vol.l, p.l43 and vol.2, pp.240-49.

42. E.A. Gait, *Report* [on Bengal], *Census of India, 1901*, vol.6, part 1, Calcutta, 1902, p.484; Asim Roy, *Islamic Syncretistic Tradition in Bengal*, pp.19ff; also his 'Social factors in the making of Bengali Islam', throughout.

43. GRPIB (1884-85), p.l8.

44. William Adam, *The Second Report on the State of Education of Bengal*, Calcutta, 1836, p.33.

45. Narendra K. Sinha, *The Economic History of Bengal; from Plassey to the permanent settlement*, Calcutta, 1956, vol.l.

46. William Adam, *The Third Report of the State of Education of Bengal*, Calcutta, 1938, pp.63-76.

47. Abdul Latif, A *Minute on the Hooghly Madrasah*, Calcutta, 1861.

48. Fazlur Rahman, pp. 43, 45-6, 54-55.

49. Quoted Khatoon, p. 83.

50. GRPIB (l857-8), p. l2.

51. GRPIB (1874-5); also GRPIB (1875-6); Khatoon, p.112.

52. *The Bengal Educational Proceedings*, Calcutta, 1881, no.l78.

53. Abdul Latif, 'Mahommedan education in Bengal', *Transactions of the Bengal Social Science Association*, 1868, parts 1-2, pp.61ff.

54. Quoted in Khatoon, p.116.

55. *Resolution of the Government of Bengal, 22 January 1884*, General Department, Education; GRPIB (l883-84).

9. The High Politics of India's Partition
The Revisionist Perspective

A REAL NEED for revaluation of the high politics of India's partition has been boldly underscored by some recent developments. One of these is the most valuable revisionist contribution of Ayesha Jalal of the University of Cambridge.[1] Whether or not the centenary years for the Indian National Congress [henceforth the Congress] witnessed any significant publications on the Congress politics, two major studies in the politics of the All-India Muslim League [henceforth the League], its 'Great Leader' (*Quaid-i Azam*), Muhammad Ali Jinnah, and the partition have come down to us in quick succession: 1984 saw the publication of Stanley Wolpert's *Jinnah of Pakistan*, [2] and the following year received Ayesha Jalal's, as mentioned above. The importance of these studies does not merely consist in the wide polarity of their approaches and views. Much greater significance is attached to the fact that their sharp difference underlines a strong and long-felt need for questioning some of the great old assumptions and myths enshrined in the orthodox historiography of British India' partition, as discussed below.

February 1988 saw the beginning of a series of developments, focusing on the politics of partition, which stemmed om the much expected disclosure of the thirty pages of Maulana Abul Kalam Azad's book,[3] left sealed for thirty years, and due to be released at the time. The delayed public disclosure of the material in early November 1988, due to some legal tangle, fuelled public curiosity and speculations about the politics of partition.[4] The contents of the excised portion, though it appeared disappointing to some for not making startling revelations,[5] deviate vitally from the book at least in one major respect. In this section, the release of which almost coincides with the birth centenary of Jawaharlal Nehru, Azad points his finger in a much more determined manner at the former's responsibility for the partition. He claims to have initiated the move for Nehru's succession as the Congress president in 1946, and regrets his decision as a 'blunder' of 'himalayan' proportion. He writes:

> I can never forgive myself when I think that if I had not committed these mistakes the history of the last lo years would have been different . . . I warned Jawaharlal that history would never forgive us if we agreed to Partition. The verdict would be that India was not divided by the Muslim League but by the Congress.[6]

These are indeed strong words, and may even seem bizarre to the multitude who have been brought up with the traditional assumptions about the partition. This brings us to what recent historical research clearly reveals as long-cherished myths of India's partition.

I

The polarity between the historical theses of Wolpert and Jalal as well as Azad's contentions touch respectively on the twin partition myths locked in a symbiotic relationship: 'the League for partition' and 'the Congress for unity'. The traditional understanding of the political process leading to partition has remained strongly rooted in these two 'unquestionable' popular assumptions, reinforced by a long and powerful tradition of academic sanctification. It would be most surprising not to find a great majority of people, having a basic familiarity with the major developments preceding the Indian partition, identifying the Lahore Resolution of the League (March 1940) with the demand for Pakistan and partition, and regarding 14 August 1947 as its logical culmination.[7] Likewise, the Indian nationalist component of this historiographical orthodoxy has been content to project partition as the tragic finale of a heroic struggle of the Indian patriots against the sinister Machiavellian forces out to destroy the sacred Indian unity. Like all myths one may find a modicum of truth to defend more moderate versions of such perceptions. But, with greater accession to our knowledge in recent times and accentuation of clarity to our perceptions on modern politics in India, such positions have become totally indefensible.[8] The traditional perspective seems desperately remiss in not conveying not merely the true nature of the high drama but also its nuances, subtleties and intricacies. This flat and linear perspective is astonishingly indifferent to or ignorant of the undercurrents as much in the League as in Congress high politics during the critical decade before partition. As early as December 1938, while moving the tenth resolution at the twenty sixth League session in Patna, repudiating the federal scheme under the Government of India Act of 1935 and investing Jinnah with the supreme authority 'to adopt such a course as may be necessary with a view to exploring the possibility of a suitable alternative which would safeguard the interests of the Mussalmans',

Maulana Zafar Ali Khan spoke about the League's 'antagonism' not 'towards the Hindus generally, but against the Congress High Command', foreshadowed the ensuing struggle between the two parties as a gigantic 'battle of wits', and expressed his concern to see 'who emerged victorious from the contest'.[9] The revisionist perspective offers a much clearer and more logical and convincing interpretation of this 'battle' between Jinnah and the Congress in which both openly stood for what they did not want, said what they did not mean, and what they truly wanted was not stated publicly but only betrayed in their vital and purposive political decisions and actions. The long persistence of orthodox beliefs in these matters has clearly been in accord with the most commonly perceived interconnections among Muslim 'nationalism', 'separatism', the Muslim League, the Lahore Resolution and partition. But 'the conspiracy of silence' resorted to both by Jinnah and the Congress in regard to the real motives underlying their respective political strategies and tactics must also be seen as largely contributing to the perpetuation of these traditional myth. The acceptance of the emerging historical truth makes a huge demand on everyone grown up with the old verity in as much as the new is totally opposed to what has so far been largely given to the world, namely, that it was not the League but the Congress who chose, at the end of the day, to run a knife across Mother India's body.

II

Jalal has initiated the much needed task of historical reconstruction by taking upon herself the challenge of demolishing the first of the twin myths which concerns Jinnah and the League's actual role in the making of Pakistan. It seems a remarkable coincidence that Wolpert's precedes Jalal's and provides a perfect foil, in its orthodoxy, to set off the critical significance of Jalal's valuable revisionist contribution which deserves a very special place in the corpus of the modern South Asian historiography on the partition of India. The academic popularity of this orthodox historiography is clearly attested by the fact that Wolpert is both preceded and followed, within the short span of a decade, by some powerful advocates of the conventional position, such as U. Kaura (1977),[10] R.J. Moore (1983),[11] and A. I. Singh (1987),[12] leaving as idea host of scholars supportive of this position but whose involvements with this issue are peripheral.

Where does one draw the line between the conventional and the revisionist positions on the issue of Pakistan and partition in relation to Jinnah and the League? On both chronological and thematic grounds the Lahore Resolution of 1940 clearly emerges as the divide between the two distinct interpretative approaches. Until then no sharp differences and disagreements seem to figure very prominently in the orthodox and revisionist analyses of Muslim politics between the two world wars. In the orthodox view, the resolution adopted at the Annual Session of the League at Lahore on 24 March 1949 was the first official pronouncement of the 'Pakistan' or 'partition' demand by the party. Though the term 'Pakistan' is nowhere to be found in the resolution, it is, nonetheless, seen to have provided for the separation of the Muslim majority areas in the north-western and eastern zones of India as 'sovereign' and 'independent states', and thereby formed the basis the 'Pakistan demand'. Along with this perceived reformulation of the League's political objectives, there is also, intrinsic to this view, an equally significant assumption of a major turn and break in Jinnah's political development: the Islamisation of the 'nationalist' and 'secular' Jinnah – 'the ambassador of Hindu-Muslim unity' emerging as the most potent and dynamic influence in partitioning British India on religious ground. Both these assumptions are challenged in the revisionist analyses: the Lahore Resolution was not meant to be the 'Pakistan demand' but a 'tactical move' and a 'bargaining counter', and hence, it implied no ideological religious metamorphosis of Jinnah, no basic changes in his political aims but a significant shift in his strategies and tactics.

In the period between Jinnah's declining influence in the Congress that led to his resignation from the party in 1920, with the corresponding rise of Gandhi and his populist politics, and the adoption of the Lahore Resolution, Jinnah and the League's political aims and objectives are commonly perceived by both orthodox and revisionist writers as seeking to ensure a secure and legitimate place for Muslims in the changing world of India as well as build up the League's position and power as central to the interests of all Muslims in India. In achieving these goals the central league leadership were internally confronted with a serious challenge of working out a delicate balance of interests and power with the growing authority and influence of the provincial Muslim political bosses in the Muslim majority areas, especially Bengal and the Punjab, reinforced by the enlarged political opportunities under the 'Montford' Reforms of 1919. Externally, their attempts, as a 'weighted minority' to secure a 'substantial' representation at the centre, were subjected to the competing claims, machinations, and much greater strength of the Indian majority represented by the Congress. Both the traditionalist and revisionist opinions find concurrence in stressing the League and Jinnah's political efforts throughout this period, towards a resolution of the Muslim problem within the constitutional framework of a united India. The detailed political analyses of the major developments of the period are aimed at revealing how, as a moderate constitutionalist and nationalist, seeking adequate safeguards for the minority interests of Indian Muslims, Jinnah's political aims were as much frustrated as was his political position undermined, in stages, during this period. The steady demise of constitutionalism and moderatism in Indian politics since 1917; Jinnah's relegation from the centre of nationalist politics consequent upon the simultaneous rise of the Pan-Islamists and Gandhi in Indian politics since 1919-20; the aggravation of communalist tendencies in politics both by the introduction of representative institutions under the 1919 Reforms, and the bitterness, frustration and confusions resulting from the collapse of the

Non-cooperation-Khilafat Movement (1922) as well as the abolition of the Khilafat (1924); the steep and significant rise in the position and influence of the provincial Muslim political bosses in the Muslim majority areas in the north-western and eastern regions in the inter-wars period; the reluctance or inability of the Congress to strengthen the hands of the 'left' faction of the League under Jinnah in the course of negotiations among the Indian political parties in the years 1926-28; the unilateral declaration by the Congress of its political goal of total independence (*purna swaraj*)– all find, in varying degrees of importance, common historiographical recognition as indicative of the predicaments of both League and Jinnah, forcing the latter to withdraw temporarily from Indian politics and move to London. The growing impotence and irrelevance of the League in the world of Muslim *real-politik, via-a-vis* the growing authority of the Muslim provinces and provincial leaders, as revealed in the subsequent developments in the Round Table Conference and the Communal Award in the early nineteen-thirties, prepared the ground for Jinnah's return, on the supplication of the League leaders of the Muslim minority areas, to resurrect the central role of the organisation and liberate it from the suffocating embraces of the provincial leaders. An essential continuity in Jinnah's aims and policies, on his return, finds general acceptance among most writers. The continuity is to be found in the common Congress and League objectives of promoting their respective national or central dominance at the expense of the provincial bases of power. Likewise, the League was not uninterested in the Congress efforts to make the British concede power at the centre which they continued to monopolise under the provisions of the Government of India Act of 1935, the ultimate League objective being a negotiated pattern of sharing power with the Congress on the basis of a substantial League representation at the centre.

The agreements between the orthodox and revisionist views are also extended to a recognition of the supreme importance of the provincial elections of 1937 held in eleven British provinces under the Act of 1935. It is, however, in regard to the nature and meanings of this significance that their divergences begin. There is no room for disputations about the crippling discomfiture of the League candidates in the election as against the overwhelming success of the Congress in the non-Muslim constituencies. Of the eleven provinces of British India, the Congress emerged with a clear majority in six and as the largest single party in three others. The revelation of the utter weakness of the League and Jinnah positively diminished their importance to the Congress, as soon experienced by the League in the growing intransigence of the Congress revealed in their post-election attitudes and dealings. For Jinnah, who had striven for Muslim political unity at the national level, the political reality of the post-1937 British India that while Hindus would dominate in all the Hindu majority provinces, Muslims seemed unable to dominate even the two largest Muslim majority provinces of the Punjab and Bengal, looked menacing. It seemed more so in view of a clear prospect of the Congress dominance at the centre as well, should the British ever decide to implement the federal provisions of the 1935 Act which offered Muslims not more than one-third of the central representation. More than ever he now clearly saw the lack of any political choice other than turning the League into the 'third' focus of power in India and the 'sole spokesman' for Muslims. 'An honourable settlement', he came to realise, 'can only be achieved between equals' and 'politics means power and not relying only on cries of justice or fair play or goodwill'.[13]

The conflicting perceptions of Jinnah's realisation are quite significant. The orthodox perception is one of a complete transformation of the mores of Jinnah's personality, ideology and policy. His old secularist idea of a Muslim minority problem to be resolved through substantial representation at the centre and provincial autonomy stood totally discomfited, and came, therefore, to be discarded in favour of the radically new demand for 'parity' at the centre based on the recognition of the Muslim claim of being a separate religious 'nation' – the much-publicised 'two-nation theory' of Jinnah. The use of religious slogans and symbols proved immeasurably useful not just in rousing sentiments against the Congress ministries in the provinces. It also helped the League in reaching the Muslim masses over the head of the provincial leaders. Jinnah's task was facilitated further by the political exigencies arising from the outbreak of the second world war. The Congress 'intransigence' drew the government closer to the League and made them realise the obvious importance of promoting Jinnah as the spokesman for Indian Muslims. Reassured by the government suspension of efforts at federation and armed with a practical veto upon any further constitutional advance offered by the government, Jinnah found the British ready to concede his demands. On 24 March 1940, Jinnah told the world what he wanted. In Jinnah's mind, so a major protagonist of the orthodox school tells us, 'partition . . . was the only long-term solution to India's foremost problem' and, having arrived at and taken this decision, he 'lowered the final curtain on any prospects for a single united independent India'.[14] From that moment Jinnah was 'set on his seven year campaign to realise the sovereign state of Pakistan'.[15] *Quaid-i Azam* had indeed forged the 'League into a political weapon powerful enough to tear the subcontinent apart.'[16] The academic judgement thus lends its weight to both the popular 'hagiology' and 'demonology' of Jinnah, the former representing the teeming millions of adoring believers whom Jinnah led to 'the promised land', while, to even greater numbers of the latter persuasion, his memory is perpetuated as a diabolical and sinister influence behind 'the vivisection of Mother India'.

The revisionist view, in contrast, envisages no real change in Jinnah's political goals but in his political strategies and tactics. His aims still continued to be to secure Muslim interests 'within' and not in total separation from India. No doubt he came to realise the grave limitations and political danger of Muslims trying to operate on the basis of the formula of a majority-minority differentiation. With the abandonment of the minority status was also discarded the notion of a simple unmodified federation which, as the 1937 election at the provincial level had clearly shown, was likely only to condemn Muslims to a virtual and perpetual dominance by the Congress. The political answer to the problem of all Indian Muslims, scattered unevenly over the subcontinent, could not have been in a total separation of the Muslim majority areas. As Muslims living in areas where they formed the majority had different needs from co-religionists in Hindu areas, Jinnah had to balance the demand for a separate Muslim state against safeguards for Muslim minorities. Viewed from this position, the Lahore Resolution, though couched in terms of separation of Muslim majority areas, did not reflect Jinnah's 'real political aims'.[17] It is simplistic, in this view, to take it as a final commitment to partition or Pakistan, if the latter term is used in its conventional sense of partition and not in Jinnah's special sense of being a strategically important embodiment of the recognition of the Muslim right and claim of being a nation – a recognition that could then be used to overcome the obvious political disadvantages of a minority status in a federal constitution. The thrust of Jinnah's political strategy underpinning the resolution was initially to secure the recognition of the Indian Muslim nationhood on the basis of acceptance of the 'Pakistan' demand by the British and Congress, and thereby gain an equal say for Muslims in any arrangement about India's political future at the centre. Once the principle of the Muslim right to self-determination, as embodied in the Lahore Resolution, was conceded, the resultant Muslim state or states could either 'enter into a confederation with non-Muslim provinces on the basis of parity at the centre' or make, as a sovereign state, 'treaty arrangement with the rest of India about matters of common concern'.[18] The resolution, in this sense, was, therefore, nothing more than a 'tactical move' and a 'bargaining counter'.[19]

III

How do these two views bear comparison on logic and evidence? The conventional view, on a close analysis, reveals serious inadequacies, and fails to accommodate certain pieces of the jigsaw.

The Lahore Resolution has given rise to three main issues, of which we have already mentioned two: the first concerns its relation to the Pakistan demand, and the second has reference to Jinnah's political aims and strategies in the most critical years between the resolution and the actual partition. There is a third question which caused some political dissent between the League and the provincial Muslim leaders, especially of Bengal, having resurfaced much later during the political conflict between West and East Pakistan. This relates to the doubts concerning the federal or unitary character of the separated Muslim majority areas as envisaged in the resolution.

Of all these three issues the last is the least ambiguous. Adopted at a time when the League's authority over the Muslim majority provinces was far from established, the resolution found it expedient to make unequivocal reference to 'independent states' rather than a single state. Only in 1946, as Jinnah needed to present a collective Muslim front to the Cabinet Mission, and also as the League and Jinnah had indeed emerged as the 'sole spokesman' for Indian Muslims, Jinnah felt himself strong enough to change the wording of the resolution from the plural to the singular 'state', providing a rather amusing justification, though no Leaguer seemed to have had the courage to ask for one at the time, that the plural was a 'misprint'. The decision was carried through the meeting of the Muslim League Council in Delhi. The provincial Muslim leaders, like Fazlul Huq, who tried unsuccessfully to resist Jinnah's centralising arm, subsequently felt bitter about this change. Huq, the mover of the resolution in Lahore, later accused Jinnah of 'betrayal' of its letter and spirit. Significantly enough the United Front, led by Huq, H. Suhrawardy and Maulana Bhasani, which decimated the Muslim League in the general election of 1954 in East Pakistan, justified its claims for the provincial autonomy, contained in its 'Twenty-one Demands', in terms of the Lahore Resolution.

The traditional understanding of and explanations for the other two seminal issues are patently uncritical and inadequate. A whole range of doubts concerning a facile equation between the resolution and the Pakistan demand as well as Jinnah's political calculations are either ignored or glossed over.

To begin with, the very omission of the word 'Pakistan' from the so-called Pakistan Resolution cannot but raise doubts in this context. Much greater significance is added to such doubts when Jinnah's initial displeasure at this equation is considered. Why did he find 'fault' with Hindus for 'foisting' and 'fathering' the word 'Pakistan' on Muslims? In his Presidential speech at the thirteenth Delhi session of the League in April 1943 Jinnah spoke his mind quite strongly:

> I think you will bear me out that when we passed the Lahore Resolution, we had not used the word 'Pakistan'. Who gave us this word? (Cries of 'Hindus') Let me tell you it is their fault. They started damning the resolution on the ground that it was Pakistan . . . . They fathered this word upon us. Give the dog a bad name and then hang him . . . . You know perfectly well that Pakistan is a word which is really foisted upon us and fathered on us by some section of the Hindu press and also by the British press. [20]

Jinnah was quite right about the beginning of this identification: the adoption of the resolution was widely reported in the Hindu and British press as the acceptance of the 'Pakistan demand'.

The second major source of doubt about the logic of Jinnah demanding partition, in 1940, stems from a consideration of the obvious and callous disregard or 'sacrifice' (*qurbani*) of less than two score million Muslim, unfortunate enough to be born and/or live on the wrong side of the 'holy land' namely, the Muslim minority areas. If anything, partition was likely to increase their vulnerability and render their position more precarious. Much of the rationale underlying Jinnah's long political career is inseparable from his anxiety to ensure a secure and rightful place for all Muslims of British India in transition. One could scarcely afford to forget that it was the Muslim minority-area leaders who made Jinnah's return from the political wilderness in London possible, and he would have been unlikely to turn his back on them, that is, as long as he could help it. He was, of course, eventually unable to help it, and the paradox of the resultant Pakistan is 'how it failed to satisfy the interests of the very Muslims who are supposed to have demanded its creation.'[21]

Thirdly, not even the interests of the Muslim majority areas were either expected to be or actually served by the partition. There is as much sense as pathos in Ayesha Jalal's most critical and searching question about the most publicised creation of the largest contemporaneous Muslim state in the world (about sixty million Muslims, leaving another thirty-five million out of it in India where it became the largest number of Muslims in a non-Muslim state): 'how did a Pakistan come about which fitted the interests of most Muslims so poorly?'[22] The situational and circumstantial differences as well as the disjunction of interests between the Muslim majority and minority areas were significant determinants of Muslim politics. The Muslim political bosses of the majority areas, who benefited most from the expanded political opportunities in the inter-war period, were both dependent on and adept in inter communal politics increasingly dominated by Muslims. Their political future was assured in a federal structure with provisions for strong provincial governments. The Lahore Resolution based on the principle of a separate Muslim nationhood communalised politics and destroyed the rationale and basis of inter-communal politics. Logically and surely, the two largest Muslim provinces – Bengal and the-Punjab – were later partitioned with all its economic, political and psychological consequences. As for the Muslims of Sind, NWFP and Baluchistan, the creation of Pakistan 'bundled them willy-nilly into a state dominated by their more numerous co-religionists from western Punjab and placed them under the tight central control ... [of] Pakistan', and the depth of their fervour for Pakistan 'can be gauged by their efforts since independence to throw off the yoke of the Punjab.'[23]

Fourthly, barring some zealots of the likes of the 'Cambridge student group', the viability of a partitioned Pakistan had been a crucial question in the minds not only of the British and non-Muslim Indian contemporaries but also of most thinking Muslims, including the *Quaid-i Azam*. Serious doubts had been expressed from time to time on the economic and defence implications of the partition, given particularly the geographic absurdity of its two major western and eastern components being separated by nearly a thousand miles of Hindu-dominated territory. Jinnah's desperate appeal for a small corridor interlinking eastern and western wings of Pakistan in the final stages of the partition-talks is a pointer to his own sharing of such doubts.

Fifthly, one of the major weaknesses of the conventional interpretation is that it offers no convincing explanations for the strange dichotomy between the rhetoric and reality of Jinnah's politics since the adoption of the resolution. His responses, in particular to the Cripps Offer (1942) and the Cabinet Mission Plan (1946), remain the weakest links in the traditional arguments. His rejection of the former as well as the acceptance (until the Congress attitudes and response forced its rejection) of the latter clearly run counter to the popular view that Jinnah craved for partition. The principle of 'secession' embodied in the Cripps Offer, whereby any unwilling province could 'opt out' of the Union, was a direct British response to the Lahore demand, providing Jinnah and the League with the surest means of fully realising the stated goals of the Lahore Resolution namely, independent and sovereign Muslim 'states'. Yet the proposals were rejected by the League, ostensibly and curiously on the ground that 'Pakistan' was not explicitly named. Most writers remain content with this tenuous explanation, regardless of the fact that Jinnah himself did not care much for the magic word and deliberately excluded it from the Lahore Resolution, as noted above. Not totally unaware of the problem, perhaps, some others have sought explanations elsewhere. Wolpert believes that the 'Muslim League were prepared to accept the offer, since it essentially embodied their Pakistan demand, but the Congress rejection left them no political option but to do likewise in order to compete most effectively for mass support.'[24] Masselos emphasises 'the political disadvantages' of the League 'being the only open supporter of the scheme in the current climate of opinion . . . .'[25] Attribution of such political concerns to the Muslim League, in the period following the election of 1937, and more so, after the Lahore Resolution, may seem more than dubious. Leaving aside the resolution itself which was a total rejection of the Congress platform and the wishes of the large majority of Indians, the League's political strategy, throughout this period, was geared to the object of reinforcing its political identity and position as the sole spokesman by exploiting every opportunity of opposing as well as discrediting the Congress. When all is said and done, the simple fact about the Cripps Offer remains that Jinnah and the League could, had they so desired, take the Muslim majority provinces out of the Indian Union. The Cabinet Mission Plan, on the other hand, categorically rejected partition – nor was Pakistan mentioned anywhere in the document – yet on 6 June 1946 the League accepted the Mission's Plan, long before the Congress indicated its 'conditional' acceptance. These two responses put together raise unqualified doubts about Jinnah's attitudes to the partition demand, the intent of the Lahore Resolution, and also the uncritical assumptions of the orthodox historiography.

Finally, the most serious objection to the conventional viewpoints relates to their inability to identify the continuity in Jinnah's political career, as already mentioned. This view is both misleading and unfair to Jinnah in presenting him as a paradox: one who had been a firm believer in Indian nationalism and also in essentially secular political values chose, in 1940, to throw away all he had striven for at a time when partition was by no means a certainty. Undoubtedly, Jinnah's politics since his shattering discomfiture in the 1937 election entered into a new phase, but the change, properly understood, is not so much one of political goals as one of tactics, as noted above. Additionally, the paradoxical view of Jinnah seems to contradict Wolpert's own psychoanalytical approach to Jinnah's politics. If Jinnah possessed those traits underlined by Wolpert – vanity, ambition, and a 'need to play the starring role' – he was even more likely to be seeking a dominant role in the much larger political arena of India, comprising about four-hundred million of which ninety-five million in the whole of India and eighty million in British India were Muslim, than his 'moth-eaten Pakistan' with its total population of about sixty million.

IV

Serious misgivings and inadequacies of this nature in the orthodox views created demands for revisionist historical research and studies in this area. Ayesha Jalal has precisely filled this disturbing historical gap, and thereby laid South Asian historiography under an enormous debt to herself. Irrespective of the enormous significance of her study, the question of the originality of Jalal's thesis needs, however, to be set in clear perspective. In his otherwise excellent review of this particular Cambridge publication in the Cambridge Journal of *Modern Asia Studies,* Francis Robinson calls Jalal's 'a novel thesis'.[26] No discerning student of the history of Indian partition should find this claim totally acceptable. Like all major works of historical revisionism Jalal's edifice is reared on an existing foundation. The centre piece both of Jinnah's political strategy in the last crucial decade before the partition and of Jalal's thesis on Jinnah has been, as already observed, the Lahore Resolution with its intriguingly 'vague' and 'amorphous' wordings. The mainspring of this thesis has clearly been a marginal, unorthodox and lesser known minority view that has long questioned the purpose of the resolution and found Jinnah's political strategy more 'a tactical move' or 'a bargaining counter' than an outright demand for partition or Pakistan.

The 'ambiguity' of the resolution drew contemporary attention. Dr B. R. Ambedkar, whose thoughts on the idea of Pakistan or partition met with Jinnah's approval, noted in 1940:

... the Resolution is rather ambiguous, if not self-contradictory. It speaks of grouping the zones into 'independent States in which the constituent units shall be autonomous and sovereign.' The use of the terms 'constituent units' indicates that what is contemplated is a Federation. If that is so, then, the use of the word 'Sovereign' as an attribute of the units is out of place. Federation of units and sovereignty of units are contradictions. It may be that what is contemplated is a confederation. It is, however, not very material for the moment whether these independent states are to form into a federation or confederation. What is important is the basic demand, namely, that these areas are to be separated from India and formed into independent states.[27]

Reginald Coupland, who met Jinnah in the early nineteen-forties, expressed similar doubts:

It was not clear exactly what this paragraph of the resolution meant. It could scarcely mean that the constituent units of the independent States were really to be 'sovereign', but that it did mean that the States were to be really 'independent' was shown by a subsequent paragraph.[28]

The notion of some ambiguities built into the resolution was juxtaposed to a less publicised but responsible view, both contemporaneous and later, that it was not intended as a specific demand for partition but as a 'bargaining point'. Penderel Moon, an observant contemporary British official, wrote later in 1961: 'Privately Jinnah told one or two people in Lahore that this Resolution was a "tactical move"; and the fact that six years later he was ready to accept something less than absolute partition suggests that in 1940 he was not really irrevocably committed to it.'[29] Hugh Tinker wrote, in 1967, that many British politicians and administrators considered the resolution as a 'deliberate overbid'.[30] Jalal herself cites several important contemporary sources casting doubts on the notion of a total separation as integral to the resolution. H. V. Hodson, as the Reform Commissioner in 1941, reported that the Muslim Leaguers 'interpreted Pakistan as consistent with a confederation.' Hodson found it the least surprising, as 'Pakistan' offered nothing to Muslims in the minority areas.[31] I. I. Chundrigar, a Leaguer who later became a Prime Minister of independent Pakistan, saw the object of the resolution as not to create 'Ulsters', but to get 'two nations . . . welded into united India on the basis of equality.' He believed that the resolution looked for an 'alternative to majority rule, not seeking to destroy the unity of India.'[32] Jinnah himself blamed Hindus, in 1943, as mentioned above, for having 'foisted and fathered' the word Pakistan on the Muslim League.[33]

All this should dispel the illusion of any claim of 'novelty' at least in regard to the core of Jalal's thesis that the resolution of 1940 had been a 'bargaining counter'. The critical importance of Jalal's work lies, therefore, not so much in presenting the resolution as a tactical manoeuvre as in her success in elevating this interpretation basically from the realm of doubts and speculations and giving it an academic authenticity, coherence and credibility. Her success in this regard is facilitated as much by her own ability as the availability of a large corpus of new documents, as mentioned above.[34] Admittedly, many of the building blocks in Jalal's edifice have been drawn from the steadily expanding store-house of historical knowledge and interpretations derived from prior researches and investigations. These are, for example, the dichotomy of interests between the Muslim majority and minority areas; the vested and entrenched position of the provincial Muslim leaders; Jinnah's aim and strategy to acquire for the League and for himself the position and the right to speak for all Indian Muslims; his determined and sustained efforts at securing theoretical and/or practical recognition of that right and position by the recalcitrant Muslim provincial bosses, the Congress and the British government; the political expediency of the transition of the League politics conducted from the vantage point of a religious and political minority to that of a nation; refurbishing the religious contents of the Pakistan idea to facilitate the League's cause; Jinnah's political calculations behind the rejection of the Cripps Offer and the eagerness to accept the Cabinet Mission Plan, and so on. But Jalal has put them all together for us into one whole coherent piece – authentically as well as creatively refined, modified and enlarged – a piece of historical study that for its thoroughness and excellence is most likely to remain for quite some time the paradigm of a revisionist thesis on Jinnah's politics in the decade before partition.[35]

The revisionist critique is logical and persuasive. Its seminal contribution consists in demystifying the politics of the League, Jinnah and Pakistan in that critical decade, as presented in the conventional historiography which is riddled with confusing paradoxes and inconsistencies, as discussed above. The essential integrity and continuity in Jinnah's long political life, subject to a significant shift in his strategy, broadly since 1937, for achieving his political aims, the overt and covert meanings of the Lahore Resolution, with the very specific contents of 'Pakistan' in Jinnah's mind, his rejection of the Cripps Offer and the intriguing wheeling and dealing with the British, his determined and persistent political manoeuvres to pull all provincial Muslim leaders into line, his eager acceptance of the Cabinet Mission Plan until the Congress forced him to reject it, and his 'continuing attempts to preserve his strategy in his many shifts and ploys' even in those closing months of the undoing of his strategy 'down to his May 1947 demand for a corridor through Hindustan to connect the two halves of Pakistan, and his June 1947 proposal that the constituent assemblies of the two new states should both meet in Delhi'[36] – are some of the major disconcerting puzzles in the orthodox versions which the revisionist historical reconstructions help to resolve so convincingly.

Jinnah's tasks, in the revisionist perspective, emerge infinitely more complex and daunting than what the traditionalists would have us believe. For Jinnah, it was far easier to aim at rousing the primordial instincts of Indian Muslims, with a view to mobilising them to achieve a division of the land, as we have so far been told, and as it eventually happened. This now seems a rather simplistic as well as distorting perception of the more mature, intricate and delicate political position of Jinnah, adept in playing a 'long, slow game'. While he undoubtedly needed the Islamic fervour to rally the Muslim masses to achieve his political aims, he could scarcely afford to push it too far to jeopardise his constant and vital objective of securing the interests of all Indian Muslims which could only have been possible within a framework of Indian unity. This was not all. Jinnah was no less interested in a strong centre than the Congress in the interests of securing and maintaining the dominant national position of the League against the provincial Muslim bases of power. But here again, Jinnah and the League, unlike the Congress, had to curb their natural instincts for a strong centre in a federal structure which would have provided a strong leverage for the Congress dominance. Thus, confronting Jinnah was a political challenge that seemed almost a 'political sphinx' and almost impossible to achieve: a Muslim nation with its 'right' to be independent, but not actually willing to break away from India, forfeiting, thereby, the control over thirty-five million Muslims to be left in a partitioned India; a strong centre essential for keeping the League in a dominant position and the Muslim provinces in line, but not without some constitutional and structural device to prevent the total Congress dominance by virtue of its brute majority. Jinnah's ideal solution lay in two federations – one Muslim – and the League-dominated, the other Hindu – and the Congress-dominated – making it in every way possible to bring the two into a system of political unity on a confederal basis or a similar structure based on treaty arrangements between them.

This view goes a long way in explaining many of those perplexities mentioned before. We understand better why the Lahore Resolution seems rather interested in the 'right' of the Muslim majority areas to be independent, and leaves every other vital concern shrouded in ambiguity. We can also see why Jinnah would not originally intend or even like the use of the word Pakistan in the resolution, though later accepted it as a 'convenient synonym' for 'this long phrase'.[37] We get the feeling that the word, which gradually came to symbolise Muslim nationhood, would recommend itself to Jinnah. Again, Jinnah's rejection of the Cripps Offer, which has been one of the weakest points in the orthodox case, provides a strong justification for the revisionist arguments.

Jinnah's strategy centring round the Lahore Resolution was almost immediately welcomed by the British Government through its 1940 'August Offer'. The Cripps Offer carried it even further by conceding, through its 'opt out' provision, the effective demands of the resolution. The League's rejection, though intriguing, is better explained from the revisionist position. Cripps' proposal contained two serious problems for Jinnah. If Jinnah was rather more interested, as noted above, in the matter of recognition of the Muslim right for self-determination

than the actual severance of the Muslim states, he was denied explicit recognition of that right – a denial given as the official justification for the League's rejection of the offer. More importantly, Jinnah, in the early nineteen-forties,
unable to assert his full authority over the Muslim majority provinces, maintained a calculated silence – quite apparent in the Lahore Resolution – on the issue of the centre, its nature and its relationship with the Muslim provinces. A
weak centre was integral to the demand of the Muslim provinces for provincial
autonomy, while the League's entire political strategy, as representatives of all
Indian Muslims, demanded a strong centre. Before such time as Jinnah could indeed become the sole spokesman for all Muslims and impose his will on the
provinces he chose not to raise the awkward question until the Cripps Offer resulted in 'flushing Jinnah out into the open and forcing him to show where he
stood on the question of the centre.' The Congress rejection of the offer made it
easier for Jinnah also to reject it and avert what seemed 'the gravest threat to his
entire strategy'.[38]

The Cabinet Mission came to recompense Jinnah for much of what was denied to him by Cripps. The compulsory grouping of Muslim provinces – leaving
Bengal and Assam in a separate grouping for ten years – offered him the effective
contents of the Muslim federation on a platter, and brought the Muslim provinces under the control of the League at the centre. It denied the principle of secession and preserved India's integrity. It stipulated for a weak centre, thwarting
the prospects for a total Congress dominance. The Mission Plan came so close to
so much of what Jinnah's political vision embraced. The offer, certainly, was not
his ideal: the prospects for the 'parity' he would have wished at the centre were
very doubtful coming from the Congress; the centre itself would not have been as
strong as he would have liked to ensure his authority over the Muslim provinces.
But the communal provisions held out the promise of a power broking role at the
centre. *Quaid-i Azam* had indeed come the closest to realising his political
dream.

Jinnah could not, however, have shown total indifference to the likely impact of the denial of a 'sovereign' Pakistan on his followers. The League acceptance of the Plan on 6 June 1946 was justified on the ground that the 'basis of
Pakistan' was 'inherent' in the plan.[39] He also had to give them an undertaking
that he would join no interim government without parity for the League.[40] In the
League's statement of acceptance there was further mention of the League's co-
operation with the constitution-making apparatus in the 'hope' that their efforts
would ultimately be rewarded with the 'establishment of a completely sovereign
Pakistan.'[41] This is an extraordinary response if one adheres to the view that Jinnah really wanted a sovereign Pakistan. How could his man, who as recently as 7
April had claimed: 'we cannot accept any proposal which would be, in any way,
derogatory to the full sovereignty of Pakistan',[42] forsake the zeal that had con-
sumed his career since 1940 for 'hope'? Rhetoric aside, Jinnah was clearly pre-

pared on 6 June to accept something less than what almost every one else knew as Pakistan.

Just as Jinnah thought himself on the verge of reaping the harvest of a long, chequered and an almost stoically determined political career, a variety of political factors and circumstances combined to snatch the cup of victory from his lips. The Congress, apparently, began the undoing of his strategy, and the 'last thirteen months of British rule', in Jalal's words, 'saw the tragic collapse of Jinnah's strategy'.[43] On 25 June 1946 the Congress Working Committee gave qualified assent to the plan; the All-India Congress Committee, under Maulana Azad's presidency, voted its approval along the same lines, on 6 July, exactly a month later than the League's acceptance of the plan. Delighted with the prospects for success, the Mission left India on 29 June. Within days Nehru took over as President and declared that the Congress was 'uncommitted' to the plan. He cast grave doubts over the grouping procedures and stressed that the central government would require some overall power to intervene in grave crisis or breakdown, warning that such central power 'inevitably grows'. He also rejected parity for the League in the Interim Executive Council. The Congress did indeed seem to be trying to make it impossible for Jinnah to use the Cabinet Mission Plan as an answer to India's political impasse. It seemed hell bent on scuttling the plan. But why?

V

The answer to this question raises the concomitant issue of the revisionist thesis: if Jinnah and the League sought to avoid partition how did it come about? It also brings us to the second myth of partition, based on a hoary assumption about 'the Congress for unity', as mentioned at the outset. If Jalal has been able to mount a successful challenge at the conventional assumptions about Jinnah and the League's politics of partition, we already have equally strong reasons and ample, though scattered, evidence enough to throw a challenge at the other 'verity' of the orthodox historiography, that is, the commitment of the Congress to Indian unity.

The Congress commitment to freedom with unity, which has been integral to the Congress ideology and politics ever since its inception, began to lose its fervour in the wake of the ineffectual and frustrating all-parties negotiations in the late nineteen-twenties, culminating in the unilateral declaration by the Congress, on 26 January 1930, of its goal of 'total independence' (*purna swaraj*). The Congress sublimated its frustration and its own share of responsibilities for the failure in resolving the Muslim Question by taking a convenient line that freedom should precede and not follow the resolution of the communal problem. It began to speak of this as a basically 'economic' problem which was incapable of being resolved in a country which was in chains. This shift of emphasis on 'freedom first' had considerable bearings on the issue of 'unity', as evident in subsequent developments where unity was sacrificed on the altar of freedom. Further, the changed League strategy, in the post-1937 political exigencies, sharpened the focus on what appears, in retrospect, the most vital, critical and determining factor in the partition namely, the nature of the central government. Provincial autonomy logically based on a weak centre had been an unchanging component of the perception of a secure future in free India among Muslims of all political shades, including the Congress Muslims. The demand for a combination of a weak centre and substantial Muslim representation therein had been a persistent item in Muslim negotiations in the pre-1937 phase. In the subsequent phase the concept of Muslim nationhood and its complementary notion of parity at the centre prompted the League to exert strong pressures on the government to revoke the federal part of the Government of India Act, 1935, which provided for a strong centre. Linlithgow obliged Jinnah by giving him a veto on India's political future.

Confronted with a choice between 'unity' and a 'strong centre', the Congress had been steadily coming to realise what might very well have to become the price for freedom, namely, division. The unqualified commitment of the Congress to a strong centre stemmed from its vision of a strong, united and modernised India. Congressmen like Nehru, with socialist streaks in them, found the concept of a strong centre inseparable from the need and demand for India's economic reconstruction based on centralised planning. The bitter communal experiences of the provincial Congress ministries after 1937 as well as that in the interim government in the nineteen-forties reinforced the Congress reluctance to seek political accommodation with the League. Finally, the Congress could hardly have been expected to overlook the supreme importance of a strong centre to ensure its own dominance in India after independence, as has been the case with what is often characterised as India's 'one-party dominance system'.[44] V. P. Menon could not have better stated the Congress case for the strong centre. Partition, he said, would 'enable Congress to have at one and the same time a strong central government able to withstand the centrifugal tendencies all too apparent at the moment, and to frame a truly democratic constitution unhampered by any communal considerations.'[45]

It is difficult to trace closely the process of the major Congress leaders in not merely coming to terms with but actually favouring the idea of partition. V. P. Menon recalled that by May 1947 Nehru was no longer averse to a proposed partition.[46] Maulana Azad's contrasting positions, as revealed in the book and the excised portion, have been mentioned above.[47] In the book he places the responsibility squarely on Lord Mountbatten, or rather, the Mountbattens:

Within a month of Lord Mountbatten's arrival in India, Jawaharlal, the firm opponent of partition, had become, if not a supporter, at least acquiescent to the idea. I have often wondered how Jawaharlal was won over by Lord Mountbatten. . . . Jawaharlal was greatly impressed by Lord Mountbatten but perhaps even greater was the influence of Lady Mountbatten . . . .[48]

Leonard Mosley held very similar views. There was, he believed, 'no doubt in any one's mind in India that the viceroy, in persuading Nehru, had performed the confidence trick of the century'.[49]

Such observations on either Nehru's or many other Congress leaders' attitudes toward the partition alternative derive credence and sustenance from an unquestioning faith in the Congress dedication to unity until the very last stage. With the arrival of the Mountbattens the patriots, in this romanticised view, seemed to gear up for the last-ditch battle, but found themselves emasculated and disarmed by the former's vice-regal charisma and charm. The historical truth seemed to lie elsewhere. There are strong reasons and evidence to suggest that long before the arrival of the Mountbattens on the scene, the upper echelon of the non-Muslim Congress leaders had been calmly calculating the distinct and pragmatic values of the partition formula. While making this assumption that it was Mountbatten who swung Nehru round to partition, Azad and others obviously ignored the possibility that the reverse might be true, and the Englishman was converted by the Indian. In a mirror-image of the dichotomy between Jinnah's professions and intentions; the Congress continued to present the facade of the ideal of unity, while it steadily and deliberately worked itself up to a position where Jinnah was forced to take his 'Pakistan' and leave the scene for good. The Lahore Resolution opened up the way for the Congress, groping since the *Purna Swaraj* Resolution of 1930 for an answer to the Muslim Question that made no demand on its 'sacred cow', that is, the strong centre.

Almost as early as the Lahore Resolution became public knowledge, most senior Congress leaders, like Gandhi and Nehru, had made known their feelings which seemed remarkably cool and pragmatic. Not many days after the Lahore session Gandhi observed:

Unless the rest of India wishes to engage in internal fratricide, the others will have to submit to the Muslim dictation, if the Muslims will resort to it . . . . The Muslims must have the same right of self-determination that the rest of India has. We are at present a joint family. Any member may claim a division.[50]

Further,

As a man of non-violence, I cannot forcibly resist the proposed partition if the Muslims of India really insist upon it . . . . it means the undoing of centuries of work done by numberless Hindus and Muslims to live together as one nation . . . . My whole soul rebels against the idea that Hinduism and Islam represent two antagonistic cultures and doctrines . . . . But that is my belief I cannot thrust it down the throats of the Muslims who think that they are a different nation.[51]

On 15 April 1940, questioned about the resolution, Nehru was reportedly

pleased, not because he liked it – on the contrary he considered it to be the most insane suggestion – but because it very much simplified the problem. They were now able to get rid of the demands about proportionate representation in legislatures, services, cabinets, etc. . . . [He] asserted that if people wanted such things as suggested by the Muslim League at Lahore, then one thing was clear, they and people like him could not live together in India. He would be prepared to face all consequences of it but he would not be prepared to live with such people.[52]

The very next day he rejoined:

Many knots of the Hindu-Muslim problem had been merged into one knot, which could not be unravelled by ordinary methods, but would need an operation . . . he would say one thing very frankly that he had begun to consider them [the Muslim Leaguers] and people like himself, as separate nations.[53]

In the confines of the Ahmedabad jail, in the early nineteen-forties, he wrote: 'wrong steps have to be taken sometimes lest some worse peril befall us . . . . . Unity is always better than disunity, but an enforced unity is a sham and a dangerous affair, full of explosive possibilities.'[54] Nehru's thoughts and attitudes to the unity proposals, as in the Cabinet Mission Plan, were clearly revealed several months before the occurrence of the plan. In January 1946, during his 'four-hour discussion' with Woodrow L. Wyatt, Personal Assistant to Cripps on the Cabinet Mission, Nehru was reported to have 'conceded that the British Government might have to declare for Pakistan . . . granted however (a) a plebiscite, and (b) territorial readjustments so that solid blocks of Hindu territory were not included, he accepted Pakistan.'[55] In a letter of the same month to Cripps, we have even positive indications that he had already seen through Jinnah's game: 'It seems clear that he [Jinnah] is not after Pakistan but something entirely different, or perhaps he is after nothing at all except to stop all change and progress.'[56] Realisation of this nature did very little for his respect of Jinnah. Duckworth, a British official covering Nehru's trip to Malaya during 18–26 March 1946, reported in April 1946, that Nehru was scornful of Jinnah and doubted very much whether he had either the intention or the power to start a revolt in India if he did not secure Pakistan.. . 'Jinnah', he said, 'rather reminds me of the man who was charged with the murder of his mother and father and begged the clemency of the court on the ground that he was an orphan'.[57]

Later in his life Nehru indicated how both age and patience might have had their share in making the minds of the Congress veterans even more receptive to the partition formula. 'The truth', Nehru told Mosley in 1960, 'is that we were tired men and we were getting on in years . . . The plan for partition offered a way out and we took it . . . .'[58] There might also have been a lingering hope in the back of their minds that they had not perhaps been committing themselves to a final and irrevocable judgement, as Nehru also admitted to Mosley, 'we expected that a partition would be temporary, that Pakistan was bound to come back to us.'[59] Elsewhere he remarked: 'The united India that we have laboured for was not one of compulsion and coercion but a free and willing association of free people. It may be that in this way we shall reach that united India sooner than otherwise and then she will have a stronger and more secure foundation.'[60]

Such sentiments were also expressed by Azad: 'The division is only on the map of the country and not in the hearts of the people, and I am sure it is going to be a short lived partition.'[61] Other front-ranking Congress leaders also are on record to lend their support to the Pakistan demand and some of them at an earlier stage than later. On 23 April 1942 the Madras Legislature passed a resolution, at the instance of C. Rajagopalachari, the Congressman with a reputation of being politically cunning, recommending a policy based on the acceptance of the Lahore Resolution. The resolution, though rejected by the All India Congress Committee, drew a significant early response from the Congress Working Committee which emphatically declared that it 'cannot think in terms of compelling the people in any territorial unit to remain in an Indian Union against their declared and established will.'[62] In early 1946 Sardar Patel, the 'strong man' of the Congress, emphatically asserted that the time had come to 'cut the diseased limb' and be done with the Muslim League.[63] V. P. Menon's claim that he converted Patel to the idea of Pakistan in early 1947 is, again, as in Nehru's case, misleading. The Sardar, in an interview with the Associated Press of America on 9 May 1947, maintained: 'Congress would like to have a strong centre . . . it was absolutely essential that there should be a strong army, and for a defence a strong central govt . . . . if the Muslim League insists it wants separation, the Congress will not compel them to remain by force.'[64] G. D. Birla, the capitalist devotee of the *Mahatma,* was also known to have favoured Partition.[65]

The Congress played the game in a masterly fashion. Jinnah's whole strategy vis-a-vis the Congress was to use the 'spectre' of the Pakistan demand which was clearly based on the assumption that the Congress would be forced, at the end of the day, to stretch itself fully to accommodate Jinnah's 'real' demands and prevent the calamity of Mother India's dismemberment. But, as Jinnah's game became apparent to the Congress, the latter chose to 'cut off the head' to get rid of the 'headache' . When all the chips were down, after Jinnah's acceptance of the Cabinet Mission Plan, the Congress called Jinnah's bluff and shattered his political strategy and ambition. Jinnah was caught in a bind because he had already presented his acceptance of the Mission Plan as a great 'sacrifice' and a proof of his 'goodwill'. By accepting something less than Pakistan, he had lost the bargaining counter which the demand for the fully sovereign Pakistan gave him.

There were the added dimensions of subtleties and dexterities involved in the Congress strategy in this regard. For the Congress High Command openly to push for partition would have been politically disastrous, and would have been viewed as an acceptance of the League's communalist view of Indian society. There was the added implication of betraying the Congress Muslims, especially when Azad remained the President between 1940 and July 1946. Azad, in his book, greets the initial acceptance of the Cabinet Mission Plan as 'a glorious event in the history of the freedom movement in India', and attributes its ultimate failure to the intransigence of the League. Nehru's press statements contributing to its destruction are glossed over as 'unfortunate events which changed the course of history.'[66] To Mountbatten he spoke of the Congress's responsibility in much more positive terms. The 'blame' for the breakdown of the Cabinet Mission Plan, he said, 'in the first place must be laid on Congress . . . '.[67] And, in the excised portion of his book, the finger he points at Nehru is unmistakable.[68]

Despite the Congress being 'on to Jinnah's game', it is conceivable that he could have gone on with his game for some more time at least had it not been for the totally unforeseen, abrupt and rapid change involving the British presence and policies in India in the aftermath of the second world war. The British refusal to impose a settlement on India and willingness to stay on until the Indians reached an agreement formed a major condition for the success of Jinnah's policy.[69] The return of a Labour Government to power, with its serious commitment to post-war reconstruction at home and demobilisation and decolonisation abroad, changed the Indian political scene rather dramatically. It was not merely the unilateral British decision to withdraw from India within a short specified period that constituted the sole threat to Jinnah. Equally importantly, or perhaps even more so, Britain appeared particularly concerned now about leaving behind a strong and centralised government in India capable of defending the British economic and political interests in the regions of the Indian Ocean. The Congress seemed keen, and looked both confident and able to take over that role. It did not take very long, in the altered conditions of time, for the British and the Congress to discover their common interests in an India with a strong centre, and the quickest way of achieving the purpose was to aim at Jinnah's 'Achilles' heel' – his Pakistan demand – to oust him by conceding his professed and not real objective.

The passion roused by the partition demand gave it a momentum too strong for Jinnah's sophisticated politics. The Pakistan idea, however vague and undefined, could not but touch a very tender point in the Muslim mind, continually nourished by dreams and hopes of an Islamic State. Jinnah's unspecified political designs, mystifying political actions, and desultory tactics left many of his followers increasingly confused and bewildered. The growing restiveness and discontent among them, especially after the fiasco and bitterness of the Cabinet Mission Plan, were bound to force his hand. Likewise, the logic and the inevitable political consequence of the Muslim 'nation' theory, with its right of self-determination, generated fear and agitation among non-Muslim minorities in the Muslim majority areas in the Punjab and Bengal, resulting in the partition of these two provinces and the further shrinkage of Jinnah's 'moth-eaten' and 'truncated' Pakistan which was destined to split even further in 1971.

VI

The revisionist perspective on the highly complex and complicated partition politics of the League and the Congress in the nineteen-forties diverge so substantially and significantly from the standard orthodox positions as to raise concern about some fundamentals of this history. There are strong grounds to challenge a few major dominant assumptions on the politics of partition, and to demand a reconstruction of the historical verities. Robinson expressed the desirability and likelihood of Jalal's work becoming 'the orthodox academic interpretation' of 'the role of Jinnah in the making of Pakistan'.[70] With greater accession to historical knowledge and, more importantly, given our willingness to forsake the comfort and complacency of the traditional and a blinkered view of the history of partition, one would like to think that the revisionist versions of both League and Congress politics of partition cannot but gain recognition as orthodox history.

Undeniably, not all doubts can be answered at the present stage of our knowledge, and again, not all the answers given are, in themselves, unquestionable. Jalal's verdict on the Lahore Resolution and Jinnah's political astuteness, for example, seem to leave some lingering doubts. The 'vagueness' and 'ambiguity' of the wording of the resolution have been universally admitted. There is also a generally agreed suggestion of its being 'deliberately vague'. Jalal moves further than this position and stresses it as Jinnah's 'strength' and political sagacity. Both the assumptions of the alleged vagueness and Jinnah's astuteness seem a little dubious. Perhaps the resolution did initially appear vague, as we have discussed above. But we have also noted that the press and public soon identified it with the Pakistan demand. Jinnah did nothing to dispel this view so that ultimately, to all concerned – the Congress, the British, and indeed to most League members and supporters, except perhaps Jinnah and a small coterie of his confidants – it dearly implied a separate Muslim homeland. The words 'autonomous', 'independent' and 'sovereign' in the resolution could not have been interpreted any differently. Without a clear acceptance of such an identification – and Jinnah himself accepted and even welcomed this identification[71] – it is absurd to think that the Congress and the British Raj could have eventually found it possible to impose Pakistan on Jinnah and the League.

This, in its turn, casts serious doubts on the soundness and strength of Jinnah's political strategy. Given his ultimate political goal of maximisation of Muslim interests within a framework of confederal or federal (under the Cabinet Mission Plan he was quite prepared to accept a federal scheme, as already noted) unity of India, comprising, ideally, a Hindu and a Muslim unit, as opposed to the idea of total separation, one has to question the rationale of his entire political strategy, centring round the resolution. No final judgement on Jinnah's politics could be offered unless we are in a position to determine the precise place of the partition formula among his political options. Was he totally opposed to the notion of partition? Or did he leave this option open, despite his preference for a solution short of partition? Answers to such questions alone can provide the true measure of his failure. Granted, however, the thrust of his policy to seek a solution other than partition, which we indeed believe to have been the case, it seems a rather dubious and self defeating tactic for Jinnah to continue, since the Lahore Resolution, to play the way he did with the 'spectre' of partition. It seems very likely, as discussed above, that the resolution sought to gain recognition of Muslim nationhood through its demand for the right of Muslim majority areas to secede. Whatever vagueness one may talk about, the resolution does not appear vague about the right of Muslim majority areas to break away and form 'independent states'. The obvious political capital to be derived from a recognition of this right induced Jinnah not to contradict the almost universal assumption about the League's association and commitment to Pakistan in the sense of partition. Were partition an unwelcome prospect, these tactics risked its achievement. It was less than political good sense and foresight not to have secured the interests of Muslims in the minority areas precisely against the strong possibility of the Congress seeking the easiest and hence the most tempting answer to this highly complex problem by trying to cut the Muslim League and Muslims out of India. The 'hostage theory' was nothing more than an after-thought – a later rationalisation calculated to offer some psychological comfort to the minorities concerned. The Lahore Resolution could afford, so it may seem, greater political tact, maturity and 'vision in attempting to integrate, openly and clearly, the demands of Muslims of the minority areas with those of their co-believers in the majority areas. Alongside the demand for the right of the majority areas to secede, could the resolution not have indicated its preference, in the interests of all Indian Muslims, for a solution avoiding partition? There is a tacit admission of failure of this strategy as well as an obvious touch of sadness when Jinnah expressed his regrets to Lord Mountbatten, in April 1947, for 'his inability to re-consider the Cabinet Mission Plan', and added: '. . . it was clear that in no circum-stances did Congress intend to work the plan either in accordance with the spirit or the letter.'[72]

One wonders about the ultimate logic of Jinnah choosing to adopt his secre-tive approach – not wanting partition and yet using the partition threat to hang, like the sword of Damocles, over the country until it was too late to be discarded. What if he tried to confront the Congress with his 'real' demands to secure the in-terests of all Muslims in India, openly rejecting the partition option, and continue to play his usual 'long, slow game'? If partition was never an option for the League and Jinnah, would the Congress and the British, even in the changed cir-cumstances in the latter half of the nineteen-forties, have found it as easy as they did to force it on eighty million Muslims of British India? Instead of this precari-ous and dangerous gamble intrinsic to 'poker', would Jinnah have done better to match the strength and skill of the Congress in an open game of 'chess'? Then, perhaps, we have hindsight on our side.

Issues of this nature will engage us in debate and discourse, as revisionist ef-forts are elevated to the status of orthodoxy. Meanwhile, revisionism on Jinnah's role in the creation of Pakistan questions the very legitimacy of the state brought into existence by the *Quaid-i Azam* as the universally acknowledged 'Father of Pakistan'.

NOTES

1. A. Jalal, *The Sole Spokesman. Jinnah, the Muslim League and the Demand for Pakistan* (Cambridge, Cambridge UP [University Press], South Asian Studies No. 31, 1985) hence-forth *Jinnah*].

2. S. Wolpert, *Jinnah of Pakistan* (New York, Oxford UP, 1984).

3. M. A. K. Azad, *India Wins Freedom* (Calcutta, Orient Longmans, 1957).

4. *The Statesman Weekly (Calcutta & New Delhi), 29 October 1988, pp. 3, 7.*

5. Ibid., 'The Maulana's Lament', Editorials, 12 November 1988, p. 9.

6. Ibid., 5 November 1988, p. 6. For a further discussion, see below.

7. '. . . there is universal agreement that Mahomed Ali Jinnah was central to the Muslim League's emergence after 1937 as the voice of a Muslim nation; to its articulation in March 1940 of the Pakistan Demand for separate statehood for the Muslim majority provinces of north-western and eastern India; and to its achievement in August 1947 . . . .' R. J. Moore, 'Jinnah and the Pakistan Demand', *Modern Asian Studies* XVII, 4 (1983), p. 529. Cf also: 'In August 1947, the Muslim League was the only party to achieve what it wanted.' A. I. Singh, *The Origins of the Partition of India* (New Delhi, Oxford UP, 1987), p. 252. See also A. Roy,

'Review' of Jalal's Jinnah in South Asia X, I (June 1987), p. I01.

8 . The most valuable recent edition of the documentary sources on the transfer of power in India is undoubtedly N. Mansergh [ed.-in-chief], E. W. R. Lumby and P. Moon (eds), Constitutional Relations between Britain and India: The Transfer of Power 1942 -1947, [henceforth TP Documents], 12 vols (London, 1970-83). In addition, the Quaid-i Azam Papers, All-India Muslim League Papers, and the 'Partition Papers' – all rendered accessible in the National Archives of Pakistan, Islamabad, together with a variety of private papers and other documentary material made available in the Indian National Archives and the Nehru Memorial Museum and Library, New Delhi, form a substantive corpus of new material on the politics of partition.

9. S. S. Pirzada (ed.), Foundation of Pakistan. All-India Muslim League Documents: 1906-1947, II (Karachi/Dacca, National Publishing House, 1970), p. 321.

10. U. Kaura, Muslims and Indian Nationalism. The Emergence of The Demand for India's Partition I929-1940 (New Delhi, South Asia Books, 1977).

11. R.J. Moore, 'Jinnah and Pakistan', pp. 529-61.

12. A. I. Singh, Origins of The Partition.

13. Pirzada, Muslim League Documents, II, p.269; also J. Ahmad (ed.), Speeches and Writings of Mr Jinnah, I (Lahore, S. M. Ashraf, 7th edn, 1968), p. 32.

14. Wolpert, Jinnah, p. 182.

15. F. Robinson, 'Review' of Jalal's Jinnah, in Modern Asian Studies XX, 3 (July 1986), p. 613.

16. S. Wolpert, New History of India (New York, Oxford UP, 1982), p. 325.

17. Jalal, Jinnah, p. 4; Roy, 'Review' of Jalal's Jinnah.

18. Jalal, ibid, p. 241. Jinnah's vision perhaps anticipated the contemporary Canadian situation in relation to Quebec. French Quebec decided against separation in 1980. In accordance with the arrangements of the-new Accord signed between the Canadian Federal Government and the Provinces, Quebec's power in the Centre has been substantially reinforced without compromising its right to contract out of Federal Programmes.

19. Ibid., p. 57.

20. Pirzada, Muslim League e Documents, II, p. 425.

21. Jalal, Jinnah, p. 2.

22 . Ibid., p. 4.

23. Ibid., p. 3.

24. Wolpert, New History, p. 335.

25. J Masselos, Indian Nationalism: An History (New Delhi, Sterling Publishers, 1985), p.206

26. Robinson, 'Review' of Jalal's Jinnah, p. 617.

27. B. R. Ambedkar, Pakistan or The Partition of India (Bombay, Thacker, 3rd edn, 1946), pp.4-5

28. R. Coupland, Indian Politics 1936-1942. Report on The Constitutional Problem of India (London, Oxford UP, 1944), p. 206.

29. P. Moon, Divide and Quit (London, Chatto & Windus, 1961), p. 21.

30. H. Tinker, Experiment with Freedom: India and Pakistan 1947 (London, Oxford UP, 1967), p. 24; also P. Hardy, The Muslims of British India (Cambridge, Cambridge UP, South Asian Studies No. 13, 1972), p.232.

31. H. V. Hodson, The Great Divide: Britain, India, Pakistan (London: Hutchinson, 1969), p. 69.

32. Quoted, Jalal, *Jinnah*, p. 70.

33. See above note 20.

34. See note 8.

35. Roy, 'Review' of Jalal's, Jinnah, p. 101.

36. Robinson, 'Review' of Jalal's, *Jinnah*, p. 617.

37. Pirzada, *Muslim League Documents, II, p.* 426. 'We wanted a word and it was foisted on us, and we found it convenient to use it as a synonym for the Lahore Resolution.' (Ibid.)

38. Jalal, *Jinnah*, p. 76,

39. Mansergh, *TP Documents*, VII, Doc. No. 469, Enclosure, L/P & J/5/337: PP 418-20, p. 837

40. Jalal, *Jinnah*, p. 202.

41. Mansergh, *TP Documents*, VII, Doc. No. 469, Enclosure, p. 838.

42. Pirzada, ibid., II, p. 509.

43. Jalal, *Jinnah*, p. 208.

44. S. A. Kochanek, *The Congress Party of India. The Dynamics of One-Party Democracy* (Princeton, New Jersey, Princeton UP, 1968); R. Kothari, 'The Congress "System" in India', in *Party System and Election Studies,* Occasional Papers of the Centre for Developing Societies, No. I (Bombay, Allied Publishers. 1967), pp. 1-18; also G. Krishna, 'One Party Dominance – Developments and Trends' in ibid., pp. 19-98.

45. V.P. Menon, The *Transfer of Power in India* (Princeton, New Jersey, Princeton UP, 1957), p. 358

46. Ibid., p. 360

47. See above p. 385.

48. Azad, *India Wins Freedom*, p. 165.

49. L. Mosley, *Last Days of the British Raj* (London, Weidenfeld & Nicholson, 1961), p.97.

50. D. G. Tendulkar, *Mahatma* (Bombay, Jhaveri & Tendulkar, 1952), V, pp 333-34.

51. Ibid, pp. 336-37.

52. *Leader,* 15 April 1940, quoted S. R. Mehrotra, 'The Congress and the Partition of India', in C.H.Philips & M.D.Wainwright (eds), *The Partition of India. Policies and Perspective 1935 -I947* (London, Allen & Unwin, I970), p. 210.

53. Ibid., 16 April 1940, quoted in ibid.

54. J. Nehru, *The Discovery of India* (Bombay, Asia Publishing House, reprint, 1969), p. 526.

55. Wavell to Pethick-Lawrence, 15 January 1946; Mansergh, *TP Documents,* VI, Doc. No. 357, L/PO/10/23, p. 796.

56. Nehru to Cripps, 27 January 1946; ibid., Doc. No. 384, L/P &J/10/59: ff. 42-4, pp. 855-56.

57. Note by Duckworth, 4 April 1946; ibid., VII, Doc. No. 54, L/P &J/8/636: ff. 3-6, p. 136.

58. Mosley, *British Raj,* p. 248.

59. Ibid.

60. M. Gwyer and A. Appadorai (eds), *Speeches and Documents on the Indian Constitution 1921-1947* (London, Oxford UP, I957), II, p. 682.

61. *Leader,* 16 June 1947, quoted Mehrotra, 'Congress and Partition', p. 220.

62. Quoted in Menon, *Transfer of Power*, p. 132.

63. D. V. Tahmankar, *Sardar Patel* (London, Allen & Unwin, 1970), p. 19I.

64. Mansergh, *TP Documents,* X, Doc. No. 375, L/P &J/10/79: f.248, p. 717.

65. Tahmankar, *Patel*, *p.* 272.

66. Azad, *India Wins Freedom*, *pp.* 135, 138.

67. Mansergh, *TP Documents, Mountbatten Papers, Viceroy's Interview* No. 14, 27 March 1947, X, Doc. No. 27, p. 34.

68. *The Statesman Weekly*, 5 November 1988, p. 6; also above, notes 3-6. It was reported that Rabindranath Roy, who was additional private secretary to Humayun Kabir, the co-author of the book, and who also typed out the manuscript, affirmed that the sealed pages contained 'no adverse comments on Jawaharlal Nehru or members of his family.' This statement was immediately contradicted by the publishers of the book, Orient Longmans saying that the excised pages 'do make critical references to Jawaharlal Nehru . . .', Ibid., 29 October 1988, pp. 3, 7.

69. Jalal, *Jinnah*, pp. 243 ff.

70. Robinson, 'Review' of Jalal's *Jinnah*, p. 617.

71. See above p. 396 also note 32.

72. Mansergh, *TP Documents, Viceroys Personal Report No. 3*, 17 April 1947, X, Doc. No. 165, L/PO/6/123: ff. 42-9, p. 301.

Index